THETIS
SUBMARINE DISASTER

Ninety-nine lives were lost—needlessly—in the "*Thetis*" disaster; but, there were also many, many more grieving families who suffered, and whose lives were changed as a direct result of that terrible day in June. A poignant story, one of many, is told by Joyce Bentley, Chair of the *Thetis* Families Association:

Our family lived in Stalybridge, Cheshire. My brother, Leading Seaman John Turner was already in the navy when I was born. I had two other older siblings, Ann and Jim. They were much older than me, so I grew up almost like an only child. On the evening of Thursday, 1st June 1939, we were all sat at home. After a very busy couple of weeks, we were just coming to the end of making all of the necessary arrangements and preparations for sister Ann's wedding, which was to be held on Saturday. I was to be one of the bridesmaids and couldn't wait to wear the dress that had been specially made for the occasion. But, less than an hour later, our happiness was shattered, when there was a knock on our front door. Mother opened it, only to find a very sombre looking policeman on the doorstep. He brought news that *Thetis*, the newly-built submarine to which brother John had been attached, had not surfaced from her trial dive in Liverpool Bay. John had been granted special leave on Saturday to come home for his sister's wedding. Dad, who was working away in Ellesmere Port at the time, was also coming over with John. Later on we received a telegram from dad—probably the first that he'd ever sent—saying that the wedding must go ahead. He also told us in the telegram that, like many other relatives and friends, he was waiting at Cammell Lairds's shipyard for further news. I could not understand why, suddenly, everything had changed from joy to sadness and anxiety. At eight years of age I just couldn't understand why dad and brother John were not coming to the wedding—it was the most special day that I could ever remember.

The wedding ceremony went ahead, but, by that time, it was known that all hope had been abandoned and that all of the men still on board *Thetis* were dead. Ann and her new husband cancelled their honeymoon.

John is buried in the mass grave in Maeshyfryd Cemetery, Holyhead.

THETIS
SUBMARINE DISASTER

DAVID PAUL

FONTHILL

*This book is respectfully dedicated to the families of all the men
who were lost on HMS* Thetis
*families whose fortitude and endurance subsequently overcame
all the odds that were stacked against them.*

Fonthill Media Limited
www.fonthillmedia.com
office@fonthillmedia.com

First published in the United Kingdom 2014

British Library Cataloguing in Publication Data:
A catalogue record for this book is available from the British Library

ISBN 978-1-78155-271-1

Typeset in 10 pt on 13 pt Sabon LT Std
Printed and bound by CPI Group (UK) Ltd, Croydon, CR0 4YY

Contents

Acknowledgements

During the course of my research for this book and its subsequent writing, I have been helped and guided by many individuals and organisations, without whom I would not have been able to complete the endeavour. I would wish to record my thanks to Mrs Joyce M. Bentley, Chair of the *Thetis* Families Association, for sharing with me her detailed knowledge relating to the events of the disaster itself and also the background to the *Thetis* Inquiry. I am also indebted to her for presenting to me all 2,000 pages of the official Inquiry – a valuable source of information which I spent many hours reading! I would also wish to record my thanks to David Stowell, submarine engineer of Barrow-in-Furness, for his help and advice regarding sources of information. Later in my research I found a book, *Silent Warriors (Volume Three)*, by Pamela Armstrong & Ron Young which gave me another detailed insight into the loss of HMS *Thetis*. I would wish to record my thanks to Pam Armstrong for kindly allowing me to use some of her diagrams, photographs and sources of information which appear in her book. I am also indebted to Tony Booth, author of *Thetis Down*, for his guidance and advice regarding copyright issues, and, like him, I would wish to state that despite prolonged and exhaustive enquiries, tracking down some copyright holders has not been possible.

The World Wide Web proved to be another valuable source of research where there are, understandably, many sites for HMS *Thetis*, far too numerous to mention. But one site in particular proved to be very informative, and that was the site of Mike Kemble http://www.mikekemble.com/ww2/britsubthetis.html. Mike was particularly helpful, extending to me the benefit of his extensive knowledge of both the *Thetis* disaster in particular, and of submarines in general. I am also grateful to him for allowing me to use some of the many images which he has of HMS *Thetis* on his web page.

I would also wish to record my sincere thanks to the staff of the Holyhead Maritime Museum, and in particular Eric Anthony (museum manager), Gerry

Thomas (museum archivist) and Vince Murtagh (museum guide) for allowing me to use many of their original photographs of the *Thetis* disaster, and whose helpful advice proved invaluable.

Finally, I couldn't end this section without thanking my son, Jon Paul, for his constant words of encouragement and helpful suggestions as to the content and title.

Sources

Internal Inquiry into loss of HMS *Thetis* ADM/116/3817
Bucknill Inquiry
ADM 116/4115 No.194,ADM 116/4311,ADM 116/4429,ADM
116/4115,ADM 116/319-22,ADM
Thetis Down, Tony Booth, Pen and Sword, 2009
Thetis – Secrets and Scandal, David Roberts, Avid Publications, 1999
The Admiralty Regrets, C. Warren and J. Benson, Harrap, 1958
Close Enough to Touch, BBC Radio 4, 1997
Death in the Bay, BBC TV documentary
Archives of the Holyhead Maritime Museum
Alexander, Count Michael, SOS *Thetis*, Franz Müller Verlag, Dresden, 1943
The Rogue's Yarn, Wendy Harris, Leo Cooper, London, 1993

Introduction

The story of His Majesty's Submarine Thetis is a long and painfully agonising one—but a story which, seventy-five years later, is still worthy of recounting.

HMS *Thetis* sank on Thursday 1 June 1939, whilst engaged on her final series of trials—which included her diving trial. There were four survivors, but the other ninety-nine men on board met their death in the disaster. *Thetis* was the third 'T'-class ('*Triton*' class) submarine to be built. The contract for the construction of the *Thetis* was placed with Messrs Cammell Lairds of Birkenhead on 28 October 1936. The contract, in accordance with practice in these matters, provided for a series of trials conducted under Admiralty supervision, lasting for some four months or more. Most of those trials took place in the company's wet basin, and included, amongst other trials, preliminary submerging trials and torpedo equipment trials. Towards the end of April 1939, *Thetis* steamed up to Gare Loch on the Clyde—the traditional trial ground for Royal Naval submarines—for her 30-hours steaming trial on the surface, and her diving trial. However, as there were some defects found in the hydroplane gear—the horizontal rudder-like gear which takes the vessel down when it is desired to submerge her—the diving trials were not conducted at that time. Also, because of serious steering gear malfunctioning, *Thetis* returned to Birkenhead for necessary remedial work in dry dock.

Both during construction and the subsequent equipment safety checks and testing programme, the submarine's bow caps were thoroughly tested—these are the 'doors' which are opened to the sea immediately before a torpedo is to be fired from the submarine.

Following rigorous scrutiny by Cammell Lairds's staff and Admiralty Overseers, *Thetis* left Birkenhead on 1 June to do her diving trial in Liverpool Bay. This was the last trial which she had to do before the 'acceptance trial'. All of the preliminary trials, except the diving trial, had taken place and the experts had been satisfied that, subject to this final diving test, she was in proper order and ready to be handed over to the Royal Navy. On a trial of this kind, in addition to the normal complement of crew, which was fifty-three Officers and Men, there would have been naval and civil personnel representing the Admiralty, representatives and employees of the contractors and one or two other supernumeraries. On the morning of 1 June, immediately before leaving the wet dock, there was some discussion as to 'trim' of the vessel—how she was 'sitting' in the water. The concern was that the boat was 'light', but she sailed anyway.

On that morning *Thetis* was accompanied by the tug *Grebe Cock*. In addition to her normal crew, *Grebe Cock* had four other personnel on board, which included a naval officer and a leading wireless telegraphist. The duties of the tug had been discussed previously by Lieutenant Commander Bolus, the captain of the submarine, and the tug's captain. Various trials were then carried out whilst *Thetis* was at sea, including the steering gear trial, and tank 'blowing'. When it was decided to move to the diving trial, the tug was informed of the diving course and told to take up her position half a mile on the port quarter of *Thetis*. The course was 310 degrees. *Thetis* signalled that she was proposing to dive at 1340 hours. It was at this point that all supernumerary personnel were meant to disembark and be transferred to *Grebe Cock*. However, nobody left the submarine. All of those on board wanted to experience the trial dive—an experience which was to cost them their lives.

Royal Naval protocol stipulates that before every submarine dives, full details must be entered at submarine headquarters, Fort Blockhouse. This requirement had been complied with, and *Thetis* was cleared for a trial dive of three hours.

The tanks were flooded in slow time, but, after this operation, the ship was found to be unduly 'light' at the forward end: furthermore, she was not diving. Various checks were then carried out, including the amount and locations of the ballast that the submarine was carrying. As part of these checks, the six torpedo tubes were checked to see if they held any ballast, but none appeared to be holding any water—during sea trials submarines do not carry any torpedoes, so the tubes can be used for ballast if required. Shortly after the checks had been completed, the rear door of torpedo tube number five was opened. This resulted in a torrent of water cascading into the compartment. It was all too evident that something was seriously wrong. Number five bow cap was open to the sea, when it definitely shouldn't have been.

The effect of flooding into this compartment was to submerge the bow of the ship; she went into a steep dive and hit the seabed. *Thetis* hit the bottom at an angle of about 40 degrees, and there she stayed for some while. It was found impossible to 'blow' the main tanks. After much discussion on board, it was considered that there wasn't any prospect of outside assistance at that stage, so attempts needed to be made to escape from the submarine. Using the recently developed Davis Submarine Escape Apparatus, men would endeavour to escape via one of the two escape chambers. By this time it was late in the evening, so it was decided to postpone any escape attempts until the morning of Friday 2 June.

It was now considerably more than three hours since *Thetis* had dived, and, as no word had been received at Fort Blockhouse as to her situation, concerns were raised. Later that evening an air and sea search was mounted, and other vessels sailed from Liverpool to assist in the search and rescue operation.

Overnight some fuel oil and some fresh water were pumped out in an attempt to increase the vessel's buoyancy. This work resulted in the stern breaking the surface. A number of unsuccessful escape attempts were made until, shortly after 0750 hours, two naval officers, Captain Oram and Lieutenant Woods, were successful. And, just at that time *Thetis* was located by HMS *Brazen*. The officers were picked up by the *Brazen's* whaler when they reached the surface. Some two hours later, Leading Stoker Arnold and Mr Shaw from Cammell Lairds broke the surface. They were the last men to escape.

Various rescue vessels were now converging on the site. A strategy had been agreed whereby it was hoped that the stern of the submarine could be further raised, thus enabling all of the trapped men to escape. Ultimately more than twenty vessels were present, all engaged, in one way or another, in trying to effect a successful rescue—they failed. At 2200 hours on Saturday 3 June 1939 it was finally acknowledged that there was no further hope of any men on board still being alive.

Throughout the short life of HMS *Thetis*, the catalogue of errors, omissions, incompetence and failure to adhere to accepted and standard procedures is only matched with the apparent complacency and indifference of the overly bureaucratic Admiralty and its procedures at the time of the disaster. It was, and still is, the worst peacetime disaster to befall a British submarine.

David Paul
Liverpool
24 August 2013

CHAPTER 1

Job N°· 1027

A pact signed on 22 April 1930 and ratified on 27 October 1930—known as the 1930 London Naval Treaty—was an agreement between five nations: the United Kingdom, the United States of America, France, Italy and the Empire of Japan. The treaty set limits on naval shipbuilding and also laid down a regulatory framework regarding submarine warfare. Under the terms of the treaty, the further development of the 'big gun' concept of submarine design was curtailed, and further distinctions were drawn between armaments allowed on 'light cruisers' and 'heavy cruisers'. However, perhaps the most significant clauses in the agreement referred to the total maximum tonnage which each of the signatory countries agreed to limit themselves to. In the case of the United Kingdom, the total maximum tonnage for the submarine fleet was restricted to 52,700 tons; also, there was a maximum tonnage limitation of 2,000 tons for any single boat. There were also armament restrictions, limiting the submarines to one 5.1 inch (130 mm) deck-mounted gun. Although the restrictions were severe, because of the United Kingdom's straitened financial circumstances, it was highly unlikely that the maximum tonnage limitation would be reached.

But, even as design work on what was becoming known as the 'Repeat Ps' was getting started at the beginning of 1934, the project itself was encountering stormy weather, with the political intervention of the then Conservative Prime Minister, Rt Hon. Stanley Baldwin. He was directly opposed to the stance being adopted by the Admiralty, in that he favoured total abolition—a view which he had expressed in the House of Commons as early as 18 November 1925 [*Hansard*: House of Commons debate on Submarines (Abolition) vol. 188 cc 381-2]. Following questioning by several members, including Mr Trevelyan, Mr Ammon, Mr Campbell and Vice-Admiral Sir Reginald Hall, the Prime Minister was asked by Mr Livingstone, directly, if the Government was in favour of the abolition of submarines as a weapon of war. The Prime

Minister responded to the effect that the Government's view had not changed since the Washington Conference of 1921, when, speaking for the British Government, Mr A. J. Balfour, Lord President of the Council, gave formal notice that he intended to bring before the open conference a proposal for the total abolition of submarines.

The Admiralty continued to argue for the retention of the submarine force, with boats significantly larger than the 250 tons/unit as was being favoured by the Government. It was argued that boats of this size would not be able to meet Britain's future needs—from both an offensive and defensive standpoint. Then, the Second London Naval Treaty of 1936 significantly moved the Admiralty's arguments further forward. The on-going design work on the 'Repeat P' project was now well advanced. The projected new class of submarine would be smaller than the Odin, Parthian and Rainbow boats which it was superseding, but it would have demonstrably improved handling capabilities—both submerged and when patrolling on the surface. Also, the new class of submarine would have a greater turn of speed when submerged. With regards to firepower, 'O', 'P' and 'R' classes were equipped with eight, eight and six torpedo tubes respectively, whereas the 'T' class, as it was later to be called, was designed to have ten torpedo tubes. When on surface patrol, six tubes would be below water level and the other four above the waterline; two located in the bows and two amidships. All torpedo tubes were forward facing. The only noteworthy negative aspect of the boats' design was that they would have a slower surface speed than their predecessors, and this was solely due to the displacement limitations imposed by the Treaty. Overall, however, the balance was strongly weighted in favour of the 'T' class submarine being infinitely better than earlier classes.

The 'Repeat Ps', which was the original designation of the design programme, were primarily designed to operate against the Japanese fleet, and were being developed to replace the nineteen earlier 'O', 'P' and 'R' classes of submarine which had been built between 1925 and 1931. These boats, having a surface displacement of 1,400 tons, were large and difficult to manoeuvre, and were thus very vulnerable when facing attack. Design development on the 'Repeat Ps' programme was completed in 1935. In June of that year the designation 'Repeat P' was dropped, and the first boat—to be named HMS *Triton*—was ordered on 5 March 1935. The keel of HMS *Triton* was laid down on 28 August 1936 at the shipyards of Vickers Armstrong in Barrow-in-Furness. HMS *Triton* was launched on 5 October 1937. It was then decided that subsequent boats would all have names beginning with the letter 'T'. Hence, the 'T' class submarine came into being. There was a total of fifty-three boats built immediately before and during the Second World War. The boats were built in three tranches; Group One boats, which were pre-war boats; Group Two boats, which were built during the Second World War, and Group

Three boats, which were also built during the Second World War. The fifteen Group One boats were of riveted construction. Only one boat, *Triton*, was ordered under the 1935 Programme. There were four boats ordered under the 1936 Programme; seven boats under the 1937 Programme, and a further three boats under the 1938 Programme. A further seven boats, the Group Two boats, were ordered under the 1939 War Emergency Programme. Group Three boats were ordered in 1941, 1942 and 1943.

Of the four boats to be built under the 1936 Programme, two contracts were awarded to Cammell Lairds; one boat, HMS *Trident*, was to be built at Vickers Armstrong, and the other contract, for HMS *Tribune*, was awarded to Scotts Shipbuilding and Engineering Company of Greenock (Of the seven boats to be built under the 1937 Programme, only one contract, that for HMS *Taku*, was awarded to Cammell Lairds, with most of the other contracts being awarded to Vickers Armstrong).

When shipyards are asked to tender for a contract, the normal process includes detailed calculations on the part of the shipyard, followed by the submission of a tender. As with all Ministry of Defence and Admiralty contracts, this is a competitive process. In the case of the tender for the building of *Thetis*, Cammell Lairds came close to losing the contract to another yard, because their tender was too high. Although no definitive figures have been released as to the projected cost for the construction of HMS

Cammell Lairds had a proud tradition of building ships on the banks of the River Mersey. Their ships were known the world-over, but very soon they would become even more well-known, but for very different reasons. (*By kind permission of Pamela Armstrong*)

Thetis, reliable estimates put the figure somewhere in the region of between £320,000 and £350,000. In the original specification, the Admiralty had called for their own engines to be used but, in an effort to reduce production costs, Cammell Lairds's initial tender had included twin Sulzer engines. As these engines were somewhat smaller than the Admiralty engines, it had the added effect of reducing the overall length of the submarine by two feet—thus further reducing the costs of construction. But, even with these figures, the then director of the Contracts and Purchase Department at the Admiralty, E. C. Jubb Esq. OBE, considered the tender to be excessive. In the fiercely competitive British shipbuilding market, Lairds's Managing Director, Mr R. S. Johnson, was determined to win the contract. After further consultations with Mr Jubb at the Admiralty, Johnson submitted a revised, and lower, tender; this resulted in Cammell Lairds being awarded the contract to build HMS *Thetis*. It was further agreed that delivery would be two years after the keel was laid.

The keel of what was to become HMS *Thetis* was laid down on 21 December 1936, and for many months to come the steel construction on the slipway was simply referred to as Job Nᵒ· 1027. The keel for HMS *Trident* was laid down on 12 January 1937, the boat being launched on 7 December 1938. Construction of HMS *Taku*, the first boat under the 1937 Programme, commenced on 18 November 1937 and the boat was launched on 20 May 1939.

The London Naval Treaty of 1936, to which Britain was a signatory, and the terms of which were accepted by the Admiralty, imposed many restrictions and limitations, but propulsion output was not one of these conditions. This proved advantageous, as the Sulzer engines each delivered 3,300 brake horsepower (bhp), whereas the Admiralty engines were only capable of delivering 2,500 bhp. It was considered that this resultant increase in speed capability would be an inestimable advantage in any conflict situation.

Because of the impending threat of war with Germany, the Admiralty were insistent that the boat must be delivered by 10 May 1938, less than two years after the start of building. This date was not achieved, but the onus of responsibility must rest with the Admiralty, having failed to deliver some of essential hull components on time.

At precisely 12.30 on Thursday 29 June 1938, Mrs. A. Power, wife of Captain A. J. Power CVO, RN of HMS *Ark Royal*, smashed the traditional bottle of champagne onto the bow of His Majesty's Submarine *Thetis*. The aim was spot on, with the bottle smashing on the first attempt—always considered to be a good omen. As the vessel slowly gained momentum down the slipway, workers and officials cheered as the submarine entered into her preferred environment, the chilling waters of the River Mersey.

Following the launching ceremony, the official guests of Cammell Lairds

HMS *Thetis* launched by Mrs Amy Power, wife of Captain Arthur John Power of HMS *Ark Royal* on Wednesday 29 June 1938. (*By kind permission of Mike Kemble*)

were taken to the Adelphi Hotel, directly across the River Mersey in Liverpool. It was traditional after every launch from the shipyard for directors and senior staff of Cammell Lairds to entertain their guests, and today was no exception! Almost two hundred guests were entertained to a lavish lunch, held in the Tracer's Room at Liverpool's premier hotel. The top table, as was the tradition on these occasions, was mainly populated by Cammell Lairds's directors and their wives. The other six rows of tables which spread out before them were filled with Admiralty personnel, including two of the Admiralty Overseers, Edward Grundy and Edward Gisborne. At another table senior personnel from the newly-launched submarine were seated, together with their wives; these included the submarine's commander, Lieutenant Commander Guy Bolus, and his wife, Sybil. Also on the same table was Lieutenant Chapman, who was to be Bolus's Number One. Because of the role that many of the shipyard's senior staff had played during the construction of the submarine, a goodly number of them had also been invited to the lunch together with their wives; indeed, without these key members of staff this day would not have been possible. Lastly, but certainly not least, a number of reporters from national and local newspapers had been invited to the celebration lunch—Mr Johnson was fully aware of the power of the press, especially in the current situation, with war against Germany almost a foregone inevitability—and Lairds definitely needed to secure as many war contracts as possible, in light

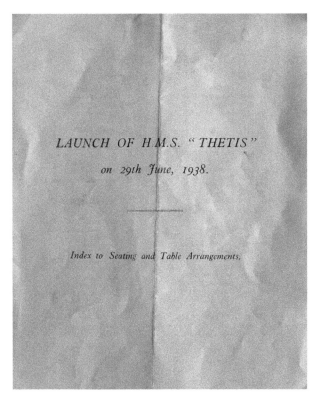

LAUNCH OF H.M.S. "THETIS"

on 29th June, 1938.

Index to Seating and Table Arrangements.

Launch Day lunch, seating plan, Wednesday 29 June 1938. (*By kind permission of Holyhead Maritime Museum*)

of their precarious financial position.

There was an air of eager anticipation around the room as the guests enjoyed their celebration lunch of a fish starter of salmon accompanied by trimmings of cucumber and mayonnaise. The main course was chicken and buttered new potatoes. Everyone then enjoyed lashings of strawberries for sweet; all-in-all, an excellent meal. But, all good things come to an end as they say, so now it was time for the formal speeches to begin. Mr Johnson, Lairds's Managing Director, rose to his feet and waited just a few minutes whilst the buzz around the room tapered off, and he had everyone's attention. His first duty was to propose a toast to HMS *Thetis*, and he deftly coupled with this the name of Mrs Power. Following this toast, Johnson went into the main content of his speech, a mixture of mirth and some hard-hitting truths about the parlous state of the British shipbuilding industry—possibly aimed at the members of the press who were giving the speech their full attention.

It appeared that Johnson had been fascinated by the name of the submarine, *Thetis*; indeed, he'd spent a great deal of time looking up the origin of the name, only to find that *Thetis* was a sea god and mother of *Achilles*—strangely enough the name of another ship that Lairds had built some time ago. Before his speech ended, Johnson made reference to the fact that *Thetis* had sought to make her son invulnerable. To perform this minor miracle, *Thetis* submersed him in the River Styx, holding him only by his heel. And this, so the story went, was where he was vulnerable. It was clear that Johnson's words had hit the spot, and the guests applauded the well-received speech.

Johnson then turned his attention to HMS *Ark Royal,* which had just been built at the yard. He made glowing reference to her captain, Captain Power, and linked with this reference the successful sea trials which had just been completed. Finally, by way of bringing Mrs Power into his speech again, Johnson thanked her for attending the launch and performing the ceremony. Mrs Power later responded by saying that she felt very honoured at having been invited, adding that she thought that *Thetis* would be a lucky ship.

Also at the reception, one of the other principal guests, the naval architect Mr F. G. John, drew some unfortunate analogies between Noah's Ark and *Thetis* in his speech, little realising that his remarks would be a harbinger of tragedy.

But the decline of the British shipbuilding industry was obviously causing Mr Johnson chronic anxiety knowing, as he did, the inroads which foreign shipyards were making in world markets—often with direct aid and intervention from their governments. Indeed, the day following the launching of HMS *Thetis*, Mr Johnson found himself back in the Adelphi Hotel after another successful launch. On this occasion a merchant ship, the *Jonathan Holt,* a general cargo ship built for the shipping company of John Holt & Co (Liverpool) Ltd, went down a slipway adjacent to the *Thetis's,* but Mr Johnson had obviously been ruminating on what was uppermost in his mind. Instead of an upbeat and witty speech similar to that which he had delivered the day before, he gave his assessment on the state of shipbuilding in Britain, and also turned the spotlight on the perceived indifference and lack of any constructive intervention strategy, with which he considered central government was viewing the situation—especially in light of the distinct possibility of war with Germany in the not too distant future. Towards the end of the speech he was quite unequivocal, stating that if shipbuilding was to survive in Britain, then there must be direct Government intervention.

In addition to Lieutenant Commander Guy Bolus, soon to become captain of HMS *Thetis*, there were two other officers and four ratings—one of whom was Leading Stoker Walter Charles Arnold—who 'stood-by' the boat from just before her launch, during the lengthy fitting-out and wet basin trials, right through until the final acceptance trials. In turn, they were joined by a further twelve senior ratings part-way through the fitting out. The purpose, like that for the personnel already on board, was in order for them to familiarise themselves with the vessel, its systems and operation. The number of crew was brought up to its full complement towards the end of February 1939, when Bolus informed Submarine Headquarters at Fort Blockhouse, that sufficient progress had been made for the remaining thirty-four crew to join the vessel.

Lieutenant F. G. Woods RN joined the crew of *Thetis* during October 1938 as Torpedo Gunnery Officer, after already having served for two years in the submarine service. By this time the fitting-out was well advanced, but major fitting work on the torpedo room, Woods' main centre of operation, had, as yet, not been started. It was deemed to be part of his training for the young, twenty-five-year-old, officer to gain valuable experience in witnessing the fitting and assembly of the bow cap operating mechanisms—the operation of which was so critical to the submarine's effectiveness.

A series of important trials were scheduled for March; these were the ballast and trimming trials—the object of which was to establish the draught and trim characteristics of the boat. Until these trials had been 'signed off', the boat would not be accepted by the Admiralty. The trials entailed submerging safely in an enclosed environment—the wet basin at Cammell Lairds—and carrying out inclining and other underwater tests, but, in order to achieve a verifiable outcome, the ultimate gross weight of the submarine had to be known. It must be remembered that these tests were to be carried out before all of the machinery and other equipment had been installed into the boat. In order to achieve this condition, it was therefore necessary to add dead-weight ballast and extra water into the tanks. In this way, design characteristics could be verified. If the boat's draught, with the compensating ballast, differed from these initial calculations, then added ballast would be needed to be incorporated in the boat's construction. Accordingly, the trim trial was scheduled for and conducted on 4 March in the presence of Mr Hill, the Admiralty Overseer; Mr G. J. Stunden, the Assistant Naval Constructor; Cammell Lairds's Forman Engineer, Arthur Robinson; Lieutenant Chapman, First Lieutenant of *Thetis* and Lieutenant Woods, Torpedo Officer of *Thetis*.

Thetis was taken down, such that the periscope brackets, deck gun and bridge were just above sea level. The exact trim was then determined by noting the difference between the draught marks on the submarine itself and the draught boards which had now been placed against the submarine. Later, in evidence to the Inquiry, Lieutenant Woods testified that he recalled tubes numbers five and six having been filled in one of the basin trials on the orders of Lieutenant Chapman, and that under his orders (Woods'), Leading Seaman Hambrook and Petty Officer Mitchell had handled the control levers of numbers five and six tubes on that occasion.

After the trials had been completed, Assistant Naval Constructor George John Stunden submitted a report of this preliminary trimming trial on 9 March. Mr Stunden stated that the submarine was submerged to a draught of approximately two feet below the top of the conning tower. Upon surfacing the draught in 'main ballast condition' was:

Forward
Port 13 feet 11¼ inches (4.248 m)
Starboard 13 feet 9½ inches (4.204 m)
Mean 13 feet 10⅜ inches (4.226 m)

Aft
Port 14 feet 7½ inches (4.458 m)
Starboard 14 feet 5½ inches (4.407 m)
Mean 14 feet 6½ inches (4.432 m)

It was thus deduced from this trial that, in water of a similar specific density, *Thetis* must have this draught for her to be in 'main ballast condition', such that by filling her main tanks she would then be enabled to submerge.

Before the trials were completed, three inclining tests were conducted, as were the final ballast and trimming trials—following the ballast adjustments which had been made earlier. During these trials, further ballast adjustments had to be made, but even then the vessel was still 'light'. Being 'light' meant that the submarine could not submerge by just relying on the hydroplanes.

Prior to the preliminary torpedo trials, which were conducted between 6 and 10 March 1939, Lieutenant Woods had drawn the attention of Cammell Lairds's staff to the fact that the clips on the watertight door between the torpedo compartment and the tube compartment were not finished to specification. The bulkhead door was secured by eighteen butterfly fittings, the bolts of which were detailed as being of equal length, but this was not the case. A casual observer might have considered this attention to detail as being pedantic, but when securing the watertight door in an emergency—as was to happen in the near future—it was essential for the door to be closed as quickly as possible. But, as fitted, the bolts hung down, thus ensuring that efficiency was impaired; the doors taking longer to close than their design requirement. During torpedo trial tests, a critical phase in any submarine's fitting-out, it was standard procedure for the equipment itself to be operated by the boat's builders, but under the direct control of Navy personnel—and there were several!

The primary purpose of these trials, which were carried out in the wet basin, was to check that everything relating to the torpedo tubes and torpedoes was in good and effective working order, and especially the torpedo firing systems and capability. The trials also included ensuring that the bow caps and bow shutters—the 'doors' in the hull which open immediately prior to a torpedo being fired—met the design specification. Because the trials were of such importance, a retired submarine officer of many years' experience, Commander Alfred Maguire, RN, was invited to be present and conduct the torpedo trials. Keeping within the legal requirements of the contract, employees of

Cammell Lairds worked the equipment during these trials. Mr H. Eccleston, one of Lairds's engine fitters, worked the bow cap levers. Also, because the tubes themselves had been manufactured at the Royal Dockyard in Chatham, personnel from that establishment were also drafted into Birkenhead to check all of their fittings and systems before the trials commenced.

Maguire observed all operations during the trials, including the loading of torpedoes into every one of the tubes. After the torpedo trials had been conducted and completed to everyone's satisfaction, Maguire noted in his report that there were sundry minor modifications and adjustments which needed to be made; perhaps the most important being to stop the ingress of water from Nos 3 and 4 bow caps. Maguire also stated in his report that the hydraulic bow cap indicator system was to be completed and tested. He also observed that there were some slight deposits of rust which had built up on the tube walls. In part this was to be expected, as the submarine had spent many months in the fitting-out basin. He suggested that, after removing any traces of rust, all of the tubes should be protected by a two-stage coating of bitumastic enamel. As Cammell Lairds did not have the necessary expertise to apply the coating, and, because it was deemed to be critical, a specialist company, Wailes Dove Bitumastic Ltd of Hebburn, was sub-contracted to carry out the work. Applying the double protective layer of bitumastic and enamel to the insides of all of the torpedo tubes was considered to be one of the most delicate and critical operations during the fitting-out process. This final preparation of the tubes was carried out on-site. The main reasoning behind the requirement of a mirror-finish on the inside of the tubes, and the special coating being applied, was to ensure the most efficient exit of the torpedoes into the open sea. Although the tubes had been manufactured by the Royal Dockyard at Chatham, the process of applying the bitumastic solution was, similar to Cammell Lairds's, not a process for which they had the requisite skills. Admiralty-approved companies, specializing in this kind of operation, were always preferred. Wailes Dove sent two, well-experienced, men to do this work—Mr Hughes, whose job it was to apply the bitumastic solution to all of the tubes, and Mr Stinson, who was in charge of the enamelling process. The work was started by the two men on a Friday morning and completely finished the following Monday evening—as Stinson was to later testify. Some weeks after the job had been completed, the Admiralty's assistant overseer, Edward Grundy, declared that after completely checking the work carried out by the workmen from Wailes Dove, he found that the rear doors in the torpedo tubes had not been coated with an enamel layer as specified. This particular detail, perhaps insignificant in itself, was to open totally divergent opinions as to what exactly did happen when the issue was raised at the public Inquiry. Wailes Dove's employee, Mr Stinson, the painter, was quite categorical in his evidence, stating the all of the work had been completed as specified in the contract. The Admiralty's assistant overseer had a diametrically opposed view, claiming that the work had not been completed. It was accepted that Grundy had little experience of checking bitumastic enamel, coupled with the fact that, at the time, he was overseeing work on another six vessels in various shipyards; the upshot being that he was only able to visit *Thetis*, perhaps, twice a week. This direct contradiction in witness testimony was to have a profound impact, affecting the findings of the subsequent Inquiry, and, it was for this reason that the dates when this work was carried out proved to be of such critical importance. What is known is that the work was carried out by Wailes Dove employees between 13 and 17 May. It was then up to Mr William Taylor, Cammell Lairds's charge-hand painter, to inspect the job on behalf of the company, and, assuming that the work was found to be satisfactory, a second and final inspection would be conducted by Mr Edward Grundy, the assistant Admiralty overseer. However, at the Tribunal, Grundy claimed that he had carried out an interim inspection of the work on 16 May, crucially, before the bitumen coating had been applied to No. 5 tube, whereas Taylor was insistent that Grundy had inspected the completed work on 17 May. The only firm conclusion that can be drawn from this evidence is that, for whatever reason, a thorough inspection of the completed work was never carried out.

It was also stated at the subsequent Tribunal that, during the torpedo equipment trials, number five tube was used for firing purposes many times. Maguire noted in his rough report—issued before he left the yard—that there were excessive amounts of dirt around all of the working parts, which he considered to be most unsatisfactory. He also made reference to the fact that much of the working gear was in an unprepared state, with several pipes being disconnected, and some not even made. He made it abundantly clear that this situation could not be tolerated.

Amongst several other points which were included in Maguire's rough report was a reference to the incomplete state of the bow cap indicator system—a point which Lieutenant Woods had made some time previously. Maguire also reinforced another observation which Lieutenant Woods had drawn attention to, and this was the rectification work needed on the bulkhead watertight door at No. 25 bulkhead. A final recommendation made by Maguire was that gauges should be fitted to every bow cap telemotor receiver, to give a clear indication of the pressure on each.

Commander Maguire in his evidence to the Inquiry stated that during the torpedo firing trials, on at least one occasion, he saw the control lever at the NEUTRAL position after an operation had been carried out, and he then gave instructions that the levers were to be put into the OPEN or SHUT position and kept there until a further order was given.

A contrary view was taken by Mr F. Shaw, an employee of Cammell Lairds. He was present at these trials of the bow caps, and was also Eccleston's foreman. He said in his evidence before the Tribunal that they did not make a practice of leaving the levers in the NEUTRAL position. They always left them in the SHUT position.

Lieutenant Commander E. R. C. MacVicker was the Submarine Command Escape Officer. On 31 March he carried out his inspection of the Davis Submarine Escape Apparatus (DSEA) on board *Thetis*. He found the equipment to be totally satisfactory. During the same inspection, Lieutenant Commander MacVicker also examined the two indicator buoys. He found these to be in position and quite satisfactory. Lieutenant Commander MacVicker, after his inspection of the escape chambers, found that the operating wheel on the after side of the after escape chamber was in such a position that it was difficult to get sufficient purchase to work it. He recommended that a suitable claw spanner be supplied in order to rectify this situation.

With regards to the carrying of DSE apparatus, there are specific Admiralty orders prescribed for diving trials. These regulations state that there should be one DSEA for each person on board during diving, plus one third of this number. Accordingly, the Admiralty provided 131 sets for the use of those on board the *Thetis* during her diving trials, making the assumption that the total complement would be ninety-eight persons—in the event there were 103 people on board that day. The Admiralty also supplied five watertight torches for use on board *Thetis*.

Having completed her initial trials relatively unscathed, the next stage in the exhaustive trial programme was the machinery trials; these were to be held in Liverpool Bay on 14 April 1939. The trials themselves were prior to full sea trials; the engines were only to be run for eight hours, as opposed to the thirty hours which was required before the formal acceptance of the vessel by the Admiralty. Partway through the trial the port engine, one of the boat's two Sulzer engines, failed. Following a thorough investigation, it was established that failure was due to a lack of cooling water circulating in the engine. This in turn was due to the circulating pump's main spindle shattering because of metal fatigue. It transpired that there was a design flaw in the pump, possibly exacerbated by Cammell Lairds having manufactured the spindle from a material different from that which had been suggested by Sulzer. Cooling water is essential in engines of this type, as it ensures that the temperature of the oil circulating around the engine is maintained at an acceptable level. More trouble was to beset the accident-prone submarine. When repairs to the circulating pump had been carried out, the vessel set out once again to complete the earlier, abortive, eight-hour engine trial. The tests being successfully completed, *Thetis* made her way back to the wet basin in the shipyard in the late evening of 18 April 1939. Unfortunately, there was another vessel berthed alongside of the north wall of the wet basin, the United Molasses tanker *Athel Duchess* (8,940 gross tons). *Thetis* collided with the ship causing damage to both. The repair costs of both vessels had to be borne by Cammell Lairds. Although there was no appreciable damage to either vessel, there was enough to cause further delays in the trials programme. *Thetis* had a spell in dry dock, where a new propeller and propeller shaft were cannibalised from *Taku* which was under construction. In this way, any delays in the completion of *Thetis* sea trials could be kept to a minimum. The damage to *Athel Duchess* was less severe, being limited to remedial work on the single propeller shaft and two blades on the propeller itself. However, the repair bill for the two vessels was still in excess of £1,000—a significant amount at the time.

Immediately before commencing her dive trials, *Thetis* needed to be issued with Cammell Lairds's certificate of seaworthiness, whereby they categorically stated that, as the boat's builders, they were satisfied that all design specifications had been adhered to, and that the boat complied with all requirements for strength, stability and all other aspects of seaworthiness, even though there were elements where the over-riding criteria which defined the term 'seaworthiness' had not been completely fulfilled. With this in mind, additional statements were added, to the effect that the vessel would be seaworthy, in all respects, before she left the Birkenhead shipyard for her dive trials which were scheduled for 30 April 1939. The certificate was signed by a senior member of Cammell Lairds's staff. On behalf of the Admiralty, final inspection of *Thetis* was the responsibility of Principal Ship Overseer, Lieutenant A. Hill, and his agreement was necessary before the certificate could be countersigned by himself, Lieutenant Commander Bolus, Mr R. D. Glenn, Commissioned Engineer, RN, and District Electrical Engineer Bowden.

On 30 April 1939, HMS *Thetis* sailed from the River Mersey, *en route* for the River Clyde. Her official sea trials for engines, steering and diving were intended to be carried out up in Scotland. The traditional trial diving ground for Royal Naval submarines is Gare Loch on the Clyde, favoured because of its natural protection. Also, the trial dives would be able to take place less than a mile offshore. However, on the voyage up to Scotland a number of events occurred which, effectively, ensured that it would not be able to conduct further trials, and especially not the dive trial. It seemed that *Thetis* was destined to be dogged with one sort of disaster or another.

Even though *Thetis* was still not, officially, a naval vessel, it was custom and practice in these circumstances for the commander designate, in this case Lieutenant Commander Bolus, to issue the commands. Accordingly, Bolus issued an order to make a change in direction to port. Immediately, *Thetis* responded by turning towards starboard. Not expecting an occurrence such as this, Bolus, making further tests, gave a command to bear starboard— *Thetis* responded by moving in a port direction. Personnel on board began to question just how the Certificate of Seaworthiness had been signed, especially having been subjected to detailed Admiralty scrutiny. It would appear that the connections on the steering gear mechanisms had been configured in some bizarre reverse manner. Consultation amongst senior shipboard personnel resulted in the decision to continue with the trials, and make any compensatory adjustments in directional control.

But, there were further setbacks and complications; it was discovered that the operating gear of the forward hydroplanes was not working satisfactorily, thus affecting the diving capability of the submarine. The Principal Ship Overseer, Lieutenant A. A. F. Hill, together with his assistant, Mr Frank Bailey, were the Admiralty's senior representatives on board, and thus bore responsibility to ensure that Cammell Lairds fulfilled their contractual duties to the letter.

For diving and surfacing *Thetis* had two sets of hydroplanes, fore hydroplanes and after hydroplanes. Following suitable ballast and trim adjustments, the after hydroplanes were raised. The forward hydroplanes were then activated, thus increasing the angle of the dive—but nothing happened! The forward hydroplanes had jammed, rendering the submarine incapable of diving. Also, the after periscope hoist press was inoperative. As Lieutenant Hill's main role as Principal Ship Overseer was to ensure compliance to contract, after a brief consultation with Lieutenant Commander Bolus, they were forced to conclude that, for now, it was imperative for the dive trials to be curtailed and *Thetis* to return so that yet more remedial work could be carried out at Cammell Lairds. Charts were called for and, in a hastily convened conference between Lieutenant Commander Bolus, Hill and Hill's assistant, Frank Bailey, it was agreed that permission be sought from the Admiralty to conduct the remaining trials in Liverpool Bay, subject to the remedial repairs being completed satisfactorily. Some days later the permission was granted by the Admiralty.

Once again, *Thetis* had to return to Birkenhead for repair work to be carried out. Commander Maguire was called back to re-assess the situation. The majority of recommendations in his earlier report had been complied with and completed, but there was still the outstanding question of the bow cap indicator light. This hydraulically operated mechanism would clearly indicate when the bow cap was fully open. During his re-assessment, he also noted that there was now some partial ingress of water through No. 6 bow cap, but stated that it would be speculation to attribute the cause—there could be any number of reasons, ranging from perished rubber seals on the bow cap to an obstruction causing the bow cap to malfunction.

The catalogue of mishaps continued when, towards the end of May, *Thetis* was being fuelled ready to resume her previously aborted trial dives. Unfortunately, as the fuel was being pumped in under high pressure, one of the pressure relief valves in the fuel line blew, causing heavy oil to be deposited in several machinery spaces, including the main control room. The area housing the submarine's batteries—which came into use during underwater propulsion—was covered in fuel oil. There was no alternative but to remove all of the batteries, weighing upwards of half a ton each, for inspection. Again, the cost of this operation and further delay had to be borne by Cammell Lairds.

When all of the remedial work had been completed, the Admiralty were sent the revised, and final, detailed diving trials and completion programme by Cammell Lairds. Although the diving trials were, by far, the most important of the trials to be completed, there were other outstanding trials which *Thetis* had yet to successfully complete, including auxiliary steering trials at full power in order to test the telemotor system; compass adjustment, some diesel-electric tests and the testing of the after hydroplanes on secondary power. It was anticipated that the programme would take a total of fourteen days, beginning with the dive trials on 1 June 1939, somewhere beyond the Bar Lightship in Liverpool Bay. The location itself was classified information for security reasons.

It was hoped that the outcome of this two-week programme would result in the final phases of preparation—victualing, gunnery inspection and cleaning—before *Thetis* was finally delivered to the Royal Navy to join the Fifth Submarine Flotilla on 15 June 1939.

CHAPTER 2

Thursday 1 June 1939

There was an early sunrise on the morning of Thursday 1 June 1939. HMS *Thetis* was berthed on the east side of Cammell Lairds's wet basin, unobtrusively awaiting the final days of construction and trialling. She was proudly flying the White Ensign, often referred to as St George's Ensign, on her masthead. Although, technically, not a Royal Naval commissioned boat as yet, it was traditional during the last weeks of construction and certainly before final sea trials were commenced, for the boat to assume, unofficially, Royal Naval status.

The day before, 31 May 1939, was also a very significant day in the life of Mr A. E. Godfrey, master of the *Grebe Cock*—a tug of 169 gross tons, owned by the Liverpool Screw Towing and Lighterage Company. Mr Godfrey had worked on tugs for more than thirty-five years, and, for many of them, as master. For the last two years he had been master of the *Grebe Cock*, one of the company's fleet of ten 'Cock' tugs. The tug itself had actually been built at Cammell Lairds some four years earlier in 1935. The orders that he was given that day required him to be at Cammell Lairds's wet basin, just across the other side of the River Mersey, at nine o'clock the following morning. After alerting his six-man crew of their task, he began to make preparation for the next day's work. His orders had been somewhat vague, merely stating that he was to attend and escort a new vessel, HMS *Thetis*, which would be leaving the shipyard to complete diving and other equipment trials. The only other instruction that Godfrey was given, was to ensure that he carried a small boat on the tug, so that non-essential personnel on the submarine could be disgorged before *Thetis* made her final dive trials; the non-essential personnel would mainly be Cammell Lairds's staff.

After months of preparation, during which time *Thetis* had encountered many setbacks, activity on board was now frenetic, with numerous last minute checks and adjustments being made—and, in the case of *Thetis*, double checks! The all-important port torpedo tubes had been closed down, the power to them turned off, and the indicator showed that they were in a SHUT position. Firm instructions were then given to ensure that they remained in this condition. Similarly, the three starboard tubes were locked in the SHUT position.

When all of the necessary engine preparations for sea had been completed, the main engines were started. However, some critical measurements still needed to be taken—the draught and trim of the boat. The Foreman Fitter of the Engineering Department of Cammell Lairds, Mr Robinson, was asked to 'blow' *Thetis's* main tanks. This was done to ensure that there was no evidence of water in the tanks. By introducing high pressure air into the tanks—'blowing' them—any extraneous seawater was forced out. Any water in tanks which were not meant to have water in would affect the draught and trim of the boat. With the tanks having been 'blown', it was now possible for Lieutenant Woods, accompanied by Lairds's Assistant Shipyard Manager, John Rowe, to accurately measure the draught and trim of the boat before setting out on her trials.

So, at quarter past nine, whilst the submarine was still in the wet basin, the final draughts were taken by Mr Rowe. The draughts were as follows:

Forward
Port 13 feet 3¾ inches (4.058 m)
Starboard 13 feet 1¼ inches (3.994 m)
Mean 13 feet 2½ inches (4.026 m)

Aft
Port 14 feet 8¾ inches (4.489 m)
Starboard 14 feet 6¼ inches (4.426 m)
Mean 14 feet 7½ inches (4.458 m)

or an overall mean draught of 13 feet 11 inches (4.242 m). Mr Rowe later told the Tribunal of Inquiry that he gave these draughts to two of the Admiralty Overseers: Principal Ship Overseer, Mr Hill, and Assistant Overseer, Mr Gisborne. Not being satisfied with these readings, as they yielded a significant list to port, Mr Gisborne asked Mr Rowe to take the draughts again when the ship was ready for leaving. The readings were taken again just before the submarine was due to sail at 1000 hours.

The following results were recorded:

Forward
Port 13 feet 8 inches (4.166 m)
Starboard 13 feet 4¾ inches (4.083 m)
Mean 13 feet 6³/₈ inches (4.124 m)

Aft
Port 14 feet 7½ inches (4.458 m)
Starboard 14 feet 4½ inches (4.382 m)
Mean 14 feet 6 inches (4.420 m)

However, instead of correcting the list to port, the 'corrections' that had been made during the interim period only served to exacerbate the problem. The submarine now had a greater list to port than previously recorded. It was suggested that by filling the starboard tubes, the problem could be rectified.

It can also be observed when looking at these two sets of readings that, between the hours of 0915 hours and 1000 hours when the submarine sailed, the mean draught of the submarine had changed—both for'd and aft. Mr Bailey commented that she was a bit 'light' aft when handed these draughts from Mr Rowe. The exact amount of water ballast that had been taken on board in order to adjust the draught was not known, but, what was known was that whilst Mr Rowe was taking the last trim readings, the Admiralty Overseers, Mr Hill and Mr Gisborne, were still having the trim of the boat adjusted ready for sailing. There was an elaborate procedure to be followed. Mr Hill gave the trim statement to Mr Robinson, Cammell Lairds's foreman fitter, for him to put the trim on the boat. In turn, Mr Robinson then handed the statement to one of Cammell Lairds's engine fitters, Mr Eccleston, and he

HMS *Thetis* being launched into the River Mersey on 29 June 1938. (*From* SOS *Thetis, Hans Müller Verlag, Dresden, 1943*)

then actually put the trim on. But, even this action was carried out under the close supervision of one of the assistant Admiralty Overseers.

Mr Rowe said that Mr Hill only came on board *Thetis* a few minutes before she actually sailed. Mr Hill remarked to the Admiralty's Chief Constructor, Mr Bailey, that they would have to fill, or that they could fill, the starboard tube or tubes. This was said after Mr Rowe had pointed out to Mr Bailey that the port side was somewhat deeper than the starboard side.

Meanwhile, leaving her berth in Alexandra Dock, *Grebe Cock* crossed the River Mersey and made her way to Cammell Lairds's wet basin for 0900 hours—the time which Captain Godfrey had been instructed to arrive; but, other than that, he was still mystified as to what his duties for the day would entail. Leaving the tug, he sought information from Lairds's dock master, Mr Taylor, but Taylor was no wiser. The only vestige of comfort which he could offer was that *Grebe Cock* would be taking a few passengers when they attended the *Thetis*. But, Godfrey needed orders as to how the *Grebe Cock* was to be deployed throughout the trials. Fortunately, as Godfrey and Taylor walked over to where the *Thetis* was berthed, they bumped into Lieutenant Commander Bolus—*Thetis's* captain. Initial introductions were made and there was a brief conversation between Godfrey and Bolus. It was a delicate discussion because, as Bolus pointed out, the trials were being carried out, technically, by staff from Cammell Lairds. Bolus did say that he wanted the tug to keep in touch with the submarine during the trials. Godfrey's next question was an important one. He asked at what speed *Thetis* would be cruising. Receiving the answer of between fifteen and sixteen knots, there was an immediate disconnect, as *Grebe Cock's* maximum speed was less than twelve knots. Bolus, having been made aware of this fact, agreed to accommodate this difference. Shortly after, when Bolus was asked if he would require *Thetis* to be towed from the basin, his answer was firm and unequivocal. He said that she would leave the basin under her own steam.

Whilst still on the submarine, Godfrey spoke to the boat's young pilot for the day, twenty-five year old Norman Willcox. He informed Godfrey as to the general area of the dive site. It was then agreed that *Thetis* and *Grebe Cock* would rendezvous at the Bar Lightship at mid-day, before moving to the dive site ready for the dive trials, which were scheduled for 1300 hours.

Before leaving Birkenhead however, *Grebe Cock* had to embark four additional members of crew; two Royal Naval personnel and two staff from Cammell Lairds. At the time of *Thetis's* dive trials, another submarine was being built for the Royal Navy at Cammell Lairds—HMS *Trident*. *Trident* had been launched on 7 December 1938 and was now almost halfway through the lengthy fitting-out period. As had been the case with *Thetis*, a number of key personnel were standing by during that time. Lieutenant Richard E. Coltart was one of the first to join her; he had served in the Royal Navy for thirteen years, the last seven in submarines. Bolus asked him to join the trials for that day and be based on *Grebe Cock*. He was to be responsible for communications between *Thetis* and *Grebe Cock*. This came a somewhat of a blow; Coltart had hoped to be on board *Thetis* during the trials, as this would have been good experience for him. The other crew member to join *Grebe Cock* from the Royal Navy was Leading Wireless Telegraphist V. J. Crosby, who was also standing by on the 'T' class submarine HMS *Trident*. He had been instructed to accompany Lieutenant Coltart on the *Grebe Cock*. Crosby, taking his orders from Lieutenant Coltart, would be required to send and receive any communications from *Thetis*. Additionally, Crosby would be required to keep an accurate log of all such messages together with the time of sending/receiving. He was also told to take his battery-operated Aldis lamp, so that radio silence could be maintained. This was an added precaution in order to ensure that no unfriendly shipping could pinpoint their position. The two Cammell Lairds staff, led by Mr E. J. Randles, were to be responsible for supervising the transfer from the *Thetis* to the *Grebe Cock* immediately before the diving trials began.

Grebe Cock slipped her moorings shortly before ten-thirty in the morning, arriving at the agreed rendezvous approaching mid-day.

Bolus had previously held discussions with Coltart regarding communications when *Thetis* was submerged; Coltart had suggested either sending small explosive charges overboard or tapping on *Grebe Cock's* hull. Both of these suggestions were dismissed by Bolus. He said that he would prefer to take a 360° sweep with the periscope immediately prior to diving, knowing full well that they would not be submerged long enough for any approaching vessel to impede them.

Coltart's involvement in the day's trials was clear; regarding his 'look-out' duties, he was to maintain *Grebe Cock* at a suitable distance from *Thetis*, and to keep watch on the submarine's mast, red flag and periscope whilst partially submerged; and, when fully submerged below periscope depth, to ensure that no surface vessels encroached into the dive area.

After commissioning, *Thetis* would join the Fifth Submarine Flotilla, whose home base was Fort Blockhouse at Gosport, Hampshire. The commander of the flotilla, Captain H. P. K. Oram, although not directly involved in the acceptance trials, had decided to pay a visit to Birkenhead, so that he could assess for himself, at first hand, the quality and general competence of the officers who would, collectively, be responsible for the boat in the future. And, as war with Germany was imminent, he also wanted to make an assessment of individual leadership qualities—as there would doubtless soon be many promotion opportunities.

Thetis was now nearing readiness for the dive trials. When she sailed, there was a total of 103 men on board. Her crew, five officers and forty-eight other ratings, were all on board and at their stations and, in addition, there was a total of nine other Royal Naval officers; five who were required to attend *Thetis* during her dive trials, coming from Submarine Headquarters, and the other four officers from other *Triton* class submarines which were being built at Cammell Lairds. There were another seven officials from the Admiralty, whose primary role was to have oversight of compliance to specification. Because of the contractual/legal requirements and the nature of the trials, whereby Cammell Lairds themselves had overall responsibility for the trials, they had deployed a total of twenty-six of their staff; including engine fitters, a number of foremen, electricians, ship fitters and a caulker, Mr W. B. Beatty, on board *Thetis*. Many of these men would not normally have been there, but, at that time, Cammell Lairds had a number of other ships under construction, and one of their most prestigious contracts—the building of the liner RMS *Mauretania* for the newly formed Cunard White Star Company— was, perhaps, the most important. Currently, she was away on trials in the Clyde, and many of Lairds's senior staff were on board. So, it was left to their deputies to carry out the required duties on board *Thetis*. There was also the additional incentive of bonus payments for the Lairds staff, which, in a time of pre-war austerity, was not to be sneezed at!

Vickers Armstrong had sent four of their employees from Barrow-in-Furness, as they had supplied some of the equipment in *Thetis*. There were another four people on board that day; an employee of Brown Bros, Mr D. N. Duncan; the Mersey Pilot, Mr N. D. Willcox, and two employees of City Caterers (Liverpool) Ltd.—the catering contractors for the day—Mr W. G. Bath and Mr G. H. Dobells. In total, 103 persons were on board *Thetis* as she left Lairds's wet basin on the morning of 1 June 1939.

Everything was now set for the trials to begin. Lieutenant Woods ordered that the gangway should be removed. On being informed of this, Lieutenant-Commander Bolus gave the order to start engines. Shortly after this *Thetis* slipped her moorings, whilst Bolus continued to issue orders through his brass megaphone. *Thetis* was now in the River Mersey and making her way to the Bar Lightship. The tide was beginning to ebb when *Grebe Cock* rendezvoused with *Thetis* at the Bar Lightship, just after mid-day. Everything was now set for the trials.

It was evident to Lieutenant Woods, from a note written at the bottom of the 'trim sheet', that all of the torpedo tubes were empty, save for the two bottom-most tubes—numbers five and six. Both of these tubes had been filled with seawater when the trim adjustments had been made in the wet basin. Vacuum tests were carried out before rendezvousing with *Grebe Cock*, and certainly before diving. The object of the vacuum test was to reveal any weak areas in the hull which might cause ingress of water when the submarine was submerged, and thus under a greater amount of external pressure from the seawater. In this test the air pressure, which was always maintained inside the submarine, was reduced. Any weakness would soon become manifest, and seepage of seawater into the internal working areas of the submarine would occur.

Sometime before the trials were due to begin, Lieutenant Commander Bolus gave Lieutenant Coltart a programme of events in the following terms:

HMS *Thetis*
Programme for Dive

Take draughts. F. A.
Disembark men not required for dive.
Open up for diving. Make diving signal.
Test H.P. blows on main tanks fitted. L.P. blowers on all tanks.
Vacuum test. Slow G.U
Submerge and obtain trim.
Test battery ventilation outboard trunks, W/T deck tubes, all T. T. drains, W.Cs and look through ship for leaks.
Surface and blow main tanks on blowers.
Stop. G.U slow.
Dive to periscope depth. Time.
Lower periscopes.
Dive to 60 feet. Close WT. doors at 60 feet.
Auxiliary drive.
Fire smoke candles.
Periscope depth 4–5 knots. Cheek by log.
Raise & Lower W/T mast.
Blow main tanks to put forward casing just awash (15 foot on gauges.).
Full speed. Cheek on log. 380 revs.
Forward Hydroplane trials.
Dive to periscope depth.
Stop end obtain trim.
Release indicator buoys.
Surface with L.P. air-take time for each tank.
Take draughts and condition of all tanks.

Also, as the officer in charge of communications between *Grebe Cock* and *Thetis*, Lieutenant Coltart ordered his wireless telegraphist V. J. Crosby, to signal *Thetis* in order to ascertain if she would be diving below periscope depth. Crosby was well-experienced in his role, having served in his current capacity for seven years on submarines.

In reply to Coltart's signal, Bolus signalled, 'No, we will have you in view with our periscope and red flag showing above the surface.'

Godfrey responded by ensuring that *Grebe Cock* was kept well astern of *Thetis*. Bolus then communicated, from his station near to the Bar Lightship, that he was about to make necessary compass adjustments. At 13.30 *Thetis* signalled that they were about to carry out the turning trials, which were to be carried out at full speed.

Preparations were now well underway on the submarine for the first dive trial to commence in slow time. The reasoning behind the dive trial being conducted in slow time was not due to any inexperience on the part of the crew; its design purpose was to ensure that all equipment and machinery functioned as it should, and complied with design specifications. Final preparations having been completed, Bolus then made it known that any people wishing to leave before the dive began should make their way to the bridge, ready to be transferred to the *Grebe Cock*. There was no response—it appeared that everyone on board wanted to experience the dive trial. That being so, Bolus ordered the diving signal to be sent to the centre of control operations at Fort Blockhouse. Finally Bolus was informed by First Lieutenant Chapman that all external vents were now closed and the engine exhaust secured. *Thetis* was shut off and ready for diving.

Before issuing his dive command, Bolus signalled *Grebe Cock*, asking her to close. He then called out through a megaphone, 'I shall not be disembarking anybody'. He asked *Grebe Cock* to take station half a mile distant on his port quarter, and stated that his diving course would be 310°.

It soon became clear that Willcox was completely disregarding specific orders which had been previously issued by the Superintendent of Pilotage, that, at the express wish of the contractors—Cammell Lairds—the pilot should be discharged at the Bar Lightship, before *Thetis* embarked on her dive trials. This order was known to the pilot, Norman Willcox, those on board the pilot cutter and Lieutenant Commander Bolus on *Thetis*. However, when the pilot cutter came closer to *Thetis* so that the pilot could disembark, it was clear from his body language and signalling that he had no intention of leaving the submarine. Pilot Bibby, in command of the pilot cutter that day, observed that *Thetis* was not flying any flag to give an indication that Willcox was leaving. And, when hailed through a megaphone, Willcox did not give any verbal response, but merely waved his arms in a gesture which showed that he would not be leaving. Bibby made a second attempt, but it was self-evident that *Thetis* was not slowing down. Orders were then given for the pilot cutter to return to port.

Shortly afterwards the bridge party, Lieutenant Commander Bolus, Captain Oram, Leading Telegraphist Allen and the Mersey Pilot Norman Willcox, made their way down to the control room. This action appeared to the observers on *Grebe Cock* to be contrary to issued protocol; namely that, upon reaching the Bar Lightship, the pilot would leave *Thetis* and be transferred to the pilot boat. Mr Randles, Cammell Lairds's representative on *Grebe Cock* commented on this, only to be told by Captain Godfrey that that was highly unlikely, as *Thetis* was now passing the pilot cutter at speed.

One of Cammell Lairds's senior members of staff who was on board, Mr Frank Shaw, a charge hand engineer fitter, had responsibility for the port engine—that is, until *Thetis* arrived at her dive station. Then, during the dive itself, he was required to remain in the control room. When *Thetis* arrived on station for the dive trial, the main engines were stopped and Shaw duly left the engine room and proceeded to his dive station as had been requested. It was then some time, perhaps upwards of half an hour, before the trial dive was attempted. During this immediate pre-dive period, First Lieutenant Chapman was instructed to check every valve in the boat which was connected, in any way, with the dive, and thorough vacuum checks were also carried out—it being critical that no uncalled-for water came into the vessel.

The lower conning tower hatch had been closed; the submarine was now secure and ready for diving. The first order of the dive sequence was issued by Bolus, that the main tanks should be flooded in slow time. Seawater came cascading into number one tank, and tank numbers four, five and six, sending plumes of exhaust air/water high into the sky. The noise of this escape could be heard on *Grebe Cock*, some half a mile away.

Whenever a submarine is about to dive, a klaxon is sounded by the captain; this alerts all crew to be ready at their designated dive station. But, as this was a trial dive, and would be conducted in slow time, there was no need to sound the klaxon. Naval personnel were fully aware of their respective dive stations. Lieutenant Woods and Able Seaman S. Crombleholme were stationed in the torpedo compartment. Crombleholme's attention was focused on number one tube's main vent, and the auxiliary vent located in the tube space. Watching the number two main vent was Able Seaman J. H. Turner. Another crew member in that area was Petty Officer E. Mitchell. He was on the telephone in conversation with Engine Room Artificer H. G. Howells, who was stationed on the after side of number 25 bulkhead.

Once the requisite tanks had been filled, the submarine should have been in a state of neutral buoyancy, whereby the submarine is neither rising nor submerging. When this state of neutral buoyancy is achieved, the fore and aft hydroplanes can be activated, and the submarine can, effectively, be driven under the water's surface. However, in the case of *Thetis*, a state of neutral buoyancy could not be attained on the first attempt—the submarine was still too 'light'. To counteract this condition, the order was given to flood the auxiliary tanks in an effort to attain neutral buoyancy. In total, more than two hundred tons of water ballast was taken on by *Thetis*, but she still, resolutely, stayed on the surface. It was evident, even at that early stage, that something was amiss.

During the whole of this period Captain Oram remained in the control room. With his expert knowledge, he was able to suggest that the major reason why the submarine was failing to dive was because of the fact that she was too 'light'. And thus the hydroplanes, both for'd and aft, were totally ineffective. Oram considered that the lightness tended to be at the for'd end of the boat. He asked Bolus if numbers five and six tubes were full of water. Somebody in the control room, not Bolus—it was never ascertained who—replied to the effect that he thought that the tubes were not full.

A clear difference of opinion then emerged. First Lieutenant Chapman stated, possibly to the unknown voice, that the submarine's log, as recorded at 10.55, noted that the order was given to flood tubes numbers five and six. The log, at 10.56, then recorded that tubes number five and six had been flooded. At this point there was a degree of confusion in the control room. Irrespective of whether or not the tubes had been flooded, it was now imperative that they were required to be in a flooded condition. Only by knowing, accurately, the state of flooding in tubes five and six, could other possible reasons for *Thetis* failing to dive be explored.

Systematically working through a diagnostic procedure, Lieutenant Woods gave orders for hydraulic pressure to be exerted on bow caps five and six. The hydraulic systems ensured that the bow caps, whilst still remaining closed, were in a state of readiness—should the need arise for them to be opened. The condition inside the tubes, whether they were flooded or not, was checked by opening the test cock in the rear doors of the respective tubes.

When number six tube was tested, the indications were that it was partially flooded, but number five tube appeared to be completely empty of any water. Now uncertain as to whether the tubes should be flooded or not, Lieutenant Woods returned to the control room to confer with First Lieutenant Chapman. After further examination of the trim chit, Chapman confirmed that the tubes should be in a flooded state. Seeking further verification, Lieutenant Woods asked Mr Robinson, one of Cammell Lairds's senior staff who was on board for the trials, whether numbers five and six tubes were meant to be flooded. Mr Robinson said that they were not meant to be flooded.

At the Inquiry into the disaster, Woods testified that typed out on the trim chit were the names or numbers of all the auxiliary and compensating tanks in the boat, and also information relating to Nos 5 and 6 torpedo tubes. Against each of the tanks was written in pencil or in ink the amount of gallons of water that was supposed to be in them, and against the words Nos 5 and 6 tubes were written in pencil or in ink the words 'FULL', although Woods later testified that he said that he did not think that they were full.

The perspective from the *Grebe Cock* was very different. After over thirty years' experience on tugs, Captain Godfrey had never experienced a submarine diving. But, even to his virgin eye, the erratic movements of *Thetis* looked somewhat bizarre to put it mildly. Godfrey and Lieutenant Coltart discussed the difficulties which were apparently being encountered by the submarine in her endeavours to dive. Godfrey had expected to see a seamlessly smooth operation when the submarine dived, but the scene which he witnessed was very different from this. The submarine undoubtedly appeared to be experiencing some extreme difficulty in diving, with the hydroplanes, seemingly, unable to perform their design function. In a valiant effort to uphold the honour of the Navy, Lieutenant Coltart diplomatically suggested that the *Thetis must be experiencing some unexpected difficulties.*

On the submarine itself, Woods' next step was to make an inspection of all of the bow cap indicators. The indicators were located on a panel between the port and starboard tubes on the forward bulkhead. At the later Inquiry, Woods was adamant in stating that all of the indicators were showing 'SHUT'. He opened the test cock for number one tube. There was small escape of air, but no water was evident.

Assisting Lieutenant Woods with these checks was Leading Seaman Walter Hambrook. The two men knew each other well, having served together before. There was an unstated trust between them, each having confidence in the other's knowledge and experience. From what they had found out to date, it appeared that only number six tube contained any water. Woods' idea was to open each of the tubes; in this way he could ensure that there was no leakage from the bow caps. The two men, working in tandem, systematically checked that the tubes were dry. They checked tubes number two, three and four. Number six tube was not tested, because Woods knew that there was some flooding in this tube.

Continuing their, now almost completed, tests, Woods opened number five test cock and found no trace of air or water. It was therefore safe to proceed in opening tube five's rear door. Leading Seaman Hambrook's role was to assist Woods to open the door, but this proved to be extremely difficult, as it was firmly secured. After having to use considerable force, Hambrook eventually got the door partially opened; a small trickle of water came out, but neither Woods nor Hambrook considered this to be unusual—thinking that it was probably water which hadn't drained away from the earlier wet basin trials.

But then, the door which Woods and Hambrook had managed to crack open burst open—all of a sudden there was an unleashed force of water being forced into the compartment. Taking cognisance of the personnel in the immediate vicinity, Woods noted that Able Seaman Crombleholme was at his station between numbers one and two tubes, charged with watching the tank vents. Lieutenant (Engineer) A. G. J. Jamison was also in the compartment—

he was standing-by *Trident* during her fitting-out, and had joined *Thetis* for experience during her sea trials. Woods frantically shouted two orders; he ordered everyone to leave the compartment, immediately; and, to Petty Officer Mitchell, who was still on the telephone, to tell the control room to 'blow' the main tanks. Engine Room Artificer Howells, also in the area, immediately followed Woods command and left the area.

Woods was to testify later that he was of the firm belief that number five bow cap was shut, and, because of this, considered that there must have been a fracture in number five tube. With hindsight, Woods accepted that, had he realised earlier that the number five bow cap was open, he might have been able to move the operating lever if it had been in the open position.

Because of injuries which Hambrook sustained during the inrush of water, Woods had to assist him out of the compartment, thus causing further delay before the port watertight door could be closed.

Whilst extreme difficulties were being experienced in the torpedo compartment, those in the control room were totally oblivious as to what was occurring just feet away from where they were. But then, all of a sudden, a strong blast of air engulfed the control room, and then, seconds later, the bow lurched downwards in an uncontrolled and erratic manner, flinging staff in all directions.

The scene being enacted on *Thetis* was being closely observed by all those on *Grebe Cock* some distance away. Leading Telegraphist Crosby also thought that *Thetis* was experiencing difficulty in diving because she was 'too light'. At one point her bow became submerged as her stern rose, but, shortly afterwards she levelled again. This manoeuvre happened for a second time—but then, unaccountably, *Thetis* suddenly plunged down and out of sight.

Although having no direct control of the submarine during the trials, because of years of experience and instinctive reactions, Oram told Bolus that the main tanks needed to be 'blown'—immediately. The force of the compressed air entering the tanks had the desired effect, in that the submarine's bow slowly began to rise again. The immediate danger had been averted, much to the relief of all 103 people on board.

Submariners are acutely aware of the dangers that they constantly face, so, when the rush of air, which was initially blowing towards the after end of *Thetis* turned and blew towards the for'd end, it became obvious to many on board that they'd failed in their attempt to avert disaster. Having expended much of *Thetis's* reserves of high pressure air, Bolus ordered a cessation of 'blowing' to the tanks in an effort to conserve the much needed compressed air. He also ordered that the five watertight doors at the bulkheads should be closed, and all un-necessary lights be switched off, so that battery power could be conserved.

The situation in the now-flooded torpedo compartment was becoming desperate. Judging from the level of water, it was clear to Woods that there was now a significant amount of water in the confined space, and that more water was rushing in as the bow slowly turned to adopt a downwards attitude. As other personnel had now vacated the area, as Woods had ordered, it was left for him to assist the injured Hambrook from the compartment before the port watertight door was closed. When questioned at the Inquiry, Woods admitted that the correct course of action would have been to have had the door closed, thus saving valuable seconds, but, in the process, surrendering the life of his colleague.

In desperate situations such as this, every second, literally, counts. It was noted at the Inquiry that Woods's noble act in attempting to save the life of Hambrook meant that for every second he was engaged in this endeavour, more water was continuing to cascade into the chamber. This act, whilst being selfless and courageous was, nonetheless totally misguided. If accepted procedure had have been followed and the bulkhead doors closed earlier, many more lives might have been saved. There were certainly enough precedents for Woods to have adopted a different approach.

The concept of survival when various compartments were flooded was well known to most personnel on board. To this end, when the torpedo compartment had been vacated, Lieutenant (Engineer) Jamison, from *Trident*, and Engine Room Artificer Howells strove to close the watertight door to stop further flooding into other compartments. This became increasingly more difficult as the bow took an even steeper angle downwards. In the original design for the watertight doors, the Admiralty had specified a quick-closing door, which was operated by a single central locking wheel. But, due to necessary cost-saving measures, the watertight doors fitted on *Thetis* were secured by a series of eighteen butterfly bolts located on the periphery of the doors. Although it was advantageous in cost terms, the use of this method of securing the watertight doors was a retrograde step. Apart from anything else, it took much longer to secure the doors—an important consideration when time was of the essence. To make matters worse, as the door in question opened towards the bow instead of away from it, the changing angle of the submarine made the task more difficult to accomplish. Try as they might, in the bitterly cold and wet conditions, it was virtually impossible to secure the watertight door, but, after much endeavour, Engine Room Artificer Howells eventually managed to get one of the eighteen clips secured. It was not enough to hold the force of water back, so water continued to cascade into the torpedo storage compartment.

As the situation deteriorated, a number of decisions had to be made—all of them critical to the well-being of the personnel on board that day. Making the decisions which would minimise the risk of losing lives was Bolus's major priority. It was a fine balance between continuing efforts to try to contain water in the areas which were already flooded, or sacrificing those areas and securing the for'd watertight compartments. In this area was the wardroom and some of the crew's quarters—but, more importantly, the battery storage room was located directly beneath the deck plates in this area. Bolus took the decision to sacrifice the areas where water had already entered, but aimed to ensure that the battery housing compartment was kept dry at all costs, knowing, as he did, that if any water reached this area chlorine vapours would soon permeate all of the surrounding areas. This eventuality would result in a slow and very painful death for all of those on board; Bolus felt that he had no option in deciding which course of action to take.

Although still in the torpedo stowage area, Woods and Mitchell were obviously aware as to everything that was happening around them. Self-preservation—a basic human instinct—assumed priority, but difficulties were encountered when trying to leave the compartment. Because of the now very steep angle of *Thetis*, they had to climb up and out of the compartment, which, in Woods's own words: 'I found great difficulty in climbing out of the compartment, due to the angle of the ship and the fact that tables, stools and boxes were falling from the aft end of the compartment on top of us. I slipped back several times, as my shoes were wet and slipping on the corticene (a linoleum-type of deck covering); Mitchell was ten seconds behind me'.

Even though it's a truism, men never want to lose their lives, so there was a scuffle as Arnold, and others, tried to shut the door—as Arnold later testified at the Tribunal. Several attempts were made to secure the door, but the men on the other side were just as intent on opening it, and thus escape to the safer side. It was quite a struggle, but eventually the door was secured when all of the men had clambered though. Even then, because of the sheer weight of the door, together with the angle at which the submarine was lodged, some difficulty was experienced in shutting it.

As a senior officer on board, and with all of the five watertight doors now closed, Woods reported the situation to the control room. As commander, it was clear to Bolus that he now needed to have an assessment made of the full extent of the damage. However, before giving orders for that operation to be expedited, he decided to run the engines at half-speed astern, hoping that *Thetis* would either surface or cause enough movement to make rescue a realistic possibility. Unfortunately, if anything, the movement which this order caused, tended to make the situation worse rather than better, as the submarine was now lodged at an increased angle. Reluctantly, Bolus gave the order to stop engines. The senior personnel on board, including Lieutenant Commander Bolus, First Lieutenant Chapman, Commissioned Engineer Glenn, Captain Oram and Admiralty Overseer Bailey then discussed the options that were still available to them. The consensus was that, one way or another, they needed to increase the ship's buoyancy. It looked as though there were two distinct possibilities here; either they could pump the water out through Number Five torpedo tube, or they could 'blow' it out using compressed air. It would undoubtedly help buoyancy if air could be 'blown' into the torpedo compartment.

As *Thetis* settled on a more even keel, Woods realized that the bow cap must have been open to allow such an ingress of water at such force. And then, immediately following this realisation, he instinctively knew that it must have been somebody under his command who had caused the disastrous error. After questioning Leading Seaman Hambrook, he (Hambrook) again confirmed that all the bow cap levers were parallel to each other, indicating that Number Five bow cap-operating lever, and the others were all SHUT. Hambrook was unequivocal in stating that all levers were parallel and 'correct'.

When *Thetis* finally settled on the seabed, the for'd and after indicator buoys were released. By way of further assessing the situation, Captain Oram made his way through to the forward escape chamber. He observed that the torpedo compartment was already more than half full of water, and the level was continuing to rise. Although one clip had been secured on the number twenty-five bulkhead door, it was having little real effect on the overall state of *Thetis*. As a submariner of many years' experience, he considered that their only option was to pump the water out—in his view, 'blowing out' under pressure was not an option. But, before any pumping could be started, it would first of all be necessary to close the rear torpedo door, and this could only be achieved if someone went back into the flooded compartment. Only then could the necessary valves be opened so that the water could be cleared from the compartment.

When later giving evidence to the Tribunal, Lieutenant Woods said that First Lieutenant Chapman had said that he would try to get through and close Number Five rear door. He wanted to make this effort on his own, even though Woods had told him that it would take two men to close the heavy door. The second part of the plan was to open up the two bilge suction valves at the after end of the torpedo stowage compartment. In this way, one valve would be able to suck water from the torpedo compartment, and the other would remove water from the torpedo tube itself.

First Lieutenant Chapman donned his Davis Escape Apparatus and went into the escape chamber—this being necessary for such an attempt to be made. It was left to Commissioning Officer Glenn to close and lock the door to the escape chamber once Chapman had entered. Having made the escape chamber secure, the 'flooding up' was started. When the valves opened, cold water entered, directly from the bay. As the depth of water increased in the chamber, Chapmen felt the pressure increasing—a pressure which was becoming unbearable, leading to severe pains in his chest and ears. The 'flooding up' had to be stopped when Chapman started banging on the door of the chamber, signalling that he needed to get out; nauseous feelings were overwhelming him.

Because of the intense pain that First Lieutenant Chapman was clearly under, the escape chamber was drained down, allowing Chapman to crawl out. It was all too evident that he was bitterly disappointed. The next attempt was made by Lieutenant Woods, accompanied by Petty Officer Ernie Mitchell. It was agreed that Woods would enter the flooded areas with a rope tied around his waist and attached to Mitchell—this was a safety measure to ensure that Woods could find his way back in the event of some unforeseen hazard.

There was a set procedure agreed before both men entered the escape chamber. They were both wearing the Davis Escape Apparatus as the chamber was 'flooded up'. As the depth of water inside the chamber increased, Mitchell indicated that he was experiencing extreme pressure on his ears, causing him some considerable pain. However, Woods did not stop the 'flooding up' process, obviously hoping that the pain would be overcome. But this did not happen; reluctantly, Woods had to give the signal to drain down the chamber again.

By this time Woods was completely exhausted, but once again he volunteered to make another attempt. He was given a little time to regain some of his lost energy before re-entering the escape chamber. This time, he was accompanied by another volunteer, from the crew; Petty Officer Smithers. The whole procedure was repeated and then the two men entered the escape chamber. The 'flooding up' process was started again, but, yet again, it was clear to Woods that Smithers was showing the usual signs of distress. Woods waited a little while before giving the signal to drain down. Some of the crew volunteered to make yet another attempt, but by this time Lieutenant Commander Bolus considered that enough was enough, and refused their request. He now thought that other ways of escape needed to be considered, namely, help from outside. Having now been firmly embedded on the sea bottom for some time, one or two problems were beginning to emerge. For one thing, the levels of carbon dioxide concentration were significantly increasing which, in a confined space such as this, would ultimately, be lethal. The temperature in the submarine was also increasing but was still bearable, and one or two significant leaks were causing more problems. To make matters worse, there was little or no food, as the compartments where food had been stored were both flooded.

Lieutenant Commander Bolus was constantly reviewing the situation, realising that as every minute passed, the men on board were facing ever-increasing risks, and were also growing more fatigued. He was also aware however that, by now, the Navy's 'Subsmash' procedure would have been activated; recognising that this was, perhaps, their best hope of survival. Unfortunately, when impacting on the seabed, *Thetis's* detection equipment had been irreparably damaged.

CHAPTER 3

Action Stations

During this time, the whole of the developing scene was being watched on the surface by the crew on board the *Grebe Cock*. As the submarine disappeared from sight, Godfrey observed that he hadn't liked the way that *Thetis* had dived. It was an observation made after many years at sea, although Godfrey's experience of watching submarines dive was limited to say the least. Lieutenant Coltart was more sanguine, stating that, had there been any problems, then *Thetis* would have released smoke signals or indicator lights, but this had not been the case. He saw no reason for concern. Lieutenant Coltart was quite convinced that *Thetis* would re-appear somewhere ahead of them.

With the passage of time, and with no discernible indicators as to *Thetis's* well-being or otherwise, Godfrey suggested to Coltart that they should move station, perhaps to somewhere in the general direction which they assumed that she would be heading; his idea being that they might just get some sign that everything was well with the submarine. But, Coltart declined this course of action. He considered that if *Thetis* did surface in the near future, then it could be anywhere in the vicinity and, by moving from station, *Grebe Cock* could end up in a dangerous position. But, as Godfrey pointed out, there was the tide to take into consideration. Because of tidal changes, *Grebe Cock* was, effectively, constantly changing her station. Coltart agreed that they should counteract the effect of these tidal changes and move station as and when Godfrey thought fit.

With the *Grebe Cock* on station and only moving to maintain her position against the tide, Mr Randles, Cammell Lairds's representative on board, together with Captain Godfrey and the two naval personnel, kept a vigilant look-out for any sightings of the submarine. But, even after many hours, no one had seen either smoke candles or indicator lights—a sure sign that the submarine was in some distress.

Later on, it emerged that *Grebe Cock* was equipped with a radio telephone, and, by using this, messages could be sent to Seaforth Radio station, and thus onwards to Fort Blockhouse, some two hundred and fifty miles distant. And, with concern now mounting regarding the well-being of the submarine, it was also evident that messages could be received from Fort Blockhouse, using the same lines of communication. Coltart immediately had a message sent to Fort Blockhouse asking for the duration of *Thetis's* dive trial—a vital piece of information which those on board *Grebe Cock* were not aware of; but, due to some unknown malfunction in the transmission equipment, there was some delay in the message getting through.

As the day progressed, there was some concern on Godfrey's behalf, in that, the tug was now drifting some way off station. Mentioning this fact to Lieutenant Coltart, they agreed that, because of the depth of the bay at that point—at least 130 feet—the two anchor chain cables could be joined end to end, thus ensuring that an anchorage could be made. The tug would normally operate in much shallower waters than this.

As his concern was rising, Coltart was anxious to make further contact with Fort Blockhouse: his intention being to alert the submarine nerve-centre, in the hope that they may see fit to activate the 'Subsmash' rescue operation; but, once again, there was difficulty in transmitting the message from *Grebe Cock*. Try as he might, all of Crosby's attempts to get a message through to the Seaforth Radio Station failed. He then tried to alert the pilot cutter at Port Lyness, in the hope that they could have a message transmitted, but again, that proved to be negative.

One of the major roles which was performed at Fort Blockhouse was to chart every single movement of all British submarines. Details were also logged relating to their dive times, dive endurance, position etc. It was the function of the Chief Yeoman of Signals to ensure that the Duty Commanding Officer was notified of any irregularities; for instance, if a submarine failed to surface on time, or failed to signal at a given time. He was also responsible for dealing with all incoming and outgoing communications.

There was a somewhat convoluted chain of command at Fort Blockhouse. The Rear Admiral (Submarines) was Rear Admiral B. C. Watson who was in overall command at Fort Blockhouse, but he was absent from the base on sick leave. Next in the chain was the Duty Staff Officer—a rotating role—which on 1 June was being filled by Commander George Barney Hamley Fawkes. However, it was the Duty Submarine Commanding Officer who was responsible for everyday issues, and on that day it was Commander Lancelot Milman Shadwell, although it should have been Captain Oram—but obviously, he was aboard the *Thetis*. However, during the day, Shadwell was aboard HMS *Winchelsea* engaged in an exercise in the English Channel, so the responsibility of command fell upon the shoulders of Lieutenant Commander Lipscombe.

Bolus's communication to Fort Blockhouse merely stated the estimated time for the dive, the duration and also the heading which the submarine was proposing to take; in fact, the bare minimum required under Naval protocol. Lipscombe received the message from the Chief Yeoman of Signals. Shadwell returned to his office sometime after four o'clock, just before Fort Blockhouse were expecting the surfacing signal to be received from *Thetis*.

Lipscombe was fully aware of the detail of the Admiralty Fleet Order which gave a prescribed and exact procedure to be adopted when a submarine could not be located when in home waters. Indeed, the time for *Thetis* to surface had now passed, but no surface signal had, as yet, been received. Keeping a watching brief on the situation, the Chief Yeoman of Signals informed Shadwell that the signal was late. He in turn put a call through to the Admiralty Operations Division at Whitehall, informing them that the submarine was, apparently, slightly overdue. He also asked if they were aware of anything further, to which the Admiralty responded negatively. Now becoming more concerned, Shadwell next put a call through to the shipyard, but they too had had no communication with *Thetis*.

The general consensus at that time was that, as the submarine was just out of the shipyard and on her first dive, any number of 'glitches' could have occurred, so there was no undue anxiety or concern from senior personnel at the Admiralty. However, the communications department at Fort Blockhouse, known as the Wireless Office, was asked to try to contact *Thetis* every few minutes in order to ascertain the situation on board. It was also at this point that Shadwell considered that he should inform Commander Fawkes—at least responsibility would then be passed upwards.

Having made an assessment of the situation after having considered all of the information available and then consulting the relevant charts of Liverpool Bay, Fawkes felt compelled to take some further action. His first action was to inform various officers and other authorities. He called the Admiralty to apprise them of the latest position, and then he contacted Watson, and also Watson's chief of staff Captain Ian Agnew Patterson Macintyre. However, Fawkes was unable to contact Macintyre and the situation was becoming more critical as time was passing—it was time for positive action.

After receiving a message from *Grebe Cock* on station in Liverpool Bay, Fawkes contacted Duty Officer Baynes at Plymouth, suggesting that he (Fawkes) was not of the opinion that an accident had befallen *Thetis*, but confessed that he had some anxiety with regards to the situation. However, Bayne's later testimony gave a distinctly different 'take' on the conversation. He was of the opinion that Fawkes had clearly stated that there was no cause for anxiety, as it was expected that the *Thetis* would surface in the near future. Baynes was aware that HMS *Brazen* was not too far from the estimated location of *Thetis* and she could be re-tasked to assist in any rescue operation. *Brazen* also had the advantage that she was now equipped with the latest submarine detection system, which would enable them to locate *Thetis* with relative ease. However, Fawkes appeared to be reluctant to take any affirmative action. As *Thetis* was now more than an hour overdue, Baynes considered that action must be taken. Fawkes was still reluctant, so, rather than taking the initiative himself, he once again contacted the relevant authority at the Admiralty in Whitehall. In fact, ultimately, it was Baynes who took the initiative in re-tasking *Brazen*. He communicated the known details relating to *Thetis,* and requested that they change course and attempt to locate her.

Coltart's message eventually got through to Fawkes. Shadwell was instructed to reply, giving Coltart the information that he had requested, namely, that *Thetis* had dived at 1340 hours, and that the dive was scheduled to last for three hours. The message, communicated via Seaforth Radio, gave no indication as to the mounting concern for the submarine which both Plymouth and Fort Blockhouse were experiencing. Indeed, the message itself was difficult enough to communicate, in that, having been received at the radio station, it then had to be forwarded to *Grebe Cock*. This task presented its own difficulties; it was not easy trying to communicate with a tugboat at sea which wasn't fitted with sophisticated telecommunications equipment. Upon receiving the message, Coltart—being a submariner of some experience—realised that, because the situation had now assumed such proportions, it would be being addressed at a much higher level than his rank warranted.

As time passed, and being conscious of Coltart's message, Fawkes became more concerned, fearing that he must, at some stage, make the assumption that some catastrophe had overtaken *Thetis*. He notified Bayne, and tentatively suggested that the time had now arrived for further action to be taken. In turn, Bayne contacted *Brazen* again, and ordered that she proceed, at full speed, to seek and locate *Thetis*.

Fawkes was then ordered to contact the Duty Commander at the Admiralty, and inform him that the personnel at Fort Blockhouse were now taking the view that some form of mishap or accident had befallen *Thetis*, due to the fact that she still hadn't surfaced. The Duty Commander at the Admiralty immediately contacted the Air Ministry who then instigated a comprehensive air-search of the Bay.

The situation was now assuming a different order of magnitude in that, according to the strict protocol which was laid down in the Admiralty Fleet Order, overall command was now vested with the Commander-in-Chief of the Home Port in whose area the accident occurred, and this was the Commander-in-Chief, Plymouth—Admiral Sir Martin Eric Dunbar-Nasmith VC, who now assumed full command of any rescue operation that might be mounted.

Soon afterwards the full-scale search and rescue operation, known as

'Subsmash', swung into operation, in compliance with paragraph five in the Fleet Orders. 'Subsmash' meant that all of the Navy's extensive resources would now be deployed in locating *Thetis* and rescuing those on board. The Mine Sweeping Flotilla was ordered to attend the scene, as indeed was the dedicated diving vessel, HMS *Tedworth*, which was moored up in Scotland on the Clyde. The Sixth Destroyer Flotilla which had underwater search equipment was also tasked to be available at the scene of concern.

When Macintyre arrived back at Fort Blockhouse, he made his own appraisal of the situation by conferring with and receiving situational reports from his colleagues. He then had HMS *Winchelsea* placed on standby, ready to make the voyage to Liverpool Bay, so that he could direct operations at the rescue scene.

With the necessary resources having now mobilised to effect a successful search and rescue operation, Nasmith's next action was to contact a former colleague of his, Commander Hubert Viner Hart, RNR (Ret.), who was the Water Bailiff and Marine Surveyor of the Mersey Docks and Harbour Board. Nasmith was aware that, in his role at Liverpool, and with his many years of experience, Hart could reach the rescue scene and give his assistance considerably ahead of any of the Royal Navy's support vessels.

Hart later recounted that when he was contacted during the evening of 1 June, he was given to understand that it was feared that some form of accident had befallen *Thetis*, and further, that in his (Hart's) role at Liverpool, he might be in a position to render immediate assistance to the stricken submarine. After that telephone conversation Hart contacted the Shore Superintendent

Lifeboats in the search area where, it was thought, *Thetis* had gone down, only to find later that the position as reported was incorrect. (*From 'SOS Thetis', Hans Müller Verlag, Dresden, 1943*)

at Liverpool and asked if he could make available the port's Wreck Master, Charles Brock, and some other staff—including divers—for a rescue attempt in Liverpool Bay. The *Vigilant*, which was one of the port's hydrographic and salvage vessels, was berthed at the port's Princes Landing Stage. Hart said that he had to sail as soon as possible, as the situation in the bay was critical. In actual fact, when the *Vigilant* sailed from the port, she did not have her full crew on board, so critical was the time factor. The remainder of the crew were brought out later on the tug *Crosby*. Also, the port's other salvage vessel, the *Salvor*, was brought in to assist with the rescue operation. Hart was aware that, should a salvage operation prove to be necessary, then 'camels' would be needed to assist in this operation. He called for two of the port's 'camels' to be readied, numbers three and four. 'Camels' were a kind of barge without having any propulsive power—they had to be towed to wherever they were required. Their use was that they worked in tandem on either side of a wreck with support wires held between the two, and also passing on the underside of the wreck to be salvaged. Hart considered that, if the submarine was unable to surface, then the 'camels' would be needed to assist in any recovery operation. Thinking ahead and taking all necessary precautions, he called for another 'camel' to be made ready as a back-up.

Just over an hour after taking the telephone call from Plymouth, the *Vigilant* was leaving Princes Landing Stage in Liverpool. Amongst those on board were Hart's deputy from the Mersey Docks & Harbour Board, Commander Eric W. Harbord; Mr C. Brock, Wreck Master who also worked for the Mersey Docks and Harbour Board and diver Frederick Orton. So, it was evident that everything that could be done was being done. To add further support to the operation, a call was sent out to locate the captains of the other two submarines which were currently being built in Birkenhead—Lieutenant Commander R. N. Garnet RN, who was to be captain of the submarine HMS *Taku*, and Lieutenant Commander T. C. C. Lloyd, who was to be captain of the other submarine being built at Cammell Lairds, HMS *Trident*. But, what wasn't known by the Admiralty when this call went out was that both captains had joined those on board *Thetis* so that they could experience for themselves the dive trials. As the 'camels' were berthed at Albert Dock, they were unable to leave the port until the high tide at midnight.

A message was received at Abbotsinch Aerodrome, home of RAF 269 squadron, from Coastal Command. The message related to a submarine which, it was thought, hadn't surfaced. The last known position of the submarine was somewhere in Liverpool Bay. The request had gone out for an airborne search, and at eight o'clock in the evening, three twin-engined Anson aircraft had taken to the air to fly the 140-mile trip to the search area. Flying low throughout the journey, the Ansons arrived exactly an hour later at 2100 hours, but sunset that night was at 2104 hours, and with darkness

The camels are towed out from Liverpool to the site of the disaster. (*From* SOS *Thetis, Hans Müller Verlag, Dresden, 1943*)

rapidly approaching, there was little chance of determining the location of the missing submarine. However, when the flight, which was being led by Flight Lieutenant John Avent, was approaching the designated search site, they were joined by four twin-engined Oxford training aircraft from Number Five Flying School based at RAF Sealand. As the search was now being augmented, Avent decided that, rather than go to *Thetis*'s last known location, he would lead his group about ten miles to the west of that position, in an attempt to maximise the daylight time available.

With a full crew on board each plane—pilot, observer, wireless operator and navigator—Avent then made the decision to cover as wide an area as possible in the time remaining that night. They were now flying at less than five hundred feet above the water, and made their wide sweeps at reduced speed. After combing this area for some time, they flew eastwards and made more, low level, sweeps. Fortunately, it was a clear night, so all seven planes were able to continue their search for some considerable time, but all to no avail.

HMS *Brazen* was now steaming towards Liverpool Bay, albeit at a very slow speed, so when Baynes's second signal was received, Lieutenant Commander Robert Henry Mills, *Brazen*'s captain, was able to give the command to proceed at full speed; this meant that all three boilers were now generating steam, and that the destroyer could cut through the waves at something more like her design speed of thirty knots.

The three Ansons arrived at the search area at, roughly, the same time as HMS *Brazen*. Having located *Grebe Cock*—the main point of reference for the search—*Brazen* moved close to the tug and inquired as to estimated location of *Thetis*, and whether the tug was in that vicinity. Coltart knew that with tide movements and a certain degree of drift, they were now only approximately in the same location as when *Thetis* had dived. Accordingly, he instructed Wireless Telegraphist Crosby to declare that they were only roughly in that area. After further consultations with Coltart, Mills decided that by searching to the west of *Grebe Cock* they would probably obtain better results. Unfortunately, as *Brazen* searched to the west of *Grebe Cock*, *Thetis* was actually lying to the eastwards side. So, even having the very latest equipment for submarine location—the ASDIC system—on board, *Brazen* was, through no fault of her own, searching in completely the wrong area.

The airborne search continued, as did *Brazen's*. And then, just before the search was about to be called off for the night, the Anson being flown by Flight Lieutenant Avent saw an object in the water. They immediately altered course and descended as low as possible in the prevailing conditions. It appeared that there was an object just under the surface which, at the time, looked as though it might indeed be *Thetis*. There looked to be a yellow buoy near to the object. As all of the indications were positive, when Avent spotted a commercial trawler some distance away, he ordered that some Very lights should be fired, indicating that they were in distress. But, for one reason or another, the crew aboard the trawler either missed seeing the lights or deliberately chose to disregard them.

Although the trawler may not have seen the Very lights, they were certainly picked up by those on board the *Brazen*. Mills then received an order requesting him to investigate the area in the region of the sighting. Rather than continue the systematic search that they were currently engaged upon, they altered course at Avent's suggestion. Ironically, had this change of search programme not occurred, there was every chance that *Brazen* could well have located *Thetis*; however, that was not to be. Unfortunately there was then another, inadvertent, error made by Avent's Anson; the navigator had made a significant error in his statement as to the buoy's location. As soon as the error was discovered, the Anson alerted Mills as to the misinformation, but by now *Brazen* was now heading away from *Thetis's* actual location. Darkness was now falling and, as the mission had been partially successful, Avent decided that it was time for them to turn and head back to Abbotsinch. Just minutes later a message came through for the Ansons to return to RAF Sealand so that they could resume their search at first light in the morning; however, Avent received the signal and flew towards RAF Sealand, but the other two Ansons had missed that particular signal and had returned to Abbotsinch.

In one of the many crucial discussions that were held on *Thetis* during those long hours, Lieutenant Commander Bolus together with senior staff on board—and that included Captain Oram—agreed, as a matter of principle, that they needed to continue the task of trying to 'blow' the front two compartments in order to change the submarine's buoyancy, but recognised that, by their own efforts alone, it might be difficult to succeed. The question remained however as to how they could secure any outside help. Another important discussion focussed around the use of the Davis Escape Apparatus. It was clearly advantageous for the men's comfort to don the apparatus straight away, but, the consensus view of the senior officers was that this would be a retrograde step, in that, if the apparatus was used merely for crew comfort, it could well jeopardise any escape attempts in the near future, and the DSEA was specifically designed to meet that function.

There followed much discussion in the control room, primarily focusing on the need to secure outside assistance, recognising that the situation was such that they could not surface through their own unaided efforts. Captain Oram, who perhaps had the most experience of submarines, made a number of suggestions. If, by their own efforts they could, even marginally, change the buoyancy of *Thetis*, then there was some prospect of the stern rising above water level—they knew the angle at which they were being held, the length of the submarine and the depth of the seabed at that position. Oram argued that, if that initiative was successful, then there was every chance that they would be located by surface vessels which everyone knew would now be being deployed. Developing his strategy, Oram then suggested that, if that was the case, then men could escape from the submarine using the Davis escape apparatus, and in doing so take with them a copy of the plan. The plan itself would necessitate a pressurised air line being attached to the submarine, and then, with the aid of those aboard, opening the necessary valves so that high pressure air could be pumped into the forward compartments and thus achieve the desired outcome; that is, changing the submarine's buoyancy and enabling her to surface. But, as the discussion developed, the view emerged that divers might be the first to arrive on the scene. This was not idle speculation, but a realistic assessment of probabilities. Those on board recognised that if the plan was to be successful, somebody having a detailed knowledge of working on submarines was required to be present—and it certainly wasn't divers. To get around this possibility, it was now seen as critical that the rescue plan should be as detailed as possible and include diagrams as to the best place to connect the air line. Also, in order to maximise the possibility of success, it was decided not to make any escape attempt until the following morning, and secondly, to have the plan strapped somewhere on the escapees body, such that, in the unfortunate event of him not being found alive, the plan could still be put into operation.

Having now agreed all of the major decisions, the action plan could be drawn up and implemented. The requirements, together with suitable sketches, were written down by Engineer Officer Glenn and then secured in watertight packaging. The notes read:

ON BOTTOM. DEPTH 140 ft TUBE SPACE AND FORE ENDS FLOODED. NO.5 BOW-CAP AND REAR DOOR OPEN. COMPARTMENTS EVACUATED. HP AIR REQUIRED TO CHARGE SUBMARINE THROUGH GUN RECUPERATOR CONNECTION OR WHISTLE CONNECTION ON BRIDGE. DIVER REQUIRED TO TIGHTEN DOWN FORE HATCH SO THAT BLOW CAN BE PUT ON FOR'ARD COMPARTMENTS WITHOUT LIFTING HATCH. STRONGBACK REQUIRED ON HATCH AS SOON AS POSSIBLE. KEEP CONSTANT WATCH FOR MEN ESCAPING THROUGH AFTER ESCAPE CHAMBER.

During the night there was frenetic activity on board, which, as it involved modifications in engineering, was fronted by Engineer Officer Glenn, the most senior engineering officer on board. The over-riding objective of the plan was to change the submarine's buoyancy. Three fresh water tanks were pumped out, even though these tanks had not been designed for such an operation. The water was eventually pumped out through the bilge suction which went out to the open sea. After this operation had been successfully completed, Glenn decided to pump out four of the six fuel tanks, two of which were located in the submarine's stern. Because of the complexities of the fuel and pumping systems, there were many piping and connection changes which needed to be made, but, by working non-stop overnight the work of emptying the fuel tanks in the submarine's stern progressed satisfactorily and, by the early hours of the morning, Lieutenant Commander Bolus was able to declare that, because of the valiant efforts of the Cammell Lairds men on board, they had finally successfully completed their task, against all of the odds. The loss in weight had had the desired effect of changing the inclination, and thus it was estimated that the stern would now be showing above the surface—obviously a help to other vessels when trying to locate the submarine. Captain Oram was convinced that the plan that had been agreed earlier still had a good chance of success.

However, by this time, it was also self-evident that the carbon dioxide levels were reaching dangerously high levels; this was reflected in the morale and physical well-being of those on board. One of the first symptoms of carbon dioxide poisoning is that those suffering have intense headaches, and also, this often leads to vomiting. As the levels of carbon dioxide continued to increase, there were other effects which began to be manifested; muscle spasms was one of the next effects, as was loss of vision, due to acid building up in the muscle tissue. It was becoming clear that if they couldn't escape in the near future then vital body organs would begin to fail and, ultimately, death would follow. It was not known just how long it would take to reach this point, but all on board knew that it would not be long, although nobody gave voice to that thought.

At the official Tribunal sometime later, Lieutenant Commander Bolus reflected that, at the time, it was clear that, for whatever reason, *Thetis* had still not been located, and that the only realistic plan for survival was to use their own ingenuity and the DSEA equipment. But, the dangers here were all too obvious; it was essential that the escape chamber must be brought into use without further delay if everyone was to escape before the effects of the carbon dioxide poisoning prohibited further attempts. Bolus estimated that, with two men escaping through the chamber at any one time, and each escape attempt taking about fifteen minutes, then the whole operation to evacuate everyone would take in excess of thirteen hours, and that was if everything went according to plan—it was an ambitious endeavour, but no other was available to them. Together with the rest of his crew, Bolus was now feeling the effects of the carbon dioxide levels in the submarine's atmosphere. But, knowing that the stern was some way above sea level, he was able to give the command to open the inboard and outboard vents for Z tank which would now be out of the water. By taking this action it would allow fresh air into the submarine's high-pressure air system. And then, if the blowers were switched on, air would be drawn through the tank into the after compartment, thus expelling some of the polluted air—at least affording some respite.

Working closely with Lieutenant Commander Bolus, Oram was convinced that there was some form of merchant vessel or perhaps a naval vessel in the near vicinity, and that their only chance of survival was to make the escape attempt now, together with the plan which they had formulated. As Oram was later to testify at the Tribunal, he offered to make the escape attempt himself; however, as a back up, if he failed or died in the attempt, he suggested that another person should accompany him. This suggestion was agreed, and Bolus asked for volunteers. There were two volunteers from the crew and later, when he had recovered some of his strength, Woods also volunteered. In making his decision, Oram weighted the experience and technical knowledge of submarines which Woods possessed and therefore chose him.

In the best traditions of the Royal Navy, before leaving the control room Oram suggested to Bolus that, because of the lack of practical experience which the Cammell Lairds and other non-naval personnel had, it would be best if the men attempted to escape in pairs—one from the Navy, who obviously had practical training with the Davis Submarine Escape Apparatus, and the other drawn from the non-naval personnel on board. He also said that the escape attempts should be made as soon as possible, as time was rapidly running out on them—information which Bolus was fully aware of!

Oram informed those present at the Tribunal that, when making their way to the after escape chamber, both himself and Woods had been helped along by the men who were now strewn on the deck plating of the submarine.

It took almost three-quarters of an hour for Woods and Oram to make the short, but extremely difficult, journey from the control room to the escape chamber, where they were met by First Lieutenant Chapman and Commissioned Engineer Glenn, who were there to help them into the escape chamber. But this in itself took some time, as both men were in need of rest after their arduous journey. And, even before attempting to enter the escape chamber, both men were smeared in grease, just like cross-Channel swimmers; a precaution taken in an attempt to reduce the impact of the icy cold seawater which they would be subjected to upon being released from the submarine. Oram had the plan safely secured on his person.

The two officers made ready to climb into the escape chamber—a practice with which Woods was very familiar, having gone through the same process on two previous occasions. Oram checked that he had the plan tied securely to his wrist, and then it was just a question of waiting for Glenn to go through the necessary procedure in order to fill the escape chamber. At this point, Oram was obviously experiencing some difficulty, no doubt due to the pressure, but nonetheless, he was resolutely holding firm as the chamber was filled. When it was almost half full, Chapman stopped the process and began to drain down. Upon being asked for his reasoning for taking this action, he merely replied that he was of the belief that the escape hatch itself was now above the water's surface, but this assumption was incorrect. The process was started again and, this time, Woods requested that the air compressors which had been switched on earlier were stopped for the duration of the escape attempt, as neither he nor Oram could hear themselves speaking.

The progress of 'flooding up' continued and, by now, both officers were becoming acclimatised to breathing the fresh oxygen from the Davis apparatus. Then, just before Oram was about to open the escape hatch, the noise of a number of small explosions in the immediate vicinity filled their ears. Without uttering any words or expletives, they looked at each other, both realising the significance of the explosions; they had, at last, been found! And, just as they were moving to escape, they could hear a spontaneous cheer coming from the men still entrapped aboard *Thetis*. It was now almost sixteen hours—painful and anxious hours—since *Thetis* had made her dive. So now, at last, it looked as though they would be rescued.

CHAPTER 4

Rescue and Escape

Mills, and many others, were now beginning to feel frustrated and dispirited by the lack of progress and success, when, as if out of nowhere, a passing merchant ship, the SS *Meath*, observed an oil slick on the water's surface. This was duly reported to the authorities and Mills was requested to investigate. Closing in on the location, Mills saw a sudden surge on the surface, followed by a mass of air bubbles; then, miraculously, he saw two figures in the centre of the disturbance—later proving to be Captain Oram and Lieutenant Woods. Orders were given for a whaler to be lowered, and shortly after both men were picked up and rowed back to *Brazen*—relieved, exhausted and thankful.

As Oram and Woods boarded the *Brazen* they were greeted by Lieutenant Commander Mills before being allowed time to recuperate. Woods then settled for some much-needed food, but Oram was more concerned with delivering the plan which he had so meticulously drawn up and secured to his person before his ascent. Lieutenant Coltart, having been made aware of the two men's escape, was then taken from *Grebe Cock* to *Brazen* to help co-ordinate the rescue plan. Initially, the major focus was to look for other men escaping via the after escape chamber, but then, sooner rather than later, they needed to put the second part of Oram's plan into action. Now that he was safely aboard *Brazen* and his plan was gaining traction, Oram's next duty was to make contact with the Commander-in-Chief, Plymouth, Admiral Nasmith, giving a résumé of events which had occurred over the last twenty hours or so, and bringing him up to date with the plans from thereon in. After this information had been conveyed, he went for a well-earned rest, as it was apparent that he was still suffering from the after effects of carbon dioxide poisoning and the general stress which the whole situation—and more latterly the escape from *Thetis*—had caused. When at 0826 hours Mills contacted responsible officers in the Admiralty, he was able to state:

'IMMEDIATE: CAPTAIN ORAM AND LT. WOODS ARE IN BRAZEN.
ALL THE REST OF THE CREW ARE ALIVE AND IN SUBMARINE AND
ENDEAVOURING TO ESCAPE BY DSEA'

When it was realised on the *Brazen* that *Thetis* had, at last, been located,
Lieutenant Commander Mills signalled *Grebe Cock* to follow them to the
submarine. The distances were small; in all of the time that they'd been
looking for *Thetis*, she was in actual fact less than two miles away from them.
At approximately the same time as Mills on board *Brazen* had seen the stern
of *Thetis* out of the water, so too had Hart aboard the Mersey Docks and
Harbour Board's vessel *Vigilant*. Realising that *Brazen* had launched a whaler
to pick up the two men who had escaped, Hart had a boat lowered, just in
case anyone else surfaced in the next few minutes. Both *Grebe Cock* and
Vigilant had been instructed not to go too close to *Thetis* as it might obstruct
any further escape attempts.

After seeing *Thetis's* stern above the water, Hart instinctively appreciated
that one possible way to rescue the men on board would be to cut an opening
into the hull of the submarine, and thus release those inside. He automatically
signalled one of his colleagues at the Mersey Docks and Harbour Board to
send oxy acetylene cutting equipment to the rescue site as soon as possible.
But, the necessary gear was stored some way from the central dock area,
and, even making all speed, it would still take upwards of six hours for the
equipment to reach the rescue site. Whilst organising this aspect of the rescue
bid, Hart was not aware that this method was being kept in reserve, just in
case either the escape chamber plan, or the pressurised air plan had to be
discontinued.

After the first two men had escaped, those remaining were at least heartened
by the fact that the rescue plan was now, in all probability, being co-ordinated
by the rescuers on the surface, and external help would soon be on its way.
Now, having proved the system could be successful, Engineer Officer Glenn
and Leading Stoker Arnold set about draining the escape chamber so that
others could escape the submarine. It was during this delicate operation that,
because of *Thetis's* precarious angle to the vertical, water spilt into the motor
room causing a short circuit in the electrical systems. The resulting smoke-
laden atmosphere necessitated men in that area either donning gas masks
or the DSEA gear. The lethargy with which these actions were undertaken
indicated the poor state of physical and mental health of the men, and—more
critically—their failing morale.

It was now becoming apparent that the carbon dioxide laden atmosphere
was beginning to take its toll. Because of this, coupled with the fact that there
was now the problem of smoke inhalation, First Lieutenant Chapman took the
initiative of asking four men at a time to enter into the escape chamber, rather

The *Vigilant*, one of the Mersey Docks & Harbour Board's salvage vessels was one of the first boats to arrive on the scene. Unfortunately, shortly after this photograph was taken, *Thetis* once again plunged below the surface. (*By kind permission of Pamela Armstrong*)

The naval whalers were in attendance shortly after *Thetis* had been located. (*From* SOS *Thetis, Hans Müller Verlag, Dresden, 1943*)

than the number which the chamber was designed for, which was two persons. Both Engineer Officer Glenn and Lieutenant Jamison considered that there was just not enough room inside the small chamber to accommodate four men—the chamber being less than seven feet high and three feet in diameter. When two men were inside the chamber wearing their Davis apparatus, there was just about enough room for manoeuvre, but, with four men, it would have been a virtually impossible task to escape. However, Chapman was the senior officer in charge, and his authority and rank had to be respected. The four men who were to make the escape attempt were two Royal Naval personnel, Stoker Wilfred Hole and Leading Stoker Thomas Kenney, and, as had been agreed in the original plan, two of Cammell Lairds's men were to join them in the chamber. There was undoubtedly some extreme discomfort, as the men were squashed together in the confined space they were now entering. When, with some difficulty, the four men eventually made it into the chamber, Arnold closed the door and made the chamber secure, ready for 'flooding up'. Exactly the same technique was used as when Oram and Woods had gone into the chamber sometime earlier. On instruction, Arnold started the 'flooding up' procedure and everything seemed to be progressing according to plan, until one of the occupants—perhaps with the thought of freedom beckoning—tried to release the escape hatch before the pressures had equalised. The pressures only became equalised when the pressure inside the chamber became equal to the water pressure of the sea outside. The design of the release hatch was such that it was impossible to open it before the pressure inside and outside of the submarine had equalised. Shortly after, a second attempt to open the hatch was made, but this too was made too early, and consequently failed. Glenn and Arnold were patiently waiting outside of the chamber whilst the escape attempt was being made, so that they, in turn, could make preparations for the next four occupants. But nothing appeared to be happening inside the chamber. They waited for five minutes, but, as the time extended past ten minutes, they were becoming increasingly concerned, as further attempts had to be made in quick succession if all of the remaining men were to escape. After fifteen minutes of waiting Arnold drained the chamber and opened the door, only to find that the men were still inside, three having already died and the fourth, Cornelius Smith, a Cammell Lairds worker, in a very poor state. Arnold later recounted at the Tribunal that he had been aware that there had been some fighting inside the chamber; not only was it extremely cramped within the chamber, but the men were, literally, fighting to stay alive as they were finding it impossible to open the hatch and thus escape. When the bodies were brought out of the chamber and others could see the fate which had befallen them, it clearly knocked morale down even further. Arnold later testified that, although nobody was able to speak by that stage, it was clear from facial expressions that morale was now at rock bottom.

In order to try to escape from the smoke-filled atmosphere, charge-hand fitter Shaw had made his way to the stern escape chamber, only to find Glenn and Arnold engaged in their gruesome task of helping Smith out of the chamber and removing the other three dead men. Cornelius Smith was one of Shaw's fitters, so he immediately went over to comfort him, knowing that Smith was now near to death. Smith was not able to say very much, but he did manage to convey to Shaw that it was because they couldn't open the hatch that they failed to escape. Although still not countermanding First Lieutenant Chapman's earlier orders, Engineer Officer Glenn and Lieutenant Jamison once again voiced their concern about more than two men entering the chamber at any one time, and this time they were listened to; in future, a maximum of two men would enter the chamber at any one time. It was Glenn that suggested that Arnold and Shaw should try to escape next. They both looked relatively fit still, and, if they did manage to escape, it would no-doubt lift the morale of the remaining men.

The main argument for the reasoning behind taking one man from Cammell Lairds and one man from the Navy was to balance lack of experience with a man who had experience. Being from the shipyard, Shaw had no experience, whatsoever, of using the Davis escape apparatus; in fact, the equipment was totally alien to him. But, the consolation was that he did have Arnold's experience to rely on; what he was unaware of was the fact that Arnold too had very little experience of the apparatus, other than a superficial academic knowledge. Arnold, being the fitter of the two, helped Shaw into the apparatus, and then explained once again exactly what he had to do when they escaped from the chamber—the most important thing being to open the exhaust tap, so that pressures could be equalised and also any poisonous gasses in the mask could escape. As he was entering into chamber, Shaw took a cursory glance around at the men remaining in the steering compartment. It was then that realisation dawned on him that, because of their exhausted state, the carbon dioxide poisoning which they were all suffering from, and the general lethargy in their actions, none could now be expected to escape through their own endeavours alone. It was apparent to him that they could only escape with intervention from outside rescuers, and, even then, time was rapidly running out. As they entered the chamber Chapman wished them good luck—a commodity they needed in abundance. One thing that Arnold took charge of was the 'flooding up' operation. This procedure could be controlled from the inside of the chamber, and Arnold wanted to ensure that, as far as possible, he controlled his own destiny. It was a critical time for both men as the 'flooding up' started. Shaw was trying to recall the lecture he'd attended at the shipyard when the Davis apparatus had been explained, but his main source of information and direction came from Arnold. But both men were experiencing, if not exactly fear, then an intrepid sense of moving into the unknown. As the chamber 'flooded up', Shaw's first instinctive reaction was to try to lift the escape hatch, but was dissuaded from this action by Arnold. However, sometime later, when Arnold gave the signal for Shaw to open the hatch, he could not release the holding clip. It was evident that he needed to wait a little longer. On the second attempt the clip was released and the hatch opened. Arnold noticed, just in time, that Shaw had not opened his exhaust valve. This oversight was corrected before Shaw made his rapid exit out of the submarine, closely followed by Arnold. On reaching the surface they were quickly spotted and picked up. Soon after boarding *Brazen* they were asked if any others were expected to escape—they answered in the affirmative! In fact, Mr Shaw and Leading Stoker Arnold had surfaced at 0950 hours, not too long after Oram and Woods had boarded the *Brazen*.

It is perhaps interesting to reflect at this point that, although Dr Ramsay Stark examined the escapees during the day, Arnold was the only one who was taken below decks to the ship's sick-bay. Also, from Ramsey's own statements, Arnold was the one who was showing markedly less effects from the carbon dioxide poisoning than the others, and yet he was the only one who was sedated. The final anomaly in this bizarre episode was that Arnold's account of events was never sought. None of the others were so completely disregarded in this manner, and nor was Arnold ever given any explanation as to why he had been treated in this way when so much was at stake.

The lesson had now been learnt, at great cost, that it really was much better for two men at a time to enter the chamber. Accordingly, the next two were prepared—one from the Navy and one from Cammell Lairds as before. The process of 'flooding up' started and, at the opportune moment, when the valve was turned to the position 'ready to open', the clip was released and the hatch duly opened. Initially, it appeared that everything was beginning to go according to plan, but, when the escape hatch was less than half way open, it became stuck. With the severely limited energy left to them, the men inside the chamber frantically endeavoured to release the mechanism, but all to no avail. The hatch would just not open any further—they were doomed. Those outside the chamber, although not realising exactly what had happened, could see that, for whatever reason, the men had not been able to escape. They were forced to drain down the chamber, and the men were helped out. Not wishing to give up hope, even at this late stage, and bow to the inevitable, two more volunteers were found and eased into the chamber. Once again, 'flooding up' started and, as had happened previously, when they came to open the hatch it stuck again in exactly the same place as the previous attempt. Try as they might, the escape hatch could not be opened any further, and it was impossible for fully-grown men to squeeze out through the aperture. It was now feared—correctly—that, because of the combination of adverse factors, the means of rescue was now out of the hands of those on board, and resided solely with the personnel on the surface who were co-ordinating and assisting in the rescue bid. Fortunately, because of the previous successful attempts, all of the rescue vessels had remained in the vicinity and, indeed, were now being augmented by other personnel having specialist knowledge. The Mersey Docks and Harbour Board Wreck Master, Mr Brock, was now at the scene, and he heard what he knew to be hammering from the inside of the submarine. From that, he was aware that not only were there men still alive on *Thetis*, but, more particularly, there was a pattern to the hammering which indicated to him that they were attempting to do something other than just attracting attention.

Part of Oram's plan had required that men on the inside of *Thetis* assisted in securing the high pressure air line which was to be fed to the submarine; but now, with all of the indications of carbon dioxide poisoning reaching its final stages, hope was fading fast. Those men on board who were not already dead were now suffering from hallucinations, sickness and confusion. The end was becoming inevitable, especially with the low levels of oxygen that were still available. But it has to be said that there was a great deal of confusion at this time—in part attributable to the successful escape of the four men—in that most of the personnel on board the rescue vessels, including the specialist personnel, were firmly of the view that more men would escape using the Davis Submarine Escape Apparatus. This confirmed to the Admiralty that the strategy to be adopted during a 'Subsmash' rescue was not only correct, but effective! Lairds's Managing Director was being kept abreast of the developing situation, and was more than satisfied with progress and the prospects for success, having been given the impression that everybody on board *Thetis* would survive.

Because of the supposed efficacy of the Davis escape equipment, there was little further activity on the surface for some time, although a constant watch was kept for any more men escaping—no-one else did escape.

The *Matabele* with Captain Nicholson aboard did, eventually, arrive at Liverpool Bay after her long journey from Plymouth. As the most senior ranking officer, Nicholson would, according to protocol, assume overall command for the rescue attempt. Lieutenant Woods, who was now in a sufficient state of recovery, made his way over to *Matabele* and informed Nicholson as to his (Woods's) understanding of the current situation. He also briefed Nicholson as to developments which had taken place whilst he was travelling up from Plymouth. In addition to making these positional statements, Woods commented on the likely state of health of those still incarcerated in the stricken submarine, knowing that the CO_2 levels would now be much higher than previously. He also expressed concern that nobody else since Arnold and Shaw's escape—now some hours ago—had escaped from *Thetis*.

Recovery work continues in Liverpool Bay. (*By kind permission of Holyhead Maritime Museum*)

As Nicholson was being apprised of the situation by Woods and others, Fredrick Orton, one of the Mersey Docks and Harbour Board's divers, was being given his instructions for the dive down to *Thetis*. The Board's Wreck Master, Brock, explained to Orton exactly what they were trying to achieve. Although an experienced diver, Orton had never worked on a submarine before, and he certainly hadn't dived to these depths in his long career. His first task would be to find the forward torpedo hatch, make it secure so that a line could be attached to pump in compressed air—without the pressure causing the hatch to blow open again. Brock explained, in great detail, what exactly Orton could expect to encounter on his way down. Also, to assist with the dive, Orton had a line connected to the submarine's decking, so that there would be no location problems—time was of the essence. This, however, did not appear to be a concept that was shared with Nicholson. His actions or, more correctly, lack of actions were later heavily criticised at the Public Tribunal.

It didn't take long for Orton and Brock to agree a priority list for tasks which he would have to do. On his descent to the submarine, Orton found a large number of wires tangled in and around the submarine, including a wire which was attached to one of the buoys. Fortunately, as he descended,

Orton found that the visibility at that depth was much better than he had expected, and he was thus able to go about his business more efficiently. One approach which Orton did take was to spend short periods of time down at the scene, rather than a more sustained longer period. Using this approach, he argued that it would avoid the necessity of having to go through the lengthy decompression process, and, as he was the only diver at the scene at that time, the longer he was able to work around the *Thetis*, then so much the better. It was perhaps at this point that a further degree of confusion and lack of firm leadership was exhibited. On what was to be his second short dive, Orton's task had been to locate the jumper stay, which was close to the forward hatch. But, even though Orton had reported good visibility at that depth, he was unable to locate the forward hatch—one of the most critical operations in Oram's plan. Returning to the surface, he took another short break before once again preparing himself to dive and locate the forward hatch. Whilst he'd been engaged on this dive, Wreck Master Brock had transferred to the *Somali* to continue his discussions with the naval personnel on board who were co-ordinating the rescue attempt. Just as Orton was about to make another dive, Brock signalled to the dive boat that they should finish diving. At that time no reason was given for this instruction, but clearly it was one which Orton needed to obey. He did question what was to happen about the guide ropes he'd already attached to the submarine, and was curtly told to just cut them. Later, he was informed of the reasoning behind the decision, and that was that it might have impaired the efforts being made in the chamber for men to escape. Orton's frustration was compounded because he still had more than an hour left to complete his main task of securing the forward hatch, especially when he was also aware that he was not, in any way, impeding any escape attempt, because he was working a long way from the after escape chamber; furthermore, many were now beginning to doubt whether there would be any further escape attempts.

There was an increasing sense of inevitable failure on board the *Somali*, as many of the senior personnel were, perhaps independently, coming to the more realistic conclusion that Oram's plan was now proving to be totally impracticable, especially given the timeframe of the operation. His plan had entailed making a strongback to secure on the forward hatch, thus ensuring that the hatch cover would not be blown off when compressed air was introduced into the submarine, but this was proving to be one task too many. The necessary strongback had been manufactured at Cammell Lairds's shipyard, but as time was now running out very rapidly, it was highly debatable if there would be any advantage in even attempting to secure it in position.

Having been subjected to the conditions on board *Thetis* and his subsequent escape via the escape chamber, Oram was still feeling the physically adverse

Rescue work was relentless, but all to no avail. (*By kind permission of Holyhead Maritime Museum*)

effects of his experience and was also exhibiting a degree of confusion. It was clear to all those on *Somali* that he was not totally aware as to the events happening all around him.

Finally, and as others had suspected for some time, Nicholson himself was now becoming increasingly sceptical as to the viability of Oram's rescue plan. He sought advice from others having more localised knowledge of the area and also the type of rescue being attempted. He crossed to the *Vigilant* and conferred with Hart as to an alternative strategy. Ultimately, in the early afternoon, a different approach to the rescue attempt was adopted. It had been suggested that *Vigilant* should try to lift *Thetis's* stern higher out of the water, in order that a hole could be cut into the exposed stern of the submarine, and thus enable the trapped men to be rescued. *Thetis* had now been submerged for more than twenty hours and everyone involved in the rescue operation was aware of the extreme hardship which the men on board would now be suffering. Nicholson gave his full support to the new initiative. Preparations went ahead, and it was during this time that rescuers heard tapping on the hull from inside; men were still alive! But neither Nicholson nor anyone else in authority thought to respond. Nicholson could not defend this lack of action when he was questioned about it at the Tribunal. If nothing else, it might have raised the morale of those on board, armed with the knowledge that help was at hand.

Although the risks were great, Wreck Master Brock volunteered to make an attempt to remove the inspection cover, which would allow access to Z tank, now well above water level. Once this plan was agreed, he was taken by whaler over to the protruding stern of *Thetis* where he was able to transfer to the submarine's superstructure. But, even if he managed to open both the inner and outer covers to gain access, there still remained the problem of the limited amount of space for the men to crawl through in order to make their escape. After a Herculean tussle, Brock managed to release the outer cover and then set about removing the four fastenings which secured the inner cover to the submarine's hull. Being new, it was an easy task to loosen them; however, just before the plate was about to be removed, there was a massive release of air under some considerable pressure. Brock's immediate instinct was to tighten up the fastenings straight away, in an effort to retain as much air in the compartment as possible. It was during his work on the hull that three more vessels joined the growing number of ships at the scene. The salvage vessel *Ranger* owned by the Liverpool & Glasgow Salvage Association arrived on scene, as did the tugs *Crosby* and *Holm Cock*, both having cutting gear on board. The *Somali* with her specialist apparatus now edged nearer to *Thetis*. Air lines were to be fed from *Somali* so that fresh air could be delivered into the submarine.

Time, as had always been the case, was now becoming a commodity in very short supply—that is, if a successful rescue was still to be mounted. As

Air compressors and other equipment is prepared to be taken out from Liverpool. (*From* SOS *Thetis, Hans Müller Verlag, Dresden, 1943*)

soon as all of the cutting and other necessary equipment had arrived on the tug *Crosby*, it was transferred to the *Vigilant*. It was at this point that, again, because of his experience, Hart organised that a cable be taken under *Thetis's* stern, near to the hydroplanes and then looped back to *Vigilant*. In this way it might prevent the stern sinking again, should the submarine cant when the tide turned. Throughout the whole of this period, there were small boats which had been launched from *Vigilant* and *Brazen* circulating in the vicinity around *Thetis's* stern just in case any other men escaped from the submarine. Wreck Master Brock was now precariously balanced on the protruding stern of *Thetis*. In this period, immediately before work continued, Brock was asked to bang on *Thetis's* hull. After many firm hammer blows there was no response from inside—the awful truth of failure was now becoming evident. But, irrespective of the lack of response from the submarine, Nicholson forged ahead, confirming that Brock was taking the correct action in ensuring that the plate was now screwed back. He'd taken this view in the absence of any information to the contrary; after all, it appeared to be the most logical course of action. However, shortly afterwards when Oram was consulted, he suggested that it was quite in order for the plate to be removed. So Brock's orders were reversed and, once again, he started to unscrew the fastenings. The tide was now turning and, because of this, *Thetis* started to cant over. It was at this point that Brock was forced to jump off the stricken submarine. As *Thetis* canted round, much of her tail buoyancy was lost. During further discussions, most notably at the Inquiry, it emerged that Hart held a different view from that of Nicholson; Nicholson maintaining that they could not possibly burn a hole low enough in the submarine's hull which would enable the men to escape, whereas Hart held the view that the vessel was far enough out of the water for a hole to be cut. With the benefit of hindsight, Nicholson's decision was a serious error of judgment.

Nicholson appeared to be totally mesmerised with the number of rescue vessels which were now on station—upwards of twenty vessels with a wide range of equipment necessary for this sort of operation. He also had around him many experienced people from whom he could seek advice as to how to proceed. He did in fact listen to Hart's considered views and advice, but perhaps for his own reasons, chose to ignore that advice. Indeed, although it was never voiced, there were now a number of people close to him who were forming the view that he just didn't know which way to turn or what to do next. Hart had wanted to hold *Thetis* in her current position until the tide turned, and then she could be raised a little further out of the water, so that a suitable hole could be burned. But, the only view that Nicholson could coherently express was that the situation was becoming desperate. And, to make matters worse, the views of Doctor G. Ramsay Stark from Holyhead didn't help. He'd arrived on site and declared that carbon dioxide poisoning was the main problem. The doctor had taken this view after having had the benefit of examining the four survivors. And, when taking into account the number of men remaining on board, coupled with his knowledge of the space available to those men, he'd calculated that there was little chance of anyone being alive for very much longer after having been subjected to such a prolonged period of exposure. Armed with this information, which he accepted without further question, Nicholson was prompted to adopt a radical course of action. So, against all other advice, Nicholson was determined to raise *Thetis's* stern. He was aiming to have the submarine raised against the flow of the tide, in order to give it more 'lift'. But, with his expert knowledge of the waters in and around Liverpool Bay and their prevailing currents, Hart was strongly opposed to this course of action and told Nicholson so in no uncertain terms. He did however state that, if Nicholson was intent upon adopting this strategy, then he would follow his orders to the best of his ability; but again reiterated that it was his considered opinion that there was very little chance of this approach being successful. Nicholson accepted that it was his ultimate responsibility, and insisted that Hart should follow these orders. The one concession that Nicholson did make however was that, in front of *Vigilant* there would be two tugs rather than a destroyer. This, it was considered by Hart, would give more pulling power, and also more manoeuvrability. Having secured the towing cables they gently eased forward, and the submarine's stern began to move a little higher out of the water.

There came a point when those inside *Thetis* really began to wonder what was happening—if indeed they possessed the faculty to wonder or were still alive. To a man, they were now all suffering from the effects of the high concentration of carbon dioxide in the fetid atmosphere within the submarine; and now, for the second time in the recent past, they were being thrown, willy-nilly around the submarine, like corks bobbing up and down on the water's surface. In actual fact, what was happening, was a last ditch attempt to rescue them. Nicholson had insisted upon the attempt being made, and Hart—against his better judgement—was duty-bound to obey his bidding. As *Vigilant* tried to raise *Thetis's* stern by gently towing the vessel, the main ballast tanks, which were fitted with holes along their bottoms, became exposed. So, as the stern was being pulled further up out of the water, trapped air came out from the holes which, in turn, allowed seawater to enter the tanks. Buoyancy was quickly lost, as more and more water entered the tanks. It wasn't long before the main tanks were completely flooded. The change in buoyancy caused the boat to slew around, breaking the towing cable. As *Thetis* swung around, she collided with *Vigilant* before sinking beneath the waves for the third time. Although the scene had been witnessed by all in the immediate vicinity, it was Hart's duty to inform Nicholson, formally, as to exactly what had occurred. He also added that, realistically, they would not be able to make any further rescue attempts until slack tide, sometime after six o'clock that evening. At the Tribunal some weeks later, Nicholson was adamant in stating that the situation was desperate and, because of that, he believed that he was fully justified in having the attempt made, even knowing the risks that were involved.

Although Hart's previous attempts to raise *Thetis* had proved unsuccessful, he was not a man who was easily beaten. Now that the burning gear had arrived on the tug *Crosby* he had it transferred to his own salvage vessel *Vigilant* and waited for low tide. He managed to have a steel cable threaded under *Thetis*'s stern and then connected to one of the camels stationed on the other side. When the tension was slowly increased on the cable, the submarine's hull could be seen to be lifting from the seabed, but, just when it looked as though they might be achieving a successful outcome, the cable failed and, yet again, *Thetis* plunged back into the dark icy waters of Liverpool Bay; this time, there would be no coming back.

It later emerged that most of the men remaining in the submarine had congregated in the area of the steering compartment and engine room—many of them having donned their DSEA apparatus. Two other men were found near to the escape chamber. It was obvious that, in a last ditch attempt, they had tried to escape. Regrettably, their quest for survival was unsuccessful. Indeed, their attempts to escape may well, inadvertently, have contributed to *Thetis*'s final demise, in that the seawater inlet valve had not been closed again after their failed attempt. This omission would have caused water to flood into the steering compartment. The salvage operation later found that much of the DSEA apparatus was left lying around—unused.

CHAPTER 5

'A Matter of Salvage'

Whilst all of this frenetic activity was taking place in Liverpool Bay, up in the Orkneys, at Scapa Flow, one of Britain's most experienced salvage experts, if not the most experienced salvage expert—Thomas McKenzie—was engaged upon salvaging the mighty German battle cruiser SMS *Derfflinger*. At the time he was the Chief Salvage Officer for the firm Metal Industries. McKenzie had salvage experience with many companies; companies such as the Liverpool & Glasgow Salvage Association, the Admiralty Salvage Section, and then, more recently, seven years salvaging experience with Cox & Danks, Ltd. When that company was acquired by Metal Industries, McKenzie continued to work for them, together with his colleague and former co-owner, Ernest Cox; undoubtedly, there was no-one in the whole of the country more experienced in this kind of work.

As chance would have it, on his way to the office, McKenzie bumped into another member of staff working at Scapa Flow. After a normal exchange of pleasantries, McKenzie was told the news that a new submarine, HMS *Thetis*, had not surfaced as scheduled during her dive trials, and was apparently experiencing some difficulties. Being conscious of the fact that, should a diving team be required to help in the rescue operation, many of the most able divers were currently working with him engaging in salvaging the *Derfflinger*, having received the news, he went straight to his office and made a telephone call to the Admiralty. He also sent a number of telegrams; again, one to the Admiralty in Whitehall, declaring that if he could be of any assistance, together with his divers, then they would be more than willing to help. McKenzie's second telegram was sent was to Cammell Lairds, again stating that he and his team were available to assist in the rescue operation if required. He added that he could also bring with him a compressed air chamber—very necessary for the divers in operations of this kind. McKenzie then found himself in a frustrating position for the next few hours, in that, the Admiralty did not immediately return confirmation of his message which, under the circumstances, was a cause for some surprise and concern. When the telegram eventually did arrive from the Admiralty, it merely thanked him for his offer, but graciously declined. A similar telegram was subsequently received from Cammell Lairds, but this time added the information that the submarine had now been located, and it appeared that all on board were safe. Without giving the matter any further thought, McKenzie returned to his normal work.

During the afternoon of Friday 2 June, Thomas McKenzie was aboard the salvage vessel *Bertha* co-ordinating operations, whilst two of his divers were more than one hundred feet below, engaged in salvage work on the German battlecruiser *Derfflinger*. They were working in difficult and trying conditions, but were both very experienced divers, and they were now beginning to make some real progress. Later that afternoon, McKenzie was handed two telegrams, one from the Admiralty, briefly stating that they now required his assistance, and requested that he should make for the submarine with all haste. The telegram gave *Thetis's* co-ordinates, but very little else. It was duly noted that this telegram was in stark contrast to the earlier message he'd received from the Admiralty.

GRATEFUL FOR YOUR ASSISTANCE. REQUEST YOU START IMMEDIATELY TO SUBMARINE IN POSITION 53° 34' NORTH, 3° 52' WEST. SUBMARINE LYING FORE PART FLOODED AND AGROUND AND TAIL JUST ABOVE WATER.

The other telegram, which was from Cammell Lairds, was a far more explicit message, stating that the position, *vis-à-vis Thetis*, was 'desperate'. The telegram also stated that there was an aeroplane waiting at Longhope to take him and his divers to Speke Aerodrome near Liverpool.

Thetis POSITION IS DESPERATE. THERE IS AEROPLANE WAITING AT LONGHOPE TO TAKE MR McKENZIE AND PERSONNEL TO LIVERPOOL—THREE OR FOUR DIVERS—CHANGING AT INVERNESS TO BE AT SPEKE AERODROME (LIVERPOOL) AT 1600 HRS.

Upon assessing this information, McKenzie immediately had his divers brought up using an emergency signal. He was fully aware that this particular signal should only have been used when there was imminent danger, however, due to the unique circumstances, he considered that he was fully justified in recalling them in this way. Upon receiving this signal the men below opened the inlet valves on their diving suits and were immediately lifted to the surface. This was not the usual practice—normally there would be a period of decompression when ascending from that depth, but today really was an exception. They were taken on board *Bertha*, and then transported to Lyness on the Orkney island of Hoy. Being now more suitably attired, they transferred to a waiting car which took them to Longhope airfield, just nine miles away. The party of seven men included McKenzie himself, one of his assistant salvage officers, three experienced divers and two attendants. The small aircraft which normally took no more than four passengers was clearly overloaded and, because of this, it was not possible to take their diving equipment with them. The light aircraft took off from the tiny airfield's grass runway, heading south across the Pentland Firth and then down to Inverness. Here there was another, faster, plane belonging to Scottish Airways which was waiting to fly them to Speke aerodrome on the southern edge of Liverpool. On his way down to Speke, McKenzie had time to discuss the proposed rescue bid with the divers who accompanied him. One issue which was on his mind, and which was of particular relevance, was the work which he and others had done on the *K-13* submarine towards the end of the First World War. He recalled that, like *Thetis*, *K-13* was also on her final sea trials in Gare Loch, again carrying a fifty-three man crew; but, on this occasion, there were only thirty-seven other people on board. But, the parallels were all too clear. *K-13* had many problems which caused her to dive without the ability to surface again. When McKenzie and his team were brought in, they were able to cut a hole through the pressure hull of the vessel using oxy acetylene equipment. McKenzie knew that the conditions in Liverpool Bay were slightly different from Gare Loch, in that *K-13* was lying in much shallower water and close to land, but, on the other hand, weather conditions in Liverpool Bay were good, *Thetis's* stern was above the water level and there was oxyacetylene equipment already at the site.

No sooner had McKenzie and his team arrived at Speke Aerodrome than they were speeding towards Princes Landing Stage in Liverpool. They were then taken directly to the rescue site, but, when they reached there, a very different scene greeted them—the stern was not out of the water any longer, and the submarine was not being held by any cables. Also, the actual location of *Thetis* was not accurately known any longer. What McKenzie did know however, was that *he*, rather than anyone else involved in the rescue bid—and that included Hart, Nicholson and Macintyre—knew more about what approach was now needed in order to save at least some of the men still held on board.

Shortly after ten o'clock in the evening—less than eight hours after leaving Scapa Flow—a high-powered conference was being scheduled aboard the *Matabele*. Earlier on, Rear Admiral (Submarines) B. C. Watson, who was in command at Fort Blockhouse, had arrived at the scene and assumed overall command. Also by that time, the Managing Director of Cammell Lairds,

Mr Robert Johnson, had arrived—now back from the sea trials of RMS *Mauretania*. In addition to Watson and Johnson, Captain Hart from the Mersey Docks and Harbour Board, and several senior Royal Naval personnel, were present at the meeting. After some lengthy discussion, during which strategy and other possibilities were discussed *ad nauseam*, it was finally and reluctantly concluded by those present that there was very little that could now be done which might, realistically, result in saving any more lives. McKenzie knew that he had been called in much too late in order for him to achieve any satisfactory outcome.

It was evident, even at that early stage that the recriminations had already begun. Hart was asked the question during one of the discussions, as to why he had taken the action on the previous day which resulted in *Thetis's* stern sinking. In response, he said that it was his understanding that the conditions aboard the submarine were such that everybody on board would be dead within the next five or six hours. He went on to say that, even though the chances were very much against success, under these circumstances, the actions taken were justified. McKenzie could not agree with this action. Nicholson, wishing to absolve himself of any culpability, endeavoured to shift the blame for the action onto Hart, stating that he (Hart) was the salvage expert, and that he had been guided by his (Hart's) decisions, when, in truth, Hart had strongly disagreed with the action which Nicholson was suggesting, and only agreed to try to raise the stern higher on the explicit understanding that Nicholson—who was in overall charge of rescue operations at that time—would accept total responsibility.

The situation had moved from one of rescue to one of recovery, although this was not openly declared at that time. Even then however, questions were being asked as to why Captain Hart had been given the responsibility of rescue, and it was increasingly becoming evident that it was due, solely, to the fact that he was an associate of Admiral Nasmith. Other names had been mentioned, most notably that of Mr George Critchley, of the Liverpool & Glasgow Salvage Association. To say that at this point that McKenzie, after having rushed his diving team down from the northern-most islands of Scotland, was frustrated would be a gross understatement. Looking at all of the so-called rescue vessels in and around the area, McKenzie was at a loss to fully understand just why the *Thetis* had not been located since sinking again earlier in the day.

Time was now inexorably moving on, and the vast majority of the senior Naval staff now assembled in Liverpool Bay were convinced that all life on board *Thetis* must have been lost. However, this was not a view totally shared by McKenzie—he wanted to make a definite check, one way or the other. He had taken the view that their lack of informed actions was because they had shrunk from the task in hand and had become, as it were, frozen. In one of the later evening discussions aboard the *Somali*, he suggested that it would be advantageous, even at that stage, to check once and for all, if there was any sign of life. This proposed course of action was agreed by all of those taking part in the discussion. As McKenzie had had to leave all of the team's diving equipment up in Scotland, due to the fact that the light aircraft which they had taken from Longhope could not carry it, he had to go to various rescue vessels to borrow enough equipment for one of his divers, Sinclair McKenzie (no relation), to make the dive. Although it was now gone midnight and there was very little light, McKenzie had the *Salvor* positioned directly over *Thetis* so that his diver could have a constant air supply. There was a strong ebb tide running, and conditions in general were not conducive to diving, but the dive still had to be made. In his heart of hearts, McKenzie knew that the men on board must be dead from the effects of the carbon dioxide by now, but his professional commitment meant that he could not leave the scene before he'd confirmed, without any shadow of doubt, that this was the case. In truth, the dive itself was merely to ascertain these facts for certain. As diver McKenzie made his descent into the now darkened waters of Liverpool Bay, his sole aim was to ascertain whether anyone aboard the submarine was still alive. His only means of establishing this was very simple; he was carrying with him a lump hammer with which he intended to tap on the submarine's hull. Some little while after entering the water he signalled to his support team above that he had reached *Thetis*. He recalled standing on the superstructure of the submarine and tapping with his hammer. He did hear some tapping coming from inside, but it was very faint, and he immediately realised that, although there were obviously some men still alive on the submarine, they must now be very close to death. With the ebb tide running as fast as it was, McKenzie was fully aware that the time he could stay on the submarine was limited. Furthermore, with the tapping from inside the submarine becoming less audible, he, reluctantly, reached the conclusion that it wouldn't be too long before the tapping ceased completely.

Later, in the early hours of 3 June, the specialist diving vessel, HMS *Tedworth* arrived from her mooring on the Clyde. The specialist diving equipment which she carried was infinitely better than the equipment which diver McKenzie had borrowed and used in his earlier dives. It was a sign of disbelief and incredulity that, even at this hour, questions were still being asked as to whether there was anyone on board the submarine who was alive; especially when all medical and technical knowledge pointed to the fact that, in conditions which were known to exist on board the *Thetis*, all life must have been extinguished some hours earlier. However, diver McKenzie, both then and at the subsequent Tribunal was unequivocal in stating that he did indeed hear tapping from inside of the submarine. Later that morning, when the tide had slackened somewhat, Thomas McKenzie's other divers, Thomson and Taylor, were sent down to see if there was any signs of life on *Thetis*. Before they had made their descent, and, irrespective of whether there was anyone still alive or not, Thomas McKenzie had instructed them to tap on the hull just in case anyone was found to be alive. He also gave them a signal which would indicate to him, whether there was in fact any life aboard. Unfortunately, they'd only been down a matter of minutes when the signal came through to McKenzie, 'no sign of life'.

This was very different from diver McKenzie's earlier finding. But, it was now clear that since diver McKenzie had gone down, all life must have now ceased. However, Thomas McKenzie was still not ready to accept the inevitable. He managed to secure enough equipment from other vessels to enable him, or rather his divers, to drill air holes through the pressure hull and, hopefully, feed fresh air into *Thetis's* hull—in fact, part of Oram's original plan.

At the high water mark, which was about mid-day on 3 June, a senior Naval officer informed McKenzie that the Mersey Docks & Harbour Board's salvage vessel, *Salvor*, with Captain Hart in command, had secured the 4½ inch cable to the *Thetis* and that, all being well, the stern should be coming up in the next few minutes. McKenzie was ordered to curtail his operations for the time being. However, the attempt to lift the stern was not successful, and because of the turning of the tide, it was decided by those in charge of the operation not to make any further attempts to pump air into the hull by connecting an airline. Needless to say, McKenzie had a very jaundiced view

With *Thetis* finally located, divers worked diligently in an endeavour to reach the trapped men. Unfortunately, by the time that this photograph was taken on 3 June 1939, all hope of any survivors had long evaporated. (*By kind permission of Pamela Armstrong*)

of how the whole rescue operation had been conducted from beginning to what was, inevitably now, the end. His view was that, if his offer of assistance had have been accepted when he sent his first telegrams to the Admiralty and Cammell Lairds's management, then the outcome would, in all probability, have been very different. He made no secret of the fact that he would have had a hole drilled into the hull at the very start of the rescue attempt. It was also well known, especially in light of what Captain Oram had said, that the stern of the vessel had positive buoyancy, and this fact could have been used to good effect, but that initiative was now completely lost.

After much soul searching and reckoning, the outcome of the last meeting held between senior staff at the rescue site on 3 June finally faced the inevitable, and had to accept that all of the many rescue attempts had abysmally failed. As the ultimate commander of the rescue operation, Rear Admiral Watson had a signal sent to the Admiralty, informing them that nobody else had been rescued from the submarine. The first duty of the Admiralty following receipt of this message was to make a public announcement. The statement which was issued was succinct and to the point, stating:

THE ADMIRALTY REGRETS THAT ALL LIFE ABOARD MUST NOW BE CONSIDERED LOST. IT IS NOW A MATTER OF SALVAGE.

The rescue now turned to being one of recovery and, technically, as the owners, Cammell Lairds would be responsible for the salvaging of *Thetis*. In the immediate aftermath of the disaster, the Mersey Docks & Harbour

Anxious relatives wait in silence and anticipation outside the gates of Cammell Lairds's on the evening of 1 June 1939. (*From* SOS *Thetis, Hans Müller Verlag, Dresden, 1943*)

Board's vessels, which were already on station at the site, were to supervise the salvage operation.

When the news of the disaster gradually spread, messages of condolence were received from around the world, including one from Herr Hitler. A copy of the telegram which had been received at Cammell Lairds's shipyard was immediately posted at the main office window. It was around this area that the families of those on board had congregated, bearing in mind that many of the men on board were local, being workers from Cammell Lairds and other local companies, such as the caterers on board that day. Pandemonium broke out when the news was posted, as there was a complete sense of disbelief and despair, with feelings raging through a wide spectrum of emotions, from sorrow right through to raw anger. Included amongst those who had been waiting was Lieutenant Commander Bolus's wife, Sybil; her loss was just as great, if not greater than the other wives, partners, mothers and sisters who had been waiting at the shipyard. She, vicariously, carried the weight and responsibility for the men who had lost their lives whilst her husband was captain on *Thetis*.

Following the distressing scenes outside the shipyard, the national mood soon turned to one of retribution. Journalists in the national press began to ask a series of detailed questions relating to the disaster, and very soon afterwards, this mood was transformed into litigation in the courts. Metal Industries Chief Salvage Officer, Thomas McKenzie, was one individual who had detailed and specific knowledge of the disaster—and hence total credibility. He voiced many of the concerns of the bereaved, by openly declaring that his approach to the catastrophe would have been very different from that which was taken by the Admiralty and those on site at the time. To begin with, McKenzie stated that as the stern was proud of the water, he would have secured it between at least two vessels and not, as Captain Hart had done, just the one. He would also have ensured that this position was held securely, such that a hole could have been cut into the pressurised hull of the vessel. The hull would have been above the waterline, and rescue would then have been a relatively simple exercise. Whilst McKenzie did not suggest for one minute that those on site took any action with malicious intent, he strongly believed that towing *Thetis* was a grave error of judgement. His considered and much publicised view was the stern could have been lifted further out of the water with the assistance of the tidal flow, and that there would have been sufficient time to rescue all of the men trapped inside. Although never made public, the Admiralty's confidential internal Inquiry, chaired by Vice Admiral Robert Henry Taunton Raikes, and convened on 6 June—shortly after the official news of the disaster was posted—came to much the same conclusion. McKenzie's views were well-known, and shared by others, and for the rest of his life he held the view that, had he have been asked for his

Everyone came to Cammell Lairds's gates, just to wait and be comforted by each other in their hour of need. The woman holding the baby is thought to be Mrs Caroline Hole, wife of Stoker W. T. Hole, one of the ninety-nine who perished aboard *Thetis*. (*From* SOS *Thetis, Hans Müller Verlag, Dresden, 1943*)

help even a few hours earlier, then there would have been a very different outcome.

Some time later, when McKenzie was called to give testimony at the tribunal, he was asked to give an account of his involvement in the rescue operation. During questioning he was also asked as to why he was of the opinion that the rescue attempt had been such an abysmal failure. He declared that, in his view, it was futile to have expected a successful outcome, given the fact that, at the time of the rescue bid, most of the people in charge of operations had insufficient salvaging experience. He was particularly scathing about Captain Hart's actions. McKenzie was cross-examined by Mr E. W. Brightman—counsel for the Mersey Docks & Harbour Board, who was, effectively, acting on behalf of Captain Hart. Brightman propounded the view that there were men of equal experience as his own, but, unlike him, they were at the site at the time. Diplomatically, McKenzie was able to explain that he held a contrary view to this. Brightman then suggested that there were bad weather conditions at the time, but McKenzie said that he did not believe that there were any adverse weather conditions prevailing at the time of the rescue bid. Following further questioning McKenzie declared in no uncertain terms that he could not understand why a small hole could not have been made in the submarine's hull. It was a fairly simple operation, and there was no specific need to rigidly adhere to Oram's plan. In McKenzie's view, the hole could have been drilled anywhere, not just near to the gun recuperator as Oram had suggested. McKenzie went on to say that, at the time, the stern was still above the water and holes could have been drilled here near to Z tank which would not only have given fresh air to the men inside the submarine, but it would have generated more time for the rescue bid. McKenzie stated that not only could holes have been cut to allow air into the submarine, but that it would have been possible with the oxy acetylene equipment available to cut a hole, in less than ten minutes, large enough for the men themselves to escape from. This statement caused quite a stir at the tribunal, and Mr Justice Bucknill appeared to be quite incredulous at hearing it. He asked McKenzie whether this was only possible with specialist cutting gear. McKenzie was quite clear in his answer, stating that given a reasonably competent operator, together with the cutting gear which was available on site, the whole operation could have been completed well before he had arrived from Scotland.

One of the other issues which McKenzie took exception to was the fact that diver Orton had been required to surface more than an hour before it was strictly necessary. This, he suggested, was perhaps also due to Hart's lack of experience. It was clear that a degree of recrimination was creeping in at the tribunal. When Captain Hart considered that his actions, together with his perceived lack of experience, were being brought into question, he stated, via a letter from his lawyers, that for a considerable time after his arrival, he had been specifically told not to get within the close vicinity of the escape hatch, as he might, unwittingly, impede any men who were attempting to escape using the Davis apparatus.

Also at the tribunal there was a major disagreement concerning just what cables would have been sufficient to support *Thetis's* stern. It was clear that Hart held to the view that a 3½-inch diameter cable was sufficient to give enough support, providing that is that the stern was still buoyant. But this had not been the case as there was, for some unaccountable reason, a change in the buoyancy of the submarine. It was apparent that most having expert knowledge of such matters tended to share McKenzie's view that, had 'camels' been supporting *Thetis* on either side, then the cables would not have broken. Hart re-iterated in the strongest possible terms that the decision to try to tow the submarine was not his, and came from higher command. He went further and stated that he was totally opposed to this course of action, but was merely obeying an order. He also maintained that it would not have been possible to cut an escape hole in the hull of the vessel at any time during the rescue operation. McKenzie disagreed with this view.

Heavy cable as used in the rescue attempts. (*From* SOS *Thetis, Hans Müller Verlag, Dresden, 1943*)

The Mersey Docks and Harbour Board's salvage vessel *Salvor* waits by one of the 'camels', carrying all of the equipment necessary for the rescue bid. (*From* SOS *Thetis, Hans Müller Verlag, Dresden, 1943*)

By Sunday 4 June, all hope had been given up of rescuing any more survivors, so, being a realist, McKenzie asked if he and his team could be released from what was now, in truth, a recovery operation. He informed Captain Hart, who was his immediate superior, that he had pressing work at Scapa Flow and had to return. It was obvious from his body language, although not articulated at the time, that he believed that the whole rescue operation could and should have had a different outcome; but, in order to have achieved this, they would have had to adopt a completely different rescue strategy, with known experts available at the appropriate time.

CHAPTER 6

Recovery

With reference to the public Inquiry regarding the disaster, it was obvious
that the feeling within the nation was such that nothing less than a full public
Inquiry would satisfy that mood. Differences arose as to when it would
actually take place. After giving a detailed summary of the events relating to
the disaster, Neville Chamberlain, the Prime Minister at the time, took the view
that in order to ascertain all of the relevant facts which led to the disaster, it
would be counter-productive to begin any Inquiry before *Thetis* was salvaged.
This view was strongly opposed by many members of the House, including the
Parliamentary Secretary, Albert Victor Alexander. He was of the opinion that
the Inquiry should start almost immediately, because the salvaging of *Thetis*
may take some considerable time due to weather conditions in Liverpool Bay
and a number of other factors. He also stressed that it was important to settle
the minds of the relatives and in some way appease their misgivings; they
were still being left in a complete vacuum with regards to why the disaster
had occurred in the first place. The information flowing from the Admiralty
had—to put it kindly—been scant; and, to express it as many people were
now stating, non-existent. Meanwhile, almost as soon as the news officially
broke that there was no hope of rescuing any more of the men on board the
vessel, the salvage operation began. After discussions between the owners of
the vessel, Cammell Lairds, and the owners of the salvage equipment on site,
the Mersey Docks and Harbour Board, arrangements were made for Captain
Hart to start the salvage operation as soon as possible. But, with the vagaries
of the weather in Liverpool Bay, this operation proved to take much longer
than originally anticipated.

The work resumed on the *Thetis* and 'camels' were now deployed on either
side in order to begin the lengthy process of recovery. But, as Chamberlain
had to report to the House just a few days later, the weather conditions in
Liverpool Bay deteriorated to such an extent that the holding cables to one

of the 'camels' failed, and the cables to the other camel had to be released. Once again, in a very short space of time, *Thetis* had plunged to the seabed. The buoyancy argument that McKenzie had forwarded had proved to be correct. His view had been that, if only the forward two compartments of the submarine had been flooded, then it would have been possible for her to have been lifted, given the remaining buoyancy. But, with the flooding as it now appeared to be, a completely different recovery strategy would need to be put in place. At this stage, many different views were being forwarded, leaving the government, and in particular the prime minister, in an invidious position. Many of the relatives of those on board were of the firm belief that those on the submarine should be left in peace at the bottom of the bay, suggesting that this would be a fitting tribute and memorial to them. It was a call echoed by many of the nation's newspapers, most notably Merseyside's local newspapers. There were however some dissenting voices at the time. Mr John Tinker, who was the MP for Leigh, was of the belief that it was essential to raise the submarine in order to find out exactly what had caused the disaster. He went further and suggested that, if the vessel could not be raised, then it would beg a whole series of other questions, not least being the one suggesting that the government, Admiralty and perhaps the makers of the submarine were in some sort of conspiracy, and had something which they didn't want to be exposed to public scrutiny. He was adamant in declaring that the submarine should be fully examined by independent assessors once she had been salvaged.

In addition to the obvious concerns which were now being voiced throughout the country, there was also much consternation at Westminster. Chamberlain was anxious to ensure that the submarine was raised, but also expressed the view that, as long as she remained on the seabed, it would be impossible to ascertain exactly what had caused the catastrophic sequence of events which, ultimately, led to the disaster. He was unequivocal in expressing the view that it would be futile to begin any public Inquiry into the disaster until the submarine was raised. And yet, only a matter of a few days later, the Inquiry was started with *Thetis* still resting on the seabed.

Other interests were now covertly coming into play. Obviously, Cammell Lairds were in constant communication with their insurers Robert Bradford & Co. of London. Their advice to Cammell Lairds was to forfeit any interest in *Thetis*. It was also indicated by the insurers that this was standard practice in such cases, but covered themselves by stating that this decision resided with Cammell Lairds's management. The vessel's builders had already submitted a claim for the entire loss of the submarine which was somewhere in the region of £350,000. However, if the company maintained an interest in the recovery, then the gross amount payable would, in all probability, be somewhat in excess of this figure. When taking advice on the situation, so that they themselves could advise Cammell Lairds, Bradford's were inclined to suggest that any further attempts by Cammell Lairds to recover the vessel should be curtailed immediately, as there was little chance of the submarine being in a condition which would enable her to be re-fitted. They, Bradford & Co., suggested that *Thetis* should be left where she was, at the bottom of Liverpool Bay. They also took the view that should the Admiralty wish, for any reason, to recover the submarine, then that would be their decision. Clearly, from an Admiralty point of view, there were many questions which needed answers, but two in particular; what to do about the bodies still in the submarine—and here opinions were divided—and the other main question, related to the reasons for her loss, so that lessons could be learned for the future.

As Managing Director of Cammell Lairds, Johnson himself was faced with many critical decisions which would need to be taken in the near future—not least of which was the question of his former employees who were now dead and incarcerated in the submarine. He made it known that he wanted all of them to receive a fitting burial, so that families and friends could lay their loved ones to rest. For this and, perhaps, other financial considerations, Johnson did not want to sacrifice *Thetis* to the insurers. A meeting was convened at the company's offices in order to answer the critical question as to whether it would be possible to salvage the submarine. During the course of the meeting Captain Hart, who was present and represented the Mersey Docks & Harbour Board, stated that he could not be involved in any further recovery attempt, as, legally, he could only be involved in such operations within a prescribed area, which was in fact within five miles of the River Mersey, and clearly, the location of the submarine in Liverpool Bay was well outside of this zone. Just so that there could be no doubt, Vice Admiral Fraser who was also present at the meeting, and represented the Admiralty, stated once again the sentiments which the Prime Minister himself had made in the Commons, which was that both the Admiralty and His Majesty's Government had an imperative that *Thetis* must be raised at all costs. But, with Hart unable to undertake the recovery operation, perhaps the only other person able to undertake such a complex operation was Senior Salvage Officer George Critchley of the Liverpool & Glasgow Salvage Association—he too was present at the meeting. There was much discussion as to whether heavy lifting salvage equipment could be utilised from the Port of London. It had already been agreed that the salvage vessels which were on site, namely the *Ranger* and *Salver* would be augmented by the Royal Navy's dedicated diving vessel HMS *Tedworth*. Watson also declared that the Navy had specialist divers on board who would assist in the operation were they to be needed. It was also thought that, should further specialist divers be needed, then McKenzie and his team at Scapa Flow could be called upon again to render further assistance. Hart's expertise, although questioned previously, was once again sought by the Admiralty. Watson asked him, directly, as to the best method to recover the vessel, given the prevailing conditions. Hart was in no doubt as to the best way to recover the vessel. He stated that one of two methods cold be utilised, either by using strong cables or, alternatively, air pressure. He suggested that cables would be much better, and that they should adopt a system well-known amongst salvage experts; the method known as 'tidal lift'. He explained to the meeting that the method involved securing cables under the submarine's hull, and then with each successive high tide, the hull could be slowly raised and gradually brought into shallower water. He did, however, caution that this may take some time to achieve recovery, adding the caveat that this was assuming there were favourable weather conditions throughout, otherwise it could take significantly longer.

There appeared to be general consensus around the table as to what method should be adopted in order to salvage the stricken submarine. However, there was not complete unanimity, in that George Critchley, the Senior Salvage Officer of the Liverpool & Glasgow Salvage Association was of the view that the best method for raising the vessel was to pump compressed air into the forward chambers of the submarine through the torpedo tubes. It was his considered opinion that, given a controlled situation, the vessel could be brought up more easily using this method, but, the ultimate decision was not his, or indeed Captain Hart's. It was up to the Third Sea Lord, Vice Admiral Fraser to make the decision on behalf of the Admiralty. He decided that Hart's 'tidal lift' method should be tried in the first instance. This view was endorsed by those present at the meeting, especially when it became known that the Port of London had a number of larger, self-propelling 'camels', capable of lifting heavier loads than the 'camels' currently on site. The fact that the 'camels' were self-propelling meant that they could be brought up from London in a matter of days.

Contact was made with the Port of London's Harbour Master, Commander E. C. Shankland. Critchley, together with one of his senior colleagues, Mr H. Thomas, left for London in order to discuss the details of the strategy with Commander Shankland. It was on their arrival that they were greeted with the news that the 'camels', which they believed were self-propelling, were similar to the 'camels' on the Mersey, in that they had no motive power of their own, although they were larger than the Mersey 'camels'. Faced with this knowledge, Critchley was left in somewhat of a dilemma. But, wishing to make some progress, his colleague, Thomas, went to view the 'camels' in Tilbury docks whilst Critchley continued his discussions with the Harbour Master. On his return to the Harbour Master's office some time later, Thomas reported that the 'camels' would not meet their requirements, in that they were not fitted with up to date equipment for securing, heaving-in and releasing the cables. It was futile continuing the discussion. It was now an incontrovertible fact that Critchley was running out of options. He considered that with additional, albeit smaller 'camels' on site, he would be able to effect the recovery. He telephoned the Mersey Docks & Harbour Board in order to obtain four more 'camels'. The proposal was considered by the Mersey Docks & Harbour Board, but, because of legal requirements which meant that they had to ensure that the Mersey was open to sea traffic at all times, they felt unable to release four of their 'camels'. Critchley had the distinct impression that, for whatever reason, the Mersey Docks & Harbour Board was loath to allow more 'camels' to be released, thus putting in jeopardy the strategy which he had devised for raising *Thetis*. However, after more cajoling and psychological persuasion they did agree to release three more of these vessels, in the knowledge that they were being used outside of the jurisdiction of the Board. But this still wasn't good enough, so Critchley's problems were by no means over as yet. He was forced to consider a different approach; indeed, an approach which he'd used before, whereby he converted a cargo vessel to salvage the wreck. Having convinced the relevant authorities that this approach was viable, Critchley, together with an Admiralty surveyor, Doctor Robb, considered many vessels which might prove to be suitable for the conversion, but eventually found one in Cardiff. The ship, a collier, had the dimensions which they were looking for, and also had sufficient space on the weather deck to make the conversion feasible. The boat, the SS *Zelo*, was owned by the Pelton Steamship Company who had their head offices in Newcastle. After travelling to Cardiff and conducting a thorough examination of the ship, Critchley and Robb agreed that the vessel met with all of their requirements, and that she could be easily converted for the purpose which they had in mind. The next step was to enter into negotiations with the company's management. In some respects they were fortunate here, in that the vessel was already under charter to the Admiralty, but, in other respects, the detailed negotiations were rather more protracted than either of the men thought possible.

After it was decided that the *Zelo* would be suitable for conversion, Vice Admiral Frazer appointed Captain Fitzroy to be in overall charge of the salvage operation. There were still lengthy negotiations to be conducted with the Pelton Steamship Company. Transferring from one Admiralty charter to another enabled the company a degree of flexibility which they took full advantage of. There was a rate fixed per month for the charter which Fitzroy, using some adroit negotiating skills, managed to have reduced; he was also able to negotiate a good rate for subsequent payments after the first month's charter. When negotiations had been successfully completed, the *Zelo* was prepared for her voyage from Cardiff to Cammell Lairds at Birkenhead so that she could be re-fitted. As soon as *Zelo* arrived at Lairds's wet basin, conversion work immediately began. A solid wooden platform was constructed on the weather deck of *Zelo* which would facilitate cables being dropped over her

SS *Zelo*, owned by the Pelton Steamship Company. The vessel played a vital part in raising *Thetis* and then taking the submarine to shallower waters. (*Michael Helm*)

sides and thus cradle *Thetis* ready for the proposed 'tidal lift' operation.

Because of the weight involved, construction was such that a so-called 'belt and braces' approach was adopted. There were several two feet square wooden beams slung across the weather deck, thus allowing for the many cables, which would ultimately suspend *Thetis* under *Zelo*. In addition to this, and giving *Zelo* even more strength, the underside of the deck was further strengthened with more beams, so that she would not fail when the dead weight of *Thetis* was lifted. Furthermore, to ensure that *Zelo* stayed on station above *Thetis* whilst the cables were attached and *Thetis* lifted, six additional anchorage points were made for totally secure anchorage. The method of initially lifting *Thetis* was to slightly lift her bow first, using a four-and-a-half inch cable before the larger nine inch and seven inch cables were secured under the keel. She could then be lowered down onto the seabed and a similar method used for the after end to be secured. The pride of the workforce at Cammell Lairds ensured that the re-fitting schedule was completed in record time. *Zelo* was once again ready to sail from Cammell Lairds on 28 June. But, once again, Fate did not favour the salvage attempt, as there were gale conditions in Liverpool Bay, and it was almost a week before *Zelo* was on station, directly over *Thetis*. It had been agreed that the divers from HMS *Tedworth* under the direction of Chief Petty Officer Dick Oliver—*Tedworth's* Chief Diver—would start work on the first part of the recovery operation. Working in pairs, the divers had, at most, half an hour to do their work. And, because of the extremely dangerous conditions under which the divers were working, Oliver had gone to great lengths to ensure that there were good communication channels between the divers and *Tedworth*—he had arranged for telephones to be placed inside of the divers' helmets, an excellent method of ensuring good communication.

Initially, it appeared as though the salvaging operation was going according to plan, but then another gale blew up in the bay, and, even with all of the precautions that had been taken, *Zelo* dragged her moorings. Tremendous strain had been placed upon the cables and much damage was done during this time. The net result was that *Zelo* had to return to the shipyards once again for repairs and even more strengthening, as it was apparent that the measures taken thus far were not adequate to cope with the unforgiving waters of Liverpool Bay. Whilst the repairs were being carried out, the opportunity was taken to increase the number of mooring points from six to ten.

The process of securing the cradle of cables under the submarine and back up the other side to the *Zelo* was dogged with a series of problems, not least of which was the weather and the tidal currents causing shifts in the seabed around *Thetis's* resting place. Thomas became increasingly frustrated with the lack of progress. It certainly didn't help matters that divers could only spend half an hour at a time working at such depths. But, after many days of arduous work and a number of minor setbacks, the cables were secure and the *Thetis* was now evenly supported throughout her length. The only thing required now was good weather and perhaps a degree of good luck, which had conspicuously been absent to date. On Friday 22 July, weather conditions were ideal and low water was at 2140 hours. Thomas gave the order that the slack should be taken up on all of the cables. This gradual operation began at 1915 hours on the ebb tide. Timing was critical, and when low tide occurred all of the cables were correctly tensioned; there was even distribution around, and now it was just a question of waiting until the tide started to rise, and thus start to lift *Thetis*. The whole operation was taking place under the glare of strong floodlights, and observations were continuously been made on all of the cables. The rising tide was now causing *Zelo* to lift and in turn that meant that *Thetis* was also coming up, with the cables taking the strain. However, number five cable did not appear to be taking the same strain as numbers six and seven cables. The strong crossbeams supporting numbers six and seven cables failed. In an effort to save the remaining crossbeams, there was nothing else that Thomas could do but release the holding tension on the other cables. This salvage attempt had spectacularly failed.

The situation, as it was now developing, was causing Thomas and his team some concern. After many weeks of arduous work in difficult conditions, it was now looking as if all of their labours had been completely wasted. The mechanical failure had led Thomas to conclude that there was no way in which any further recovery attempts could be made. The tidal conditions had meant that divers could only spend a very limited amount of time on site, and it was imperative that the positioning of the cables needed to be checked and possibly adjusted in light of the earlier failure. Their despondency was soon communicated to staff at Cammell Lairds, and, in particular, the Managing Director, Mr Johnson. Reluctantly, he came to the view that it was perhaps better to let the submarine lie on the bottom and declare that it was a total write-off. Irrespective of the financial loss involved, he formed the opinion that maybe it was a fitting tribute to allow the men on board to rest in peace. However, this view did not prevail, and, within a very short space of time, *Zelo* was back at Cammell Lairds undergoing extensive modifications. The robust wooden structure on the deck was completely dismantled and replaced with an even stronger steel structure, able to withstand much greater stresses than had previously been envisaged. The Admiralty surveyor, Doctor A. M. Robb had made many of these new calculations, and it was his firm belief that with all of the additional strengthening, then it would still be possible to lift *Thetis* using the 'tidal lift' method. He did however concede that there was a distinct possibility that the submarine might well be subjected to stresses beyond her normal limits, but added that as high tensile steel had been specified for the hull's construction, there should not be any problems.

Divers poised and ready to start their work of recovery. (*By kind permission of Holyhead Maritime Museum*)

As if to underline the extreme conditions that the divers were working under, when Dick Harknett and Petty Officer Henry Otho Perdue, both divers from *Tedworth*, went down to make an assessment on the condition of *Thetis's* propeller shaft and stern before the lift commenced, they encountered more difficulties. Having finished their reconnaissance work, they signalled that they were coming up to the surface; however, Perdue became entangled on some of the cables around the submarine. Fortunately, Harknett had seen his colleague's predicament and went back to assist him. Both men reached the surface sometime later. Petty Officer Jack Dymond, who was observing proceedings from *Tedworth's* after end, noticed that something was amiss. For some reason, Perdue's dive suit looked as though it was over-inflated, which meant that the diver inside was unable to move. Straight away Dymond went to Perdue's assistance, bringing him on board and releasing the pressure on his faceplate. But, it was now becoming obvious to Dymond that the diver was in agony. As an experienced diver himself, he made the assumption that it must be the 'bends'. Perdue was immediately taken to *Tedworth's* decompression chamber. Both Perdue and Dymond were helped into the chamber. Because of the dire situation, Dymond had been asked to go into the chamber so that he could be on hand to assist if necessary. And that help was soon required as, once inside, Perdue collapsed. The pressure inside of the chamber was increased, such that it became equal to the pressure Perdue had experienced on the seabed. At this point Perdue's breathing became easier, but he was still unconscious. There was nothing for it, but to have the chamber brought back to normal atmospheric conditions, so that the ship's doctor could make an examination. Even whilst the doctor was making his examination, Perdue's condition deteriorated, and, in less than fifteen minutes he lay dead. *Thetis* had claimed her one hundredth innocent victim. At the later post mortem examination, it was discovered that the primary cause of death was not the 'bends' as had been assumed, but an undiagnosed case of tuberculosis earlier in the diver's life. He should not have been diving, as the tuberculosis had irreparably damaged his lungs.

Even given these tragic circumstances, it was imperative that work to recover *Thetis* continued unabated. And so it was on Monday 28 August that *Zelo* was back on station and ready for another salvage attempt to be made. It was deemed too dangerous to send divers down at this point, so tugs were employed to secure the cables under *Thetis*. A total of eight cables were secured under the submarine, some forward of the conning tower and some towards the after end of the submarine. With the newly reinforced structure on the *Zelo* together with the lessons that had been learnt from the previous abortive attempts, *Thetis* was gradually, very gradually, raised from the seabed. Using the 'tidal lift' approach, it took a total of nine lifts over the space of a week to take her above the low tide mark in Anglesey's Moelfre

Bay. There was an ironic twist, perhaps not fully appreciated at the time, that the final successful lift took place on Sunday 3 September 1939, the very day that the Prime Minister declared that England was at war with Germany. But, the Government's wish, and the Admiralty's wish had been fulfilled, in that the *Thetis* had been raised. The main question remaining was what was going to happen to the now salvaged *Thetis*?

It was also time for Cammell Lairds to face a deluge of letters and other correspondence offering comprehensive advice, recovery and burial services—in fact, the extensive correspondence covered the whole gamut of requirements for the gruesome task that lay ahead of the authorities. It was evident after reading the letters that many of the offers were genuine, and many of the correspondents did have relevant experience. But, on the other hand, many of the offers of assistance were received from people having some ghoulish interest in finding out, at first hand, exactly what had happened, and how matters were being resolved. Perhaps one of the first genuine letters to arrive at Lairds came from a clerk and ex-sick berth attendant, who was now working at Devonport Dockyard, Mr Albert Tucker. From the tone of his letter he was obviously acquainted with many of the nauseous scenes which would confront anyone involved in recovering the bodies. Other letters came from all over the country, with the correspondents having varying degrees of knowledge, experience and genuine concern.

With the list of correspondents steadily increasing day by day, Cammell Lairds, following detailed discussions with the Admiralty, wrote letters to all of the people who had offered their services, in whatever capacity, gently declining their offers of assistance. It was becoming clear that the operation of removing the bodies would not involve any civilian assistance. This, according to the Admiralty, was a matter for the naval authorities and the naval authorities alone. However, before the difficult and delicate work of removing the bodies could begin, the submarine had to be taken some way further up the shoreline at Moelfre Bay.

More than three months had elapsed since *Thetis's* fatal dive in Liverpool Bay, and now, for the first time, her badly battered conning tower was once again above the waterline. Although the *Tedworth* had now departed the scene, three of her divers had remained to render any assistance necessary. Also, divers from Chatham Dockyard were transported up to augment the dive team— knowing that theirs was a recovery operation rather than a rescue operation. Working with divers from the Liverpool & Glasgow Salvage Association, a plan evolved which, it was hoped, would enable recovery work to begin on the submarine. The idea was to block all of the open outlets except the stern. The submarine could then be 'blown' with compressed air, thus forcing water out. Again, it was hoped that, as a result of this action, the stern would become exposed once more. But, before this work could begin, the hatch to the engine room needed to be opened. Preparations steadily went ahead in order to put the plan into action. Diver Keys, together with his other colleagues from *Tedworth*, were given the task of sealing the hatches and ensuring that the engine room compartment was prepared in readiness. It was during this work, in dark and cramped conditions that one of the divers, quite inadvertently, placed his hand on the face of a body which had become exposed. It later transpired that this was the body of Torpedo Gunner's Mate Ernest Mitchell. He had been, at the time of the sea trials and the onset of the disaster, trying to close the watertight door at number twenty-five bulkhead. This gruesome revelation caused immediate and lasting damage to the diver. He was taken to the surface and later transferred to a Royal Naval hospital, where he was to remain for many months; his mind having been seriously affected by the devastating experience that he had, inadvertently, been subjected to.

The stranded *Thetis* was still at the mercy of the weather, even so close inshore at Moelfre Bay. Indeed, even though much of the preparation work had been completed, the actual recovery work could not proceed for another two months because of the adverse weather conditions. When it was possible for further preparation and recovery work to continue, the divers were forced to gain access to the submarine via the engine room compartment. They then had to check that all of the watertight doors were open and that any necessary valves were closed. But, before they could start on this aspect of the plan, they were faced with the most horrendous scenes which any person could be faced with. With their torches switched on to help guide their way, they soon saw and encountered the flaccid bodies of more than sixty men whose watery grave they were now entering. For some inexplicable reason, many of the bodies were naked or half-naked, and their facial expressions of fear and ultimate despair were, even now, too vivid to even begin to describe. Faced with this currently insurmountable obstruction, the divers were forced to abandon any further attempts at progress for the time being.

With the difficulties that the divers were now encountering, there was mounting speculation as to the condition of the bodies trapped inside *Thetis*. Some three months after *Thetis's* fateful dive trials, one of the Admiralty's top medical advisors, Surgeon Commander S. G. Rainsford, attempted to give an explanation as to the state of the bodies inside the submarine. He made reference to a similar occurrence in the United States when one of their submarines, USS *S-4*, had sunk with all hands, when she collided with a United States Coast Guard cutter. That accident had occurred late in 1927, when the submarine had been on dive trials off Massachusetts. Indeed, on that occasion, because of the difficulties in recovering the submarine, the bodies had actually been left for almost five months. However, when they were finally recovered, they were in as good a condition as could possibly have been expected after such a lengthy period of exposure. Surgeon Commander Rainsford expressed

A submarine tube space, similar in dimension and layout to that of *Thetis*. (*From* SOS *Thetis, Hans Müller Verlag, Dresden, 1943*)

HMS *Thetis* lying in Moelfre Bay, Anglesey. (*By kind permission of Holyhead Maritime Museum*)

Workmen continue their task whilst *Thetis* lies in Moelfre Bay. (*By kind permission of Holyhead Maritime Museum*)

no qualms when advising the Admiralty as to what they might be expected to find.

Because of the delicacy of the situation, it had been declared that, upon reaching Cammell Lairds's shipyards once again, the submarine would then, and only then, be opened and the bodies removed. This would be the direct responsibility of officers of the Royal Navy. It was further declared that, having removed the bodies, they would all—Royal Naval personnel, and also non-Royal Naval personnel—be taken to Liverpool's Anglican Cathedral to lie in state. However, there was one dissenting voice to this plan, and that was the Managing Director of Cammell Lairds, Mr Johnson. He was adamant that no bodies would be removed from the submarine at Cammell Lairds. As the shipyard was not a Royal Naval yard, the Admiralty were powerless to countermand this directive; the matter, in this one respect, was outside of their jurisdiction. They reacted by issuing a statement which declared that *Thetis* would be taken to dry dock at Holyhead where the bodies would be removed.

Surgeon Commander Rainsford held to the view that, similar to the men on board USS *S-4*, the men on board *Thetis* would also be in a good state of preservation; that is, providing that the bodies had not been exposed to the atmosphere. He cautioned that, should the bodies have been exposed to the atmosphere for any prolonged period of time, then they would become putrefied, thus making any post mortem examination extremely difficult, if not impossible, to perform. There was the added but practical complication that, under these conditions, it was likely that the bodies would become swollen beyond recognition. This condition would also make it difficult to remove the bodies through the hatches. The decision was taken that before any further salvage work could be continued, it was imperative that the bodies were removed. This task proved somewhat more difficult than had been anticipated, as the bodies were horribly swollen as had been feared. In fact, the whole gruesome and delicate process took upwards of three weeks, and even then the work could not be completed. It was proving impossible to remove the bodies that were held in the steering compartment, as the hatch door to that area, for some unknown reason, was not yielding.

Paying due respect both to the dead men and also to their families and friends, a tug flying the Red Ensign at half-mast carried the bodies that had been recovered to Holyhead further around the island. There then followed the grim task of identifying the bodies—as far as possible that is. Obviously, Leading Stoker Arnold was detailed to render every assistance in this respect. Also, in the period immediately before the sea trials commenced, two of the naval ratings from *Thetis* had been transferred onto other duties, but they knew many of the submarine's crew. For this reason, they too were drafted in to assist Arnold. It was relatively easy to name many of the officers on board—if, that is, they were still in uniform. Similarly, many of Cammell Lairds's staff could be identified

Preparations being made to have *Thetis* taken to Holyhead. (*By kind permission of Holyhead Maritime Museum*)

by the works number which was marked on their overalls. Even though all three did the best they could, the task was proving too much. It was clear that additional support was needed. Headed by Superintendent W. E. Jones, a small team from the Anglesey constabulary was brought in. Their task was to sift through personal effects; clothing, any papers that were still intact and any items of personal jewellery—indeed, anything that might assist in identifying the bodies. But, because of the general state in which the men had been found, this too proved to be a difficult, if not impossible, task. Even when family members were called upon to help in the identification process by detailing any physical characteristics of the dead men, the task still proved daunting.

Anglesey's coroner, Doctor E. R. Hughes, was called upon to conduct an autopsy on Torpedo Gunner's Mate Ernest Mitchell. His body, like the others being recovered, had been taken to Holyhead's main hospital, Stanley Hospital. Upon recovery, his body was found to be relatively well preserved, but, inevitably, having been exposed to the atmosphere, the body rapidly decomposed. Hughes, being a consummate professional, approached his task in a detached but totally correct manner, giving a highly detailed report of exactly how Mitchell had met his end, paying particular reference to the collapsed lungs and the bulging eyes—clear indications of the rapidity of death.

The following day Surgeon Commander Rainsford arrived together with

Workmen aboard HMS *Thetis*, preparing her to be taken to dry dock at Holyhead. (*By kind permission of Holyhead Maritime Museum*)

his colleague Consulting Pathologist W. W. Woods, but they decided that an autopsy was out of the question, as Mitchell's body was now in an advanced state of decomposition. Furthermore, when Rainsford was informed that a further four bodies were to be available for post mortem examination on 9 September, he decided, in consultation with other medical colleagues, that because of the decomposing state of the bodies, he would be able to gain all of the information necessary from conducting one post mortem examination. It was difficult to give a positive identification for Torpedo Gunner's Mate Ernest Mitchell, although he did have several tattoos on both of his arms and also on his right leg. Mitchell was found to be still wearing his DSEA apparatus. During the examination, Rainsford found that Mitchell had not died due to drowning; this he was able to confirm by noting that there was a complete lack of water in both the trachea and bronchial tubes, and further, that there was little or no water in the stomach. Armed with this evidence, and the fact that the rapidly decomposing body had been examined barely two hours after being taken from the submarine, Rainsford suggested that any further attempts at post mortem examinations would be futile. He formally recorded that Mitchell's death had been caused by asphyxiation through carbon dioxide poisoning. Bearing in mind the circumstances in which all of the men had died, he then attributed the cause of death for all of them as asphyxiation through carbon dioxide poisoning.

As Cammell Lairds had declined the Admiralty's request for the bodies to be taken from the submarine at the shipyard, they were then forced to rely upon the good offices of the Liverpool & Glasgow Salvage Association. The Admiralty also made the company responsible for ordering the specially made coffins for all ninety-nine bodies. After much deliberation, it was eventually decided to have all of the coffins zinc-lined. This was primarily to ensure that no fluids seeped out of the coffin at any point. Also, because of the bloated nature of the bodies, the coffins had to be made in sizes which were approximately twice the size of normal coffins—the cost of the coffins was also significantly higher than would have been paid for normal sized coffins, but this item of expenditure was met by the Admiralty. Having completed the formidable task of having to identify all of the ninety-nine bodies, relatives of the dead men were then, officially, informed by telegram of the loss of their loved ones. The Admiralty then issued next-of-kin with two third-class rail warrants in order that they could attend the funeral in Holyhead. However, where relatives had requested a private funeral, arrangements were made by the Admiralty to have the coffins transported to the station nearest to their home address.

For obvious reasons, the Admiralty went to great lengths to dissuade relatives from seeing the state in which their loved ones had been found. However, some couldn't bear the thought of never seeing their nearest and dearest again. This

Now looking very different from when she sailed out of the shipyard on 1 June 1939.
(*By kind permission of Holyhead Maritime Museum*)

experience proved to be extremely harrowing for all involved—both relatives and
navy personnel. Leading Stoker Arnold and his two former colleagues from *Thetis*
gave support and comfort where they could, as did staff from Cammell Lairds.

There were still many more distressing specifics which had to be addressed.
It was decreed that, once recovered, all clothing should be removed from
the bodies before being transferred to the mortuary for further detailed
examination. The police force also had a significant role in this part of the
recovery process. It was delegated to them to ensure that all valuables and
money found on the bodies should be returned to their loved ones. The police
force in Anglesey then made arrangements for all of these items to be sent to
local police stations up and down the country—a difficult task at the best of
times, but, even more difficult at the outset of war. But, human nature being
what it is, a small number of relatives complained that some or all of their
relations' belongings had not been returned. One such person falling into this
category was Mr Alfred Mortimer whose son, telegraphist Thomas William
Mortimer, died in the disaster. Mr Mortimer thought that his son must have
been wearing his watch on the day of the trial dive, but, although he had
received some of his son's other belongings, he had not received his watch.
Later on, when Cammell Lairds had completed their cleaning and clearing
of the submarine, Mr Mortimer received a letter from the shipbuilders baldly
stating that his son's watch had not been recovered nor indeed had any more
personal items of his son's been found.
The grim work of removing all of the bodies from the submarine, once started,

Forlorn in the waters of Moelfre Bay. (*By kind permission of Holyhead Maritime Museum*)

continued unabated for some considerable time. And then, on 14 September 1939, just eleven days after Chamberlain had informed the nation that we were at war with Germany, the first seven men were buried with full military honours in a brick-lined mass grave at Holyhead's Maeshyfryd Cemetery. The funeral cortège made its slow journey, first passing through the town of Holyhead and then on up to the cemetery overlooking the town itself and the Irish Sea. Many of the town's shops which lined the route were closed for the day as a mark of respect, and a goodly number of the townsfolk quietly stood on the sidewalks as the lorries passed by. First in the cortège came the naval firing party and directly behind them were the four lorries carrying the seven coffins all draped in Union Flags; masking, in part, the unusually large coffins. All of the coffins were festooned with wreathes and other floral tributes. Directly behind the coffins were the family members and officially invited guests; the Admiralty had decreed that no other persons would be allowed to be present at the funerals. Having arrived at the cemetery, the funeral service was conducted at the graveside by ministers from all the denominations to which the dead men had belonged. The culmination of the service was when the naval firing party fired three volleys over the grave. This was followed by the buglers sounding the Last Post and Reveille.

The next funeral was scheduled to take place on 27 September. It was to follow much the same format of the earlier funeral, but, because there were so many coffins of this occasion, it was considered more respectful by the Admiralty for the coffins to be taken to the cemetery prior to the committal;

Being laid to rest with full military honours at Maeshyfryd Cemetery, Holyhead. (*By kind permission of Holyhead Maritime Museum*)

in this way, family members could lay their wreaths and pay their final respects to their own loved ones with dignity and in privacy. Before the service commenced, there had been a naval guard placed around the coffins—a fitting tribute to the dead men.

Coinciding with the time of the funeral, Holyhead's pilot boat was towing out into the Irish Sea a small fishing vessel; this too was witnessed by many of the townspeople who were, respectfully, lined along the harbour wall as the boats sailed out. There were two zinc-lined coffins on the deck of the fishing smack, both draped in the Union Flag and having a guard of honour of six naval rating stood nearby. The coffins were those of Lieutenant Commander Guy Bolus, *Thetis's* captain and Mr Arthur Stanley Watkinson, the Engineering Manager of Cammell Lairds, who was also on board *Thetis* on that fateful day. Both families had thought that a burial at sea was more fitting for their loved ones. In addition to the six-man guard of honour, Leading Stoker Arnold was on the vessel as was Mr Watkinson's grieving widow, Mrs Marjorie Watkinson. Lieutenant Commander Bolus's sister was also on the boat, as his wife could not be present.

The two vessels made their way out to the designated spot some miles out into the bay, where the flags were taken from the coffins and replaced with wreaths. Then, with dignity which was fitting for the occasion, the two coffins were given to the sea, without further ceremony or any religious act. The only

The conclusion of the memorial service held directly over the location where HMS *Thetis* had sunk. A naval party on board HMS *Seagull* fired a ceremonial volley from the foredeck. The memorial service was held aboard HMS *Hebe*, directly ahead. (*From* SOS *Thetis, Hans Müller Verlag, Dresden, 1943*)

discernible reference was the wreaths, which remained on the water's surface as a transient symbol of the men's sacrifice.

It was with a certain degree of irony, which appears to have been lost on the Admiralty, that many of the relatives who made the journey to Holyhead for the mass funerals were billeted in a bed and breakfast boarding house known as 'The Sailor's Rest'. However, Mrs West, who was the owner of the property, did everything in her power to comfort the distraught relatives in their hour of need, especially when so many of them were a long way from home and familiar surroundings and at such a traumatic period of their lives.

But, even at this stage, there were still many bodies remaining on *Thetis*; these were the bodies of the men who were entombed in the steering gear compartment. Because of the difficulties which would be encountered when removing the bodies from this area, it was considered that the boat needed to be taken to Holyhead before this final recovery could be made. However, before that operation could be completed, there was still some further survey work which needed to be conducted, and, like so many other events associated with *Thetis*, this too took an inordinate amount of time. It was then, and only then, that 'blowing' re-commenced, and the next phase of the recovery operation could finally begin. Indeed, it was not until 23 October that 'blowing' enabled, first, the stern to break the surface and then, a little while later, the bow. *Thetis* was afloat again after almost five months, but

Just some of the many floral tributes laid at the memorial service honouring all those men who died in the *Thetis* disaster. (*From 'SOS Thetis', Hans Müller Verlag, Dresden, 1943*)

it was not until mid-November that she was finally secured in dry dock at Holyhead.

Faced with the prospect of having to recover the bodies remaining in the submarine, the task was not nearly as complicated as it had been for the divers in their earlier attempts. Because the *Thetis* was no longer beneath the waves, it was now possible for the Admiralty to call upon the services of some of the specialist teams around the country. The concept of rescue teams such as these was first developed following several mining disasters in and around the Shropshire, Staffordshire and Yorkshire mining areas. Hedensford Mines Rescue Station in Cannock, Shropshire, was contacted by the Admiralty to see if they were willing to undertake the task of recovering the bodies which were still entombed in the submarine. However, it was the rescue team from Gornall Colliery in Staffordshire who eventually had to face the gruesome task, with support from a number of volunteers from HMS *Drake*. But, on further reflexion, officials from the Admiralty considered that extricating bodies from a submarine would not be a particularly edifying experience for naval personnel. So, 'when push came to shove', most of the remaining bodies were removed by seven local Holyhead policemen.

After gaining entry via the escape chamber, the volunteer team,

The royal naval burial party marching up Holborn Road, Holyhead to Maeshyfryd Cemetery on Saturday 29 September 1939. (*By kind permission of Holyhead Maritime Museum*)

The monument at Maeshyfryd Cemetery, Holyhead. Forty-four of the men who died in the *Thetis* disaster are buried here. (*Author photograph*)

understandably, found even more decay than the divers had previously. They also discovered bodies slumped against the engine room bulkhead door—thus giving an explanation as to why the divers had been unable to gain access to that area during their recovery missions. Starting their own recovery operation, when each of the now grotesquely swollen bodies had been secured, they were carefully enfolded into an oversized canvas bag. A crane was then used to lift each body out of the submarine via the escape chamber, and then they were laid to rest on the quayside. When the last body, that of Leading Seaman Walter L. Hambrook, was lifted from the submarine on 12 November, *Thetis* was thoroughly cleaned and, as far as humanly possible, the accumulation of noxious fumes was removed before further surveys and investigations were continued.

The painstaking, heartrending and delicate task was finally over—*Thetis* had reluctantly released the last of her captives.

The third and final funeral was held at Maeshyfryd Cemetery on 16 November 1939. As had previously been the case, the general public were excluded from the ceremony. Fitting tributes were paid by Canon Hughes of Holyhead and Archdeacon Morgan of Bangor, who jointly led the service. The Commander-in-Chief (Western Approaches) was represented by Captain Kitson, and Commander Shadwell stood in for Rear Admiral (Submarines) Bertram Watson who, for obvious reasons, remained in his office. Similarly, it was left to Mr J. Watters, Assistant Shipyard Manager, to represent Cammell Lairds.

Maeshyfryd Cemetery, Holyhead. The monument lists every man who was lost in the *Thetis* disaster. (*Author Photograph*)

CHAPTER 7

The Inquiries

After it was finally confirmed and announced that there could be no more survivors from the *Thetis* tragedy, two quite different and separate inquiries began. The first Inquiry, conducted at the behest of the recently appointed Commander-in-Chief (Portsmouth), Admiral Sir William M. James, was an internal and highly confidential Inquiry for the Admiralty and commenced its work on 6 June 1939. The second Inquiry, which was ordered by His Majesty's Government, was prompted, in the view of many observers, by the public and spontaneous outcry relating to the 'authorities' abysmal failure to rescue the ninety-nine men remaining on board *Thetis*. The public Inquiry, chaired by the Honourable Mr Justice Bucknill, started its hearing on Monday 3 July 1939, just a few days after the internal naval report, the so-called Raikes report, had been delivered to Admiral Sir William M. James. The findings in the Bucknill Inquiry were, in parts, very different from those in the Raikes report.

Admiral James had commanded that a full, thorough and confidential Inquiry should be initiated, immediately, to examine and assess exactly how *Thetis* was lost. The swiftly convened Inquiry was chaired by Vice Admiral Robert Henry Taunton Raikes who had extensive knowledge of submarines and procedures to be adopted in all emergencies on board. His other two fellow-committee members were Rear Admiral William Frederick Wake-Walker, from the Royal Naval War College at Greenwich, and Captain Claud Barrington Barry, who was commander of the submarine depot ship HMS *Medway*.

Frenetic activity followed for the next three weeks, whilst the Inquiry interviewed in excess of fifty experts of one sort or another, including the four *Thetis* survivors. On 29 June 1939, less than one month from the day of the disaster, and exactly one year since the submarine had been launched, the confidential Raikes Report, officially entitled, 'Finding of the Board of Inquiry into the Loss of HMS *Thetis*' was delivered to Admiral James. The most important of the several findings related to the conduct of senior officers, at all levels, in the search and rescue operation, the report also brought into sharp focus, and was critical of, certain aspects of submarine design and naval training as it related to submarines. However, it must be remembered that this Inquiry began its work when *Thetis* was still on the seabed, so critical forensic evidence was not available for consideration at that time.

Raikes castigated Lieutenant Commander Bolus for many of his actions and also for failing to act in certain circumstances. When examining the issue as to the number of people on board at the time of the disaster, Raikes conceded that it was generally the case for vessels on equipment trials to carry additional, specialist staff to monitor those trials. The engine trials on *Thetis* were no different from this. On the day of the dive trials, engine trials were also to be carried out on *Thetis*. However, the engine trials were to be carried out prior to the dive trials and, after completion, the personnel not specifically required for the dive trials were to disembark. For this reason, it was written into the construction contract that the contractors would provide a suitable vessel for staff to disembark to. So, immediately before the dive trial, Captain Bolus had requested that any personnel wishing to disembark should leave the boat and transfer to the *Grebe Cock*; however, none did, and, perhaps more significantly, Bolus did not give any definite instructions for them to do so. It was also acknowledged that it was custom and practice at such times for officers standing by other similar vessels being fitted out to be allowed to participate in the engine and dive trials to gain valuable experience. As the submarine building programme meant that two other vessels were currently being built at Cammell Lairds, Lieutenant Commander Garnett from *Taku*, and Lieutenant Commander Lloyd from *Trident*, were on board *Thetis* for her dive trials. In light of this there was some question as to whether the number of Admiralty representatives could have been reduced to a smaller representative figure. On this point, the Raikes Inquiry was particularly scathing, stating quite categorically that a number of the Admiralty staff on board for the diving trials could have been disembarked. The report concluded that the representatives of the Rear Admiral (Submarines) need not have been on board, nor indeed the representative of the Engineer-in-Chief, and probably the three Admiralty Overseers. The report also concluded that the number of officers from other submarines was excessive, suggesting that a maximum of two officers should have been on board. They did however exonerate Captain Oram's presence, as he was the Commanding Officer of the flotilla which *Thetis* was to join.

The Raikes Inquiry had then gone on to consider other personnel on board during the dive trial, and specifically those people working for Cammell Lairds. It was accepted by Lairds Managing Director, Mr Robert Johnson, that, perhaps, there hadn't been the need for quite so many of his employees on board. Raikes, however, was quick to distance himself from stating just

Working to prepare the submarine before she was moved to Holyhead. (*By kind permission of Holyhead Maritime Museum*)

how many Lairds staff should have been on board; it was a Lairds decision, and not an Admiralty decision. The final example of personnel who were surplus to requirements as quoted by Raikes was the Mersey Pilot, Mr Norman Willcox—there was a pilot cutter waiting to transport him back to Liverpool, but he had waved it away, contrary to all instructions.

It is perhaps worth noting that, when the Bucknill report was later published, there were some marked and significant differences between that report and the confidential Raikes report; one of the most significant differences being the lack of detailed questioning at the Public Tribunal with regards to the numbers of men who were actually on board the submarine during the dive trials. The first trials, which were held up in Gare Loch in April 1939, had a relatively small number of crew on board, whereas the trials in Liverpool Bay had 103 people on board. It was suggested that, because of legal requirements, this number of personnel was required to comply with the three-watch rotation system. It was also suggested at the Public Tribunal that the number on board could not have been reduced any further, but this line of questioning ended at that point, whereas Raikes' had not!

It was stated that Lieutenant Commander Bolus had 'blown' tanks numbers one, two and four. He had also ordered tank A to be 'blown', although he didn't order numbers five and six tanks to be 'blown'. It was suggested, that, had this have been done, the location of *Thetis* might have been found a good

Making final preparations before the move to Holyhead. (*By kind permission of Holyhead Maritime Museum*)

while earlier. Also, it would have negated the need for Cammell Lairds staff on board to change the internal piping; an exercise which, not only cost a great deal of time but, perhaps more importantly, a good deal of valuable air.

Speculation was rife as to why Bolus had taken this decision; the most likely reason being that he didn't want to use too much air at that time, because further compressed air might have been needed at some future time. Alternatively, he may have thought that it might have needed somewhat more than just 'blowing' tanks to ensure that the stern of the submarine broke the water's surface. Raikes, however, opted for an alternate view, suggesting that it would only have taken a small amount of compressed air to significantly increase the submarine's buoyancy. It was thought to be inconceivable that Bolus, given his experience and knowledge, did not opt for this decision, i.e. to 'blow' numbers five and six tanks.

There was conjecture as to if Bolus had 'blown' the tanks when *Thetis* sank, he might have been able to have kept the stern above water level, thus enabling air to be piped in, and crew members lives saved. It remained an unsolved mystery as to why Bolus did not adopt this approach. One explanation which was offered was that the crew, including Bolus, was absolutely exhausted and suffering from the effects of carbon dioxide poisoning, and thus unable to take either actions or critical decisions.

Lieutenant (Engineer) Jamison, First Lieutenant Chapman and Petty Officer

Smithers, in a gallant and unselfish action, had attempted to enter the flooded compartment and shut the rear door of number five tube; the object being to prepare the compartment for removing the water. They all suffered severe effects. The attempt actually failed, but, even had they succeeded, the act of clearing the flooded compartments was not going to restore the submarine's buoyancy. The Inquiry team considered that it was not known whether the senior personnel on board, including Lieutenant-Commander Bolus, Captain Oram and Lairds's senior staff, had a full understanding of how unstable the submarine was, or would indeed become if certain compartments were 'blown'. Again, it was not known if senior staff on board had any understanding of the complex 'blowing' different compartments would require in order to restore buoyancy.

When evidence had been taken with regards to the part played by Lieutenant Woods, Raikes was scathing and unequivocal in his condemnation of the officer. The committee, if nothing else, was meticulous and thorough in its Inquiry, especially when the question of the opening of the rear torpedo door of number five tube by Lieutenant Woods was considered. One of the first questions that Woods was asked was whether or not he had used the rimer to check whether there was any water in the tube. When the door is about to be opened, a lever is pushed up from the locked position to the unlocked position. In turn, this aligns two holes, one being in the door itself. When the two holes are in alignment, a small brass pin, about four inches in length (10 cm)—known as a rimer—is passed through the holes to check that there is no extraneous matter in the immediate vicinity of the holes. If there is any water in the interior of the tube which is above the level of the holes then it will come out from the tube through them. Similarly, if the tube is full of water and under some pressure, then, when the rimer is used, water will spurt through the aligned holes. Woods declared that he had not used the rimer. The committee concluded that there was no evidence to indicate that Woods was given any instruction as to the use of the rimer during training. Also, it was considered that sufficient importance was not attached to the presence and use of the rimer as part of the safety arrangements of the tubes. Woods was not held to blame for this oversight, the committee attributing blame to shortcomings in the Royal Navy's training. Even so, Woods was severely criticised for opening the rear door of number five torpedo tube. After this first and major criticism, the Inquiry had then focused on how it could be possible for the bow cap to be open at the same time as the torpedo rear door. The committee had heard Woods's categorical assertion that when power was put on the bow cap operating panel, all the indicators showed that the bow caps were shut. That statement had led the committee to conclude that, if that were the case, then the bow cap would have closed when the power was put on it, if it was not already closed. Not making absolutely definitive statements—as they could

More work on *Thetis*. (By *kind permission of Mike Kemble*)

not—the committee nonetheless thought that the balance of probability was against so many highly trained and experienced submariners making such an obvious error as not knowing that the bow cap was open.

The question as to the reasons for the error was then deliberated on, and it was considered that the unfortunate positioning of the bow cap indicators was a possibility—as they could not all be seen at the same time. Also, confusion might have been caused because the 'SHUT' position on the indicators was different for different tubes. But, again, this theory was discounted because, as Raikes concluded, it would have meant that a remarkable series of errors had occurred, and it was highly unlikely to make a mistake concerning the bow cap operating levers and then to compound it by making mistakes with the bow cap indicators.

Following the evidence of expert witnesses, the committee ultimately considered that there might have been two possible reasons for the bow cap being open. Firstly, the bow cap could have been partially open because of jamming or some other obstruction which might have caused this state; or secondly, there could, conceivably, have been a failure between the bow cap and the telemotor ram because of some sort of mechanical failure. The committee heard that any degree of movement of the bow cap was magnified on the indicator itself, but this was not evident. The committee was forced to conclude that either there was a mechanical failure which meant that the indicator was showing 'SHUT' when, in fact, the bow cap was actually 'OPEN', or, Lieutenant Woods had read the indicator incorrectly.

As to the actual closing of the watertight door in number twenty-five bulkhead, both the crew of the submarine, and also the Admiralty themselves, came in for severe criticism. Undoubtedly, there was a delay in the closing of this door. The lower clips were hanging down, and were jamming between the coaming and the door. The crew who were stationed in that compartment should have ensured that all clips were positioned correctly in their holders. Woods was quite categorical in stating that if they hadn't been hanging down, then the compartment could have been isolated and lives saved. The Admiralty were seen to be culpable in this respect; due to a late design change which they had insisted upon, the original quick-closing design was modified—possibly due to cost considerations—to a design with eighteen butterfly clips. Indeed, Raikes attributed more blame to the Admiralty rather than crew error.

Consideration was then given to the checking of the automatic inboard vents before opening the rear door of the tubes. The function of the automatic inboard vents is to prevent the submarine from losing any depth when a torpedo is fired. The automatic vent allows the tube to flood up immediately after a torpedo is released, thus preventing any loss in depth. Woods was also absolved for not checking this device before opening the rear torpedo door— as there weren't any torpedoes loaded on the submarine during the trials.

One of the significantly more controversial statements that was made in the Raikes's report, which, remarkably, was not referred to in the Bucknill report, was the fact that, under normal circumstances, there was no danger attached to opening the rear doors when working with the torpedoes. But, as there were no torpedoes on board during the trials, so the rear doors would be regarded as safety fittings. Raikes's report stated: 'We consider that in these circumstances there was no adequate reason for Lieutenant Woods opening the rear doors and he was not justified in doing so without instructions'.

When considering evidence relating to the acquisition of oxy-acetylene

Still lying on her side, *Thetis* beached in Moelfre Bay, Anglesey. (*By kind permission of Mike Kemble*)

burning equipment, the committee heard a number of contradictory statements. The Admiralty asserted that at 2300 hours on 1 June, they were in communication with the Liverpool and Glasgow Salvage Association. This was some eight hours after the *Thetis* went down. They informed the Association that their services would, in all probability, be required, and that oxy-acetylene burning equipment would be needed at the scene of the disaster. However, Mr Critchley, the joint manager of the Liverpool and Glasgow Salvage Association categorically refutes that this message was received. It was Mr Critchley's assertion that, had the message been received, then oxy-acetylene equipment would have been sent out on the company's salvage vessel *Ranger* and would have been available within a few hours of receiving just such a message—his company, being the largest in the country, would not have neglected or overlooked such a call. In private correspondence, Mr Critchley stated that the call was received on 2 June. Being so incensed with the manner in which the disaster had been dealt with by the Admiralty, Mr Critchley refused to participate in any further investigations or discussions relating to the submarine disaster.

The Inquiry then turned to how Captain Hart, Marine Surveyor and Water Bailiff of the Mersey Docks and Harbour Board on board the salvage vessel *Vigilant*, and Captain Nicholson on board HMS *Somali*, had handled the situation. Captain Nicholson had arrived from Portland at about 1040 hours on the morning of 2 June, and, under the terms of the 1934 Admiralty Fleet Order, he was now the senior ranking officer on site, and therefore assumed overall command of the rescue and salvage operations. Hart had immediately gone aboard *Somali* in order to brief Nicholson as to progress and also to discuss and agree a proposed course of action. At that point, the plan being followed was the one which Captain Oram had brought with him, namely that they were to keep away from the escape area until they could connect an air-pipe. It was considered, even at that stage, that men would be able to escape via the escape chamber. However, with both men, Nicholson and Hart, aboard the salvage vessel, *Vigilant,* the decision was taken to pull the submarine horizontally, in order to try to lift the stern. But, this move resulted in the submarine 'slewing'. The Inquiry considered that this reaction to the towing should have been anticipated by Captain Nicholson, even though the decision to tow was taken on the advice of Captain Hart. The Inquiry further concluded that the only course of action with any chance of success was to have attempted a direct vertical lift.

Both Hart and Nicholson had taken the view that, due to the force of the tide, *Thetis* was being kept under the surface, but, at 'slack' water, about 1800 hours, she would re-appear. This assumption was incorrect. At this stage, the submarine was at an angle of approximately 60° and there was an additional 12° list. The Inquiry made reference to the fact that this angle would not have assisted the men inside *Thetis* who were already in a much weakened state. When the focus of attention turned to the escape procedures, and in particular when the decision was taken to put four men into the escape chamber, the committee rapidly reached the conclusion that this was a very precarious action to have taken, and not at all likely to have been successful. The report roundly criticised First Lieutenant Chapman for taking this action. The only mitigating circumstance could have been that he had suggested this approach in order to save time; however, the committee was clear that the decision was totally wrong, and further, that not only had it caused considerable delay, but it clearly had affected the morale on the submarine—a view which was later endorsed by Leading Stoker Arnold.

Before leaving the subject of escape via the escape chambers, the committee found that there were shortcomings in the design, and that there needed to be further design work on these chambers. The committee found that on *Thetis*, the drains were open drains, and that because of this, there was a danger that water might have fallen onto electrical equipment and be an added hazard. In the case of *Thetis* there had indeed been an electrical fire, as a direct result of this design oversight.

With reference to the actual overall direction of the rescue attempt, Raikes was particularly critical, with Captain Nicholson being singled out for severe criticism. It was clear that Nicholson had not fully grasped the magnitude of the situation, and further, when he did, it was too late to take remedial action. There was also the series of compounded errors which, as officer in command, he should not have sanctioned; the most notable being the decision to attempt to lift the stern in the manner in which it was lifted. There was the

Waiting in the Escape Chamber wearing the DSEA equipment. Mariners always insisted that it was very claustrophobic inside. (*By kind permission of Pamela Armstrong*)

breaking of the towing wire and the proposed cutting of a hole in the body of the submarine—but no oxy-acetylene equipment had arrived at that stage.

It was clear to the committee that during the attempted lifting operation, the submarine had lost a considerable amount of buoyancy. Some weeks later, at the public Inquiry, Mr Thomas McKenzie, Chief Salvage Officer for the firm of Metal Industries, confirmed that basic salvage precautions had not been taken. The committee reiterated that decisive action needed to be taken, but that towing in the manner in which they had attempted to tow *Thetis* was unsound, to put it at its mildest, and that the alternative of a vertical lift should have been attempted.

Captain Ian Macintyre, who was Chief of Staff to Rear Admiral (S) and, effectively, in total command of the attempted search and rescue operation, had travelled to the scene of the disaster by boat, even though air transport was readily available, and even in light of the known gravity of the situation. This was considered to be a gross miscalculation on his part. He was, quite rightly, severely criticised for this action. But, the strongest criticism levelled at him in this area was the fact that, until he could reach the scene of the disaster, he hadn't seen fit to appoint officers who had relevant knowledge and experience who would be able to deal with the developing situation.

At the public Inquiry, which was held some time later, Macintyre said that, whilst time was a critical issue, the most important consideration, in his mind, was to ensure that he kept in touch with all those concerned with the rescue. He then went on to say that, before he had left to travel to Liverpool, he was of the belief that there were two, very experienced, submarine captains on hand. This was not the case.

When Macintyre made his comments relating to having two senior and experienced officers at the scene, he was totally unaware that both Lieutenant Commander Garnett, who was to be captain of the *Taku*, and Lieutenant Commander Lloyd who was to be captain of the *Trident*, were actually on board the *Thetis* during her dive trials—both *Taku* and *Trident* were being built at Cammell Lairds during the time that *Thetis* was being fitted out. Macintyre had

Until *Thetis* could be returned to her home in Birkenhead and completely rebuilt, the deck gun would never fire in anger. (*By kind permission of Mike Kemble*)

contacted Lairds in order to ensure that these two officers were available to assist in the rescue attempt; indeed, Cammell Lairds confirmed that they were not on the *Thetis* during the dive trials. In fact, the truth was very different from this. Both men, in order to gain further experience of submarine trials, were actually aboard *Thetis*—and, like so many more, they actually died aboard *Thetis*.

Technical data were also considered by the Inquiry, and, specifically, the fact that *Thetis* was not equipped—perhaps on grounds of cost—with an air purification system. The calculations had been made that, under normal sea-going conditions, with a standard crew, each person on board would have approximately four hundred cubic feet of air, meaning that, about 0.7 cubic feet of carbon dioxide would be being accumulating every hour. The calculation then went on to demonstrate that this would yield a safe submerged time of in excess of sixteen hours. After that duration, the atmosphere on board would have reached the critical three percent carbon dioxide level, which was considered to be saturation level. Any figure above three percent would impair operational efficiency.

It was known that when *Thetis* sailed, the number on board was almost twice as many as would be the case during normal sea-going operations. This would have the effect of reducing the amount of air for each person to less than two hundred cubic feet. However, it should be borne in mind that this was under 'dive' conditions, and when *Thetis* sailed from Birkenhead, it was assumed that many of the supernumeraries would be disembarked to the *Grebe Cock*. A further complication was known about which would, in turn, reduce yet further the amount of air available to each man, and that was the fact that there were two flooded compartments which, under normal circumstances, would not have been flooded.

The calculations which were made assumed that although four men had escaped from the submarine, there was still an excessive number on board. The cubic feet of air which was available was known to be significantly reduced, and, distressingly, it was thought that the remaining ninety-nine persons on board would only have about two hours of life left.

The Admiralty took a particularly hard line with regards to the rescue attempts, stating that, to the best of their knowledge, if a partially flooded submarine was unable to surface unaided, any rescue attempts would, in all probability, be too late to ensure that lives could be saved. So, apart from the DSEA equipment now available on all submarines, it looked as though this was the only effective means of escape. There were however some dissenting voices with regard to this policy. Captain Oram himself considered that rescue from the surface could not be discounted. When the Raikes final report was delivered, the possibility was raised of having an interlocking mechanism fitted between the bow cap and the rear door of the torpedo tube. The Inquiry had noted that, currently, there was nothing to stop another similar disaster happening in the future, as there was no physical mechanism which would prevent the bow caps being opened at the same time as the rear doors. However, the report included a caveat which stated that no mechanical interlocking mechanism could be regarded as being one hundred percent reliable, and did not therefore recommend that they be fitted.

Raikes did recommend that the current quick-opening mechanism for the doors be retained, but that a safety clip should also be fitted, and that the clip should be designed in such a way that if no water comes out, the clip can be released and the door opened. The fitting of the clip became mandatory on all submarines as, with the clip fitted, it was impossible for it to be taken off until the door was free. The clip became known as the *Thetis clip*.

In summary, a brief assessment of the Raikes report would suggest that it had a bias towards the onus for the disaster to be placed firmly upon the shoulders of individuals, rather than, in general, the procedures that were adopted. Raikes considered that there were five significant lines of Inquiry which needed to be pursued; 'Why were so many extra people on board the boat at the time of the disaster?'; 'Why was it that the reporting of the location of the marker buoy had been so inaccurate?'; 'Why weren't deep sea divers sent for earlier and why was no suitable equipment provided?'; 'Why was it that 'camels' were not sent to the general area where *Thetis* was thought to be, rather than waiting for her to be found?'; and, 'Would it have been preferable to have made earlier attempts at rescue, rather than placing too much reliance upon the efficacy of the DSEA equipment?'

When the Bucknill Inquiry started its proceedings on Monday 3 July 1939, Bucknill was fully aware of the findings of the Raikes Inquiry, and also of the pertinent questions which Raikes had posed.

However, this was a far more formal Tribunal than Raikes's had been, and, it was being held in public. The scope of the Inquiry might also have been somewhat different from the earlier Admiralty Inquiry. Indeed, the very first page of the transcript of the tribunal made it abundantly clear as to the remit of the Inquiry, which stated:

Thetis immediately before being taken from Moelfre Bay around to Holyhead. (*By kind permission of Mike Kemble*)

TRIBUNALS OF Inquiry (EVIDENCE) ACT, 1921

Royal Courts of Justice
Monday 3 July 1939.

MINUTES

of a

TRIBUNAL OF Inquiry

into the circumstances attending the loss of

HIS MAJESTY'S SUBMARINE

Thetis

and the subsequent attempts to save the lives
of those in the ship.

Judging from the statements above, there was no doubt as to the remit of the Tribunal, and the Hon. Mr Justice Bucknill, who chaired the Tribunal. Captain G. C. P. Menzies, RN, Captain A. H. Ryley and Professor T. B. Abell, OBE, M.Inst.N.A, M.Inst.M.E—acting as assessors—ensured that the remit was fully adhered to. There was also a very impressive array of top barristers and other legal representatives who would be allowed to question and cross-question all of the witnesses, starting with the Attorney-General who would be representing His Majesty's Government. Indeed, to a large extent, Bucknill was guided by the Attorney-General as to the general procedures which might be adopted, but, as to the scope and emphasis, he (Bucknill) had his own, very definite, agenda.

After the initial introductions and formal proceedings were completed, Mr Justice Bucknill turned to the Attorney-General and addressed him as follows: 'Mr Attorney-General, can you help me at all as to the best course that we can adopt for the purpose of getting the evidence of the Inquiry?'

The Attorney-General replied as follows:

My Lord, as your Lordship knows, when the Prime Minister announced the setting up of this Inquiry, he stated that; 'Of course, the Government will give the tribunal, all the assistance in its power, and as a considerable amount of preliminary work will be necessary before the Inquiry can be opened, the Treasury Solicitor has been instructed to place his services at the disposal of the tribunal for the purpose of collecting all the evidence and other material which the tribunal may require to have submitted to them.' In carrying out those instructions, the Treasury Solicitor has collected a great deal of evidence and explored, so far as may be, all matters which appear, or might appear, to be relevant. I have those statements of the witnesses, which I have read, and my purpose, and the purpose of those with me, Mr Willink and Mr Cyril Miller, is to assist in putting that evidence before you in such manner as your Lordship thinks proper. What I was prepared to do, if your Lordship thought it convenient, was to make an opening statement indicating the order in which I thought it would be convenient to call the witnesses, and giving your Lordship a short outline of the events, because I think it will assist in considering the evidence as it is called if your Lordship has in mind the main outline of the facts which will be proved by the witnesses. Naturally, I am not proposing, at this stage, to suggest hypotheses. I then propose to put before you in as concise form as possible the sequence of events, and then to proceed to call the witnesses.

Mr Justice Bucknill agreed that the process which the Attorney-General had outlined 'would be a very convenient course'. So, the tribunal proceeded along the lines which the Attorney-General had outlined and to which Mr Justice Bucknill had agreed. But, before moving to the substance of his introductory remarks, the Attorney-General first thanked his learned friends and colleagues for their assistance during the preliminary investigations which had, thus far, been made. He then opened by stating that the *Thetis* sank on 1 June 1939, during her final trial, which was her diving trial. He said that there were four survivors, and that the other ninety-nine men on board met their death in the disaster. The *Thetis* was the third Submarine of the *Triton* class to be completed. The contract for the construction of the *Thetis* was placed with Messrs Cammell Lairds, of Liverpool—stating that they, Cammell Lairds, would be represented by Mr A. T. Miller.

Local villagers view the stranded submarine as the tide continued to ebb and flow.(*By kind permission of Mike Kemble*)

The Attorney-General first outlined the order in which he was proposing to call the witnesses. Firstly, he would take evidence from each of the four survivors, and that, he stated, would be direct evidence as to exactly what had happened. Following the initial four witnesses, he would take evidence as to the general procedure with regard to the trials of the vessel under construction, detailing the evidence of previous trials and the relevant history prior to her last voyage, that is up until leaving Birkenhead on 1 June 1939. He then suggested that evidence should be taken with regards to the Davis Safety Apparatus, and that the instruction which personnel had received in this connection would be critical. Following this, he proposed to take evidence from witnesses who, on the day, were stationed on the support tug, the *Grebe Cock*. The Attorney-General then considered that evidence should then be taken from personnel on board various vessels and aeroplanes which had been despatched to search for the *Thetis* and give assistance when she was found. Following this, there would be evidence relating to the end of the successful search which had been at 7.50 a.m. on Friday 2 June. The tribunal would then hear of the subsequent actions of vessels in the location seeking to save lives. The Attorney-General did not propose to take any evidence after the time when all attempts for saving life were clearly hopeless. A significant head of evidence would then be evidence received from the Admiralty as to their general policy with regards to the safety of those who serve in submarines. Emphasis was stressed here on the careful and repeated consideration which had been given to this matter, as to the best method of saving life from a submarine in cases where it is possible. The Attorney-General noted that the vessel had been built with two escape chambers, to be used in conjunction with the Davis Safety Apparatus. His further remarks stated that, where necessary, witnesses could be recalled at a later stage.

Then, after these introductory remarks and what transpired to be a very lengthy 'outline of the events'—the phrase used by the Attorney-General—the first four witnesses, the four survivors from the disaster, were called. They were firstly questioned by the Attorney-General and then cross-questioned by other Counsel.

And so, the lengthy process of witness statements and testimonies followed, with every sentence being meticulously logged into what was to become the Inquiry transcript, which ran to more than two thousand pages.

When all of the witnesses had been questioned and cross-questioned, and all of the evidence had been collected and digested, Mr Justice Bucknill's lengthy Inquiry into the circumstances attending the loss of His Majesty's Submarine *Thetis* and the subsequent attempts to save the lives of those in the ship drew to a close. The report of the Inquiry was completed on 31 January 1940 and subsequently given to the Right Honourable Neville Chamberlain, His Majesty's Prime Minister. The Prime Minister presented a summary report to parliament in April 1940.

CHAPTER 8

The Report of the Pubic Inquiry (Parts 1–3)

In the opening paragraphs of his report, Mr Justice Bucknill stated that at about 3 p.m., British Summer Time on 1 June 1939, HMS *Thetis* with 103 men on board sank in Liverpool Bay, whilst engaged in the operation of a trial dive. At the outset he categorically declared that the immediate cause of the casualty was the opening of the rear door of No. 5 torpedo tube when the bow cap was open to the sea.

The report continued: About 7.50 a.m., on the 2nd, HMS *Brazen* and SS *Vigilant*, while searching for the *Thetis* sighted her stern above the sea level. Shortly afterwards Captain Oram and Lieutenant Woods, and about two hours afterwards, Leading Stoker Arnold and Mr Frank Shaw, a charge hand engineer fitter of Cammell Lairds, came to the surface by using the Davis Submarine Escape Apparatus (DSEA), and were picked up. Attempts were made to salve the ship and to save the lives of those on board, but about 3.10 p.m., her stern sank and disappeared. These are the cardinal facts relating to the loss of the *Thetis* and of ninety-nine lives on board.

Bucknill's report then went on to state that there were at least six facts acting in sequence which produced the full extent of this disaster:

i.   The complete blocking of the test cock in the rear door of No. 5 torpedo tube with bitumastic enamel.

ii. The opening of the rear door at a time when the bow cap of the tube was open to the sea. The precise moment when the bow cap opened is the critical and most obscure point in the case.

iii. The failure of those on board the *Thetis* to effectively close the port water tight door in the bulkhead between the torpedo tube compartment and the torpedo stowage compartment.

iv. The failure of those in the *Thetis* to expel the water from the two flooded compartments.

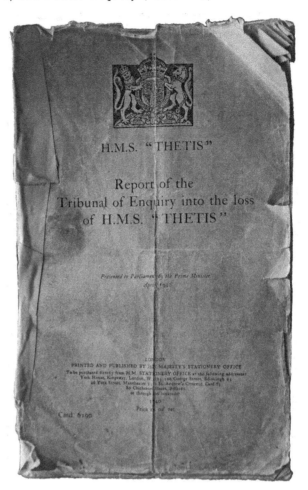

The report of the
Tribunal of Enquiry
into the loss of HMS
Thetis as presented to
Parliament by the Prime
Minister in April 1940.
(*By kind permission
of Holyhead Maritime
Museum*)

    v.   The failure of those outside the *Thetis* to render effective assistance.

    vi. The failure of those on board the *Thetis* to escape by the Davis Escape
Apparatus.

Mr Justice Bucknill's report to the Prime Minister was in five separate sections.
The first three parts of the report, which are summarised in this chapter, gave:

1.   an explanation of the structure of the *Thetis* (the section also gave a
detailed account of certain work done on *Thetis* before the vessel left
Birkenhead on 1 June 1939).

2.   an account of the disaster as witnessed by the survivors.

3.   a detailed account of the events which occurred outside the *Thetis*
relating to her loss and the attempts to render assistance.

The dimensions and layout of the tube space of *Thetis* were very similar to those of HMS *Alliance*, as seen in this photograph. It was in this space that the caterers had laid out tables for the celebration lunch of sandwiches and soft drinks. (*By kind permission of Pamela Armstrong*)

Summary of Part 1.
An explanation of the structure of the *Thetis*

(The section also gave a detailed account of certain work done on *Thetis* before the vessel left Birkenhead on 1 June 1939).

HMS *Thetis* was one of a number of submarines being built for the Royal Navy immediately prior to the outbreak of the Second World War. The submarine, like its sister ships, *Trident* and *Taku* was being built at the shipyards owned by Cammell Lairds on the banks of the River Mersey at Birkenhead. Other ships (or boats as submarines are normally designated) were being constructed at the shipyards of Vickers Armstrong in Barrow-in-Furness, some sixty miles away further up the Lancashire coast, and at Scotts in Greenock.

    Thetis is 275 feet long (about 84½ metres), and is divided into six main compartments

      1.   Torpedo Tube Compartment
      2.   Torpedo Stowage Compartment
      3.   Mess Space
      4.   Control Room

5.   Main Engine Room
6.   Steering Compartment

There are six torpedo tubes, arranged in two tiers of three each, Nos 2, 4 and 6 being in the port tier and Nos 1, 3 and 5 being in the starboard tier. No. 5 tube is about 21 inches in diameter. Its mouth is closed by a circular bronze plate called the bow cap. When the bow cap is opened it swings back into a position in which it lies fore and aft with the midships of the vessel, thereby leaving a free path for the torpedo from the tube to the sea.

Each bow cap is opened or shut by telemotor power which is operated by a lever. The bow cap of No. 5 tube is always below the sea level when the ship is afloat.

The after end of the tube is in the torpedo tube compartment. This compartment has a narrow alleyway between the starboard tier of tubes and the starboard side of the vessel. There is also a narrow alleyway amidships between the two tiers of tubes.

The lowest tube on the starboard cluster of tubes is the No. 5 tube. The bow cap operating levers, which are about eleven inches long, are located in the alleyway between the boat's inner skin and the bank of torpedo tubes. The opening and closing of each bow cap is activated by operating the bow cap operating lever for any particular bow cap. So, bow cap No. 5 is opened or closed by means of No. 5 bow cap operating lever. The three levers on the starboard side, arranged in a vertical configuration, are, from top to bottom, the bow cap operating lever for No. 1 tube; the bow cap operating lever for No. 3 tube; and, the bow cap operating lever for No. 5 tube.

The simple operation of pushing the bow cap operating lever forward to 45 degrees from its initial vertical position is enough to open the relevant bow cap. The telemotor operation ensures that from a neutral position to a fully open cap takes somewhere in the region of six to seven seconds. When the bow cap is required to close, the operation is carried out in reverse; passing through vertical and pulling the lever back to 45 degrees; thus, the bow cap operating lever traverses through an included angle of 90 degrees, from the forward 'OPEN' position, through the neutral position to the aft 'SHUT' position.

Each of the six levers has an indicator pointer which moves in conjunction with the lever itself. A vertical line on the indicator dial shows the neutral position. When the lever is aligned with the pointer in the neutral position, the telemotor continues to move the bow cap to either 'OPEN' or 'CLOSED.'

However, after the salvaging of *Thetis*, it was demonstrated that by pushing the No. 5 lever forward by as little as 12 degrees from the vertical neutral position towards the 'OPEN' position enabled enough oil to pass through the valve, such that the telemotor came into operation and caused the bow cap to creep open until reaching its fully open position.

The levers have a small wheel on either side. By turning the wheel, power is admitted to the control valve. So, by turning these wheels—together with operating the lever—specific bow caps can either be opened or closed. As a 'fail safe' there are also two isolating valves, located in the torpedo stowage compartment, immediately abaft of the tube compartment. The isolating valves can be used to isolate the telemotor power from the whole of the tube compartment.

In between the two tiers of the torpedo tubes are six mechanical indicators. They are located at the forward end of the alleyway and situated one above the other. The number five indicator is the lowest of the six, with its lower edge about nine inches above deck level. The indicator immediately above is the indicator for number six tube. The six mechanical indicators are connected to six rams which actually open and close the respective bow caps. The six mechanical indicators are, in essence, a dial and a pointer. The face of the dial has stamped onto it the words 'OPEN' and 'SHUT'. The positioning of these words is, rather confusingly, different on different dials. For example, in the case of the mechanical indicator for number five tube, 'SHUT' is shown as being at five o'clock and 'OPEN' is at seven o'clock. Whereas, in the case of the mechanical indicator for number six tube—directly above the dial for number five tube—'SHUT' is shown at eleven o'clock and 'OPEN' is at two o'clock. This means that when the pointer on number five dial is to the right of vertical, the bow cap is shut, whereas on the dial directly above, the number six dial, when the pointer is to the right of vertical, the bow cap is open—very confusing. Also, because of a horizontal bar immediately abaft of the number five tube mechanical indicator, which obstructs a direct line of vision, that particular dial is difficult to see.

The dial pointers on the indicators start to move whenever there is movement of the bow cap. So, if number five bow cap was opening from a shut position, the pointer on the dial would move anti-clockwise from its 'SHUT' position at five o'clock, through twelve o'clock, ending at the 'OPEN' position at seven o'clock—describing an arc of some 300°. But, as was pointed out at the Inquiry, because of the horizontal bar, there would be some movement of the pointer which would not be visible to anyone standing directly in front of the indicator. For each of the six tubes in the torpedo tube compartment there is a hydraulic indicator. The sole purpose of the indicator is to show when the bow cap is fully open. The indicator for the number five tube is in the starboard alleyway, and is located about four feet forward of the operating levers. The indicator itself has a window, and, when the bow cap is fully open, a 'tell-tale' is shown in the window with the words 'safe to fire' displayed. The 'tell-tale' operates on the last movement of the bow cap to fully open. The window on the indicator is blank at all other times. It was noted during the Inquiry that the tell-tale requires close observation in order to be seen.

There are two levers fitted to the rear door of number five tube. The larger lever is the operating lever and the smaller lever is the test cock lever. When the test cock lever is pointing downwards, then the rear door is locked, and when the lever is pointing upwards then the door is unlocked. Also, as another safety feature, the lever can be operated in such a manner as to automatically indicate whether the tube is more than half full of seawater. In the attachment of the test cock lever to the rear door, there is a hole drilled of about ⅜ of an inch (just less than 1 cm) diameter. There is also a similar hole drilled in the rear tube door itself. In order to open the door, the lever must be pushed up from the locked position to the unlocked position. During this movement there is a point when the holes coincide. It is at this point that a rimer can be passed through into the inside of the tube. The rimer is used to ensure that nothing, such as seaweed, is blocking the two coincident holes. The rimer itself is a brass pin about four inches (10 cms) long. It is attached to the lever attachment with a brass chain. The rimer is kept in a housing in the lever attachment when not in use.

If there is seawater inside of the tube and above the level of the coincident holes, then it will spurt out. If the tube is full of seawater and under pressure, when the holes are coincident, seawater will spurt out horizontally.

There are two ways in which the tube can be filled with water. The bow cap for that tube can be opened, thus causing water to enter the tube; but also, there is a cock in the tube which connects to a tank beneath the tube. This tank, called the 'Water Round Tube' tank (WRT), has a valve which opens directly to the sea, and the tube can be filled by opening this valve and the cock in the tube. The tube has a drain cock at either end. The purpose of the drain cocks is to show whether the tube is empty of water or not.

The layout of the submarine is important, and especially the positioning of the watertight doors. Almost immediately behind the rear doors of the torpedo tube compartment is number twenty-five bulkhead, which also has watertight doors. The watertight doors separate the torpedo tube compartment and the torpedo stowage compartment. Number twenty-five bulkhead has two pairs of two doors, making a total of four doors. On 1 June, when *Thetis* sailed from Birkenhead, only the port door was open. The door itself is closed by securing eighteen 'turnbuckles' bolts with butterfly nuts screwed onto them. When it is required to close the door, all eighteen bolts are placed in the corresponding iron hasps which have U-shaped ends fastened to the bulkhead. To make the door watertight, the butterfly nuts are then tightly screwed up. The bolts and nuts are held with stowage spring clips which are fitted to the door, and remain there until the watertight door is required to be closed. The Inquiry took note of the fact that the bottom of the watertight door is on a level with the centre of the middle pair of torpedo tubes.

It was known that the weight of water required to fill the torpedo tube compartment was about forty-five tons, when the torpedo tubes were empty and the rear doors closed. And, similarly, the weight of water required to fill the torpedo stowage compartment—which is the compartment immediately behind the torpedo tube compartment—is about ninety tons. It was stated during the Inquiry that, if the bow cap of number five tube was opened thirty degrees or more when the rear door was opened, then water would flow into the tube compartment at the rate of, approximately, two tons per second.

The Inquiry heard that *Thetis* was fitted with the latest equipment for communicating with surface vessels. This equipment, not specifically named at the Inquiry, was to be used in the event of the submarine being unable to surface. However, when *Thetis* struck the seabed, the equipment was irreparably damaged, and was therefore totally ineffective.

As an integral part of her safety equipment, *Thetis* carried two indicator buoys. The buoys are used to indicate the vessel's position in the event of an emergency when the submarine is submerged. The spherical wooden buoys are painted red and are approximately twenty-seven inches in diameter. The buoys are stored in cages on the main deck. When a holding catch is released from the inside of the submarine the buoys float out of the cage to the surface, tethered by a length of 350 feet of wire. Each buoy has a flag pole to which is attached a red flag.

Other safety equipment carried as standard included three smoke candles. In an emergency they are fired out of an ejector tube in the submarine. Upon reaching the surface, the candles produce a column of smoke which, in normal weather conditions, lasts for about three or four minutes. *Thetis* also carried twenty-five indicator lights. They are normally used with practice torpedoes, but, in an emergency, they can be fired out of the smoke candle tube. In good visibility, the light emitted from these indicator lights can be seen from a distance of two miles.

All submarines are fitted with adequate means of escape in the event of a disaster or some other emergency whilst the vessel is submerged. *Thetis* was fitted with two escape chambers, one towards the forward end of the submarine, and one towards the stern. The forward escape chamber was built into the bulkhead immediately abaft and behind the torpedo stowage compartment, and the after escape chamber was built into the bulkhead immediately forward of the steerage compartment. Both chambers are similar, being cylindrical in form and about three feet in diameter (just less than one metre), and six feet and nine inches (slightly more than two metres) in height. There are two entrance doors, one on each side of the watertight bulkhead. The top of the chamber has a hatch, about thirty inches (about 75 cm) in diameter. This hatch is opened from inside of the chamber and is held on hinges. When the hatch is open, the top of the chamber is directly open to the sea.

A set, and well-rehearsed, sequence of events is required to be carried out if men are to escape from the vessel via the escape chamber. The most important part of the escape procedure is for the escape chamber to be totally flooded, thus equalising the water pressure inside the chamber with the water pressure of the sea itself. There is a pipe leading from the sea to the escape chamber. The pipe has a master valve controlling the entrance of seawater, and a valve which controls the entrance of the water into the chamber itself. The rate at which the chamber becomes flooded is controlled by a lever inside of the chamber. There is also an outboard vent, whereby air can escape and be displaced by the water flooding into the chamber. After an escape has been effected, there is a drain pipe and valve which enable the chamber to be drained down and become ready for further escape attempts. Fail-safe devices are built into the escape system, and for this reason, the valve system can be activated from either the compartments on either side of the bulkhead or from inside of the chamber itself.

The escape hatch at the top of the chamber is normally held in its seating by clips inside the chamber and one external clip. Before opening the hatch, the internal holding clips are released, and the external clip is released by a lever, which can be operated from either inside the escape chamber or from one of the adjacent compartments. There is also a wheel and gearing system which is used to close the hatch after it has been opened.

The engine room space in HMS *Alliance*, seen here, was similar in size to that on *Thetis*. Sixty-seven men waited in this area for rescue which never arrived. (*By kind permission of Pamela Armstrong*)

Before entering the escape chamber, however, the Davis Submarine Escape Apparatus (DSEA) had to be donned by anyone wishing to escape. This equipment enabled men who were themselves completely submerged to be sustained by a supply of oxygen until reaching the surface. The escape apparatus included a rubber breathing/buoyancy bag which contained a cylinder of compressed oxygen, goggles and a nose clip. The nose clip was meant to ensure that the man breathed only through his mouth. The breathing/buoyancy bag had a non-return valve which meant that air could escape from the bag as the wearer was ascending to the surface and the water pressure was decreasing.

The mouthpiece, which must be properly fitted, is connected to the buoyancy bag by a flexible corrugated hose. As the man breathes out, the exhaled air passes through a canister filled with soda lime—the soda lime helps to purify the air by absorbing the carbon dioxide. From there the air passes to a rubber bag being worn on the man's chest. Oxygen is then released from the small cylinder which is attached to this bag—the amount of oxygen being regulated by the wearer by means of a simple tap. In order to start the process, the cap on the oxygen cylinder must first be broken by screwing the plunger into the cap until the seal is broken.

At the after end of the steering compartment there is another watertight bulkhead (No. 146). This bulkhead is nineteen feet (5.8 metres) forward of *Thetis*'s stern. The Z tank is immediately abaft of No. 146 bulkhead. There is a manhole door in No. 146 bulkhead. The watertight door is secured by nuts and bolts which are located on the forward side of the bulkhead. The head of the rudder is housed in Z tank, as are numerous pipes and tubes.

The Admiralty contract to build the submarine HMS *Thetis* was awarded to the Birkenhead shipbuilder, Cammell Lairds & Co. Ltd. *Thetis* was the third submarine of her class, built under the 1936 programme. On the day of the dive trials in Liverpool Bay, seven Admiralty and Overseeing Officers were on board *Thetis* including the Admiralty constructor of *Thetis* Mr F. Bailey, the Principal Ship Overseer, Mr A. A. F. Hill, and two of Mr Hill's assistants, Mr E. Gisborne and Mr H. Horsman.

One of the critical criteria built into any submarine design is the ability to be able to dive quickly when required to do so. When a submarine is sailing on the surface, the main ballast tanks are empty. However, when the submarine is required to dive, the main ballast tanks are filled with seawater, causing the submarine's buoyancy to change—and hence diving begins. Submarines are designed such that, when fully equipped and crewed, diving begins as soon as the main ballast tanks are filled. This state of buoyancy is referred to as 'standard condition', and, when in 'standard condition', the trim of the submarine is referred to as 'main ballast trim'. When sailing in seawater of normal density, officers on board are fully aware of the necessary draught of the submarine to maintain 'main ballast trim'. Because of varying density of seawater, and also the different dead weight of the submarine at different times, 'main ballast trim' cannot always be achieved without having to make some adjustment in water ballast. The condition of the submarine when on her initial dive trials is obviously very different from her normal condition, in that, the number of staff on board is very different, and the weight of the submarine itself is very different—with the absence of torpedoes and other equipment for example. The calculations necessary to ensure that there is sufficient ballast in the auxiliary tanks to attain 'main ballast trim' is, necessarily, complex.

The Inquiry was told that, for sea diving trials, it was important that the submarine should not be over-weighted or lacking in buoyancy when the main ballast tanks were filled. The aim was to have ample margins of buoyancy before the main ballast tanks flooded, such that, when they were flooded the submarine would not submerge either too deep or too quickly.

In order to determine whether any additional permanent ballast is required to ensure that the submarine is in 'main ballast trim', a preliminary dive is made in the shipyard's wet basin. Accordingly, the trim trial was conducted on 4 March in the presence of Mr Hill, the Admiralty Overseer; Cammell Lairds's Forman Engineer, Arthur Robinson; Lieutenant Chapman, first lieutenant of *Thetis* and Lieutenant Woods, torpedo officer of *Thetis*.

Thetis was submerged to a depth such that the deck gun was just above water level. In evidence to the Inquiry, Lieutenant Woods testified that he recalled tubes numbers five and six having been filled in one of the basin trials on the orders of Lieutenant Chapman, and that under his orders (Woods's), Leading Seaman Hambrook and Petty Officer Mitchell had handled the control levers of numbers five and six tubes on that occasion.

Assistant Naval Constructor George John Stunden submitted a report of this preliminary trimming trial on 9 March. Mr Stunden stated that the submarine was submerged to a draught of approximately two feet below the top of the conning tower. Upon surfacing the draught in 'main ballast condition' was:

Forward
Port 13 feet 11¼ inches (4.248 m)
Starboard 13 feet 9½ inches (4.204 m)
Mean 13 feet 10⅜ inches (4.226 m)

Aft
Port 14 feet 7½ inches (4.458 m)
Starboard 14 feet 5½ inches (4.407 m)
Mean 14 feet 6½ inches (4.432 m)

It was thus deduced from this trial that, in water of a similar specific density,

Thetis must have this draught for her to be in 'main ballast condition', such that filling her main tanks would then enable her to submerge.

Lieutenant Commander E. R. C. MacVicker was the Submarine Command Escape Officer. On 31 March he carried out his inspection of the Davis Submarine Escape Apparatus (DSEA) on board *Thetis*. He found the equipment to be totally satisfactory. During the same inspection, Lieutenant Commander MacVicker also examined the two indicator buoys. He found these to be in position and quite satisfactory. Lieutenant Commander MacVicker, after his inspection of the escape chambers, found that the operating wheel on the after side of the after escape chamber was in such a position that it was difficult to get sufficient purchase to work it. He recommended that a suitable claw spanner be supplied in order to rectify this situation.

With regards to the carrying of DSE apparatus, there are specific Admiralty orders prescribed for diving trials. These regulations state that there should be one DSEA for each person on board during diving, plus one third of this number. Accordingly, the Admiralty provided 131 sets for the use of those on board the *Thetis* during her diving trials, making the assumption that the total complement would be 98 persons—in the event there were 103 people on board that day. The Admiralty also supplied five watertight torches for use on board *Thetis*.

On 30 April 1939, HMS *Thetis* sailed from the River Mersey, *en route* for the River Clyde. Her official sea trials for engines, steering and diving were intended to be carried out up in Scotland. The traditional trial diving ground for Royal Naval submarines is Gare Loch on the Clyde, favoured because of its natural protection. Also, the trial dives would be able to take place less than a mile offshore. However, on the voyage up to Scotland a number of events occurred which, effectively, ensured that it would not be able to conduct further trials, and especially not the dive trial. Upon Lieutenant Commander Bolus giving a command to steer to port, the submarine immediately turned to starboard. And, when giving a command to turn to starboard, *Thetis* turned to port. It would appear that the connections on the steering gear mechanisms had been fitted the wrong way around. But, there were further

Thetis almost buoyant and ready for the journey around to Holyhead. (*By kind permission of Mike Kemble*)

setbacks and complications. The operating gear of the forward hydroplanes was not working satisfactorily, thus affecting the diving capability of the submarine. The Principal Ship Overseer, Lieutenant A. A. F. Hill, together with his assistant, Mr Frank Bailey, were the Admiralty's senior representatives on board, and thus bore responsibility to ensure that Cammell Lairds fulfilled their contractual duties to the letter. Following consultation with Lieutenant Commander Bolus, they were forced to conclude that, for now, the diving trials had to be postponed until remedial work could be carried out at Cammell Lairds.

After further discussion between Lieutenant Hill, Mr Frank Bailey and Lieutenant Commander Bolus, it was agreed that permission be sought from the Admiralty to conduct the remaining trials in Liverpool Bay, subject to the remedial repairs being completed satisfactorily. The permission was granted by the Admiralty.

The torpedo equipment trials took place between 2–6 May. During those trials, the tubes, their doors, bow caps and apparatus for opening and shutting them were all fully tested. The Admiralty inspector stated in his report that the hydraulic bow cap indicator system was to be completed and tested, and that the insides of the tubes were to be coated with bitumastic solution and finally coated with enamel. It was also stated that during the torpedo equipment trials, number five tube was used for firing purposes many times.

For the purposes of the torpedo trials, a retired submarine officer, with many years' experience, Commander Maguire, RN, conducted the firing. Keeping within the legal requirements of the contract, employees of Cammell Lairds worked the equipment during these trials. Mr H. Eccleston worked the bow cap levers. Commander Maguire, in his evidence to the Inquiry, stated that during the torpedo firing trials, on at least one occasion, he saw the control lever at the neutral position after an operation had been carried out, and he then gave instructions that the levers were to be put into the 'OPEN' or 'SHUT' position and kept there until a further order was given.

A contrary view was taken by Mr F. Shaw. He was present at these trials of the bow caps, and was also Eccleston's foreman. He said in his evidence before the tribunal that they did not make a practice of leaving the levers in the neutral position. They always left them in the 'SHUT' position.

One of the most significant pieces of work in the whole story of the *Thetis* was the application of a bitumastic solution to the torpedo tube walls and rear doors, followed by bonding of a hard layer of enamel. The two-stage operation is completed with a blow-lamp to ensure that the two layers are fully bonded and smooth. The smooth finish is critical, as the sole reason why the tubes are coated with this bitumastic/enamel layer is to ensure that, when fired, the torpedoes have a smooth, and thus speedy, passage to the sea. The job of applying this coating is a very specialised one—a job that would not be undertaken by Cammell Lairds. It was alleged that tenders for the work were sent, with Admiralty approval, to three companies specialising in this kind of work, but that the contract was only ever going to be awarded to one company—the Wailes Dove Bitumastic Company Limited. The truth of this allegation has never been verified. However, it remains a matter of fact that Wailes Dove was awarded the contract for this specialist work. The Inquiry was told that work started on Saturday 13 May when an employee of Wailes Dove started to paint the inside of all six torpedo tubes with a bitumastic solution. Following completion of this work another employee coated the solution with enamel and smoothed the work with a blow-lamp. The report from the Inquiry then states that on the following day, Sunday 14 May, the enameller applied the bitumastic solution to the insides of the rear doors of the six torpedo tubes, finishing about mid-day then, at about three o'clock in the afternoon started to apply the enamelling. He stopped work at five o'clock in the afternoon. The Inquiry did not report whether the surfaces were smoothed off with the blow-lamp on Sunday afternoon or Monday morning. It was noted in the subsequent report that the work on the rear doors was completed sometime on Monday 15 May.

The chronology of events, as recalled by Mr Hughes and Mr Stinson, the two employees of Wailes Dove Bitumastic Company Limited who were sent to do the job, is a little different from that described above. According to Hughes, who was responsible for painting on the bitumastic, work started on the Friday and, after working all weekend, was completed by Monday night. Hughes recalled that as he completed spreading the bitumastic on each tube, he then went on to the next one. Meanwhile John Stinson, his work colleague, prepared the enamel for application. Enamel was delivered in solid bars, and first had to be thoroughly heated through before reaching a liquid, and thus useable, state. Stinson was at pains to state that the work could not be rushed, as that could cause burning and leave an unsatisfactory finish.

Apart from the obvious difference in the dates when the work was done, it is at this stage that the differences arose between the accounts of what work was done and when it was done arise. The employees of Wailes Dove have a particular understanding of the work which they did, and when they did it, whereas the Admiralty Assistant Overseer, Mr Grundy tells a different version of events. The enameller, Mr Stinson, testified that he took no steps to prevent the solution choking the test cock holes when the solution was applied to the rear doors, but, as a precaution, he twisted some cotton waste into spools, soaked them in oil and then used them to plug the test cook holes. He said that he did this to prevent the waste from adhering to the sides of the hole, and to prevent the enamel entering the hole. He also said that when he had finished cleaning up the surface with the blow-lamp, he removed the cotton waste plugs. Mr Stinson gave this evidence before *Thetis* was raised.

In his evidence to the Inquiry, Mr Grundy, the Admiralty Assistant Overseer, stated that he inspected the rear doors of the torpedo tubes on Tuesday 16 May and that, at that time, there was no bitumastic solution or enamel on the insides of the rear doors. He also declared that he was awaiting a further call from an employee of Cammell Lairds to inspect the work on rear doors when it was finished, but that he was never called.

In his evidence to the Inquiry, Mr Taylor, Cammell Lairds's charge hand painter, who was directly responsible for overseeing the work of the sub-contractors, said that the foreman of the sub-contractors, Wailes Dove, who were applying the bitumastic solution and enamel, reported to him (Taylor) on Tuesday afternoon, 16 May. He said that the work was now completed and ready for inspection. Mr Taylor examined the tubes and also took note that the insides of all the rear doors had been painted. He went on to say that on the following day, Wednesday 17 May, he arranged to meet with Mr Grundy in the torpedo compartment to make his inspection, having informed Grundy that all of the tubes, in their entirety, doors and all internal surfaces, were ready for him to survey. He continued his evidence by saying that it was on that day, 17 May, that Mr Grundy in the presence of himself (Taylor) had inspected the tubes from the rear doors which were open, and that on the same day a gauge was passed through the tubes. The Inquiry's report concluded that, on this point, it believed the evidence of Mr Taylor. Both Mr Taylor and Mr Grundy gave this evidence before the *Thetis* was raised.

Before all the remedial work had been completed, *Thetis* was removed to the shipyard's dry dock so that work could be done on the bow caps—there had been some minor leakages. When the work was completed, checks were made on the time taken to open and close the bow caps. It was found that the bow caps could be fully opened, starting from a fully closed state, in a matter of six to seven seconds after the lever had been pushed to the 'OPEN' position. It was also calculated that, when submerged, the bow caps would take another two seconds to open because of the water pressure against the tube. Before the tests were finished, the hydraulic indicators for the bow cap shutters were also tested. They were found to be in a satisfactory working order.

It must be noted that this work was completed on 18 May and that, after that date, no further work was done on either the torpedo tubes or the bow caps. The bow caps were not opened again before *Thetis* went out on her dive trials, nor were the torpedo tubes flooded again before the trials.

The Contractors submitted to the Admiralty a diving trial schedule on 24 May 1939. The following is an extract from that schedule:

Thursday 1 June DIVING & DIESEL ELECTRIC TRIALS ETC.

Leave Basin 9.30 a.m. (H W.11.32 a.m.—27 feet 4 inches)
Proceed to Bar Lightship and adjust compasses.
Proceed to Diving Position, about 15 miles due west of Bar Lightship,
carrying out on way:
After Hydroplane Trials on secondary power and local control
And Auxiliary Steering trials at full power on ship's telemotor and local
control
Diving trials to commence at about 1.30 p.m.
After completion of Diving Trials, carry out Diesel Electric Trials on passage
back
Enter basin 10.30 p.m. (HW 11.52 p.m.—28 feet 1 inch).

The programme was approved by the Admiralty.

The question was asked during the Inquiry whether Liverpool Bay was a suitable place to hold the diving trials. In answer to this question it was reported that the mouth of the Thames was used for similar trials, and that was quite satisfactory. The Inquiry was told that there were no particular dangers in the diving trials. The only significant difference was that, because the equipment was new, the trials were always carried out in 'slow time'. It was reiterated that Liverpool Bay had no peculiar features which would make it a dangerous place for a submarine to dive.

The Inquiry was given specific legal information relating to the terms of the building contract. It was clear from the contract that any trials which were necessary to be made could only be conducted at such places and over such courses as may be approved by the Admiralty. Then another clause, Clause 8 of Schedule B of the Contract, was quoted. This clause stated that 'the Contractors are to work main and also any auxiliary machinery which may be required for and during the trials ... In accordance with the practice in submarines, assistance in working the main and auxiliary machinery and appliances will be afforded by the crew free of charge to the Contractors but without prejudice to the Contractors' entire responsibility.'

The following clause, Clause 9, stated that 'the diving, trimming and submergence trials, and all the trials underway, will be carried out by naval officers and crew, but the Contractors shall work the main and auxiliary machinery, &c., as provided for in Clause 8, and provide a pilot with an attendant vessel.'

On 30 May, Lieutenant Commander Bolus checked with Mr Watters, the Assistant Shipyard Manager at Cammell Lairds, that everything would be as stipulated in the contract. He was keen to ensure that the shipyard would have a suitable boat to transfer those not required for the dive trials back to the support tug—the tug was also being supplied by the shipyard.

The rear doors of the torpedo tubes were again opened and finally shut by Mr Wolfe, Cammell Lairds's Assistant Foreman Ship Fitter, in the presence of and with the assistance of Mr Horsman the Admiralty's Ship Fitting Overseer on the afternoon of 31 May. Mr Wolfe gave evidence that when he left the *Thetis* about 4.30 that afternoon, all the control levers were at 'NEUTRAL' i.e. in the vertical position.

On the same day, the watertight doors were examined and the bolts of No. 25 bulkhead doors were all found to be properly stowed in their clips.

The mechanism of the two indicator buoys was also tested. The smoke candle ejector was tested by filling the pipe with water and blowing it out. In each case the mechanism was found to be in order.

On the morning of Thursday 1 June 1939, the Foreman Fitter of the Engineering Department of Cammell Lairds, Mr Robinson, was asked to 'blow' *Thetis's* main tanks. After this, at quarter past nine, whilst the submarine was still in the wet basin, the final draughts were taken by the Assistant Shipyard Manager, Mr Rowe. The draughts were as follows:

Forward
Port 13 feet 3¾ inches (4.058 m)
Starboard 13 feet 1¼ inches (3.994 m)
Mean 13 feet 2½ inches (4.026 m)

Aft
Port 14 feet 8¾ inches (4.489 m)
Starboard 14 feet 6¼ inches (4.426 m)
Mean 14 feet 7½ inches (4.458 m)

or 13 feet 11 inches (4.242 m) mean. Mr Rowe told the Inquiry that he gave these draughts to two of the Admiralty Overseers, Principal Ship Overseer, Mr Hill, and Assistant Overseer, Mr Gisborne. Not being satisfied with these readings, Mr Gisborne asked Mr Rowe to take the draughts again when the ship was ready for leaving. The readings were taken again just before the submarine was due to sail at 1000 hours. The following results were recorded:

Forward
Port 13 feet 8 inches (4.166 m)
Starboard 13 feet 4¾ inches (4.083 m)
Mean 13 feet 6⅜ inches (4.124 m)

Aft

Port 14 feet 7½ inches (4.458 m)
Starboard 14 feet 4½ inches (4.382 m)
Mean 14 feet 6 inches (4.420 m)

It is easy to observe when looking at these two sets of readings that, between the hours of 0915 hours and 1000 hours when the submarine sailed, there was a mean increase of about one-and-a-quarter inches, and, of more concern, a forward increase of nearly four inches. Mr Bailey commented that she was a 'bit light' aft when handed these draughts from Mr Rowe.

It was not known what the exact amount of water ballast taken on board to adjust the draught was, but what is known is that whilst Mr Rowe was taking the last trim readings, the Admiralty Overseers, Mr Hill and Mr Gisborne, were having the trim of the boat adjusted ready for sailing. There was an elaborate procedure to be followed. Mr Hill gave the trim statement to Mr Robinson, Cammell Lairds's foreman engineer, for him to put the trim on the boat. In turn, Mr Robinson then handed the statement to one of Cammell Lairds's engine fitters, Mr Eccleston, and he then actually put the trim on. But, even this action was carried out under the close supervision of one of the assistant Admiralty overseers.

Mr Rowe said that Mr Hill only came on board *Thetis* a few minutes before she actually sailed. Mr Hill remarked to the Admiralty's Chief Constructor, Mr Bailey, that they would have to fill, or that they could fill, the starboard tube or tubes. This was said after Mr Rowe had pointed out to Mr Bailey that the port side was three-and-a-half inches deeper than the starboard side.

The final draught figures taken on 1 June, immediately before *Thetis* sailed, can be compared with her draughts in 'main ballast condition' on surfacing on 8 March:

8 March	1 June
Forward	Forward
Port 13 feet 11¼ inches (4.248 m)	Port 13 feet 8 inches (4.166 m)
Starboard 13 feet 9½ inches (4.204 m)	Starboard 13 feet 4¾ inches (4.083 m)
Aft	Aft
Port 14 feet 7½ inches (4.458 m)	Port 14 feet 7½ inches (4.458 m)
Starboard 14 feet 5½ inches (4.407 m)	Starboard 14 feet 4½ inches (4.382 m)

It is easy to see that the submarine had virtually the same draught aft on 1 June as on 8 March, but, for some reason, she was four inches lighter forward.

Mr Wolfe, Cammell Lairds Assistant Foreman Ship Fitter, was asked about the routine followed by Cammell Lairds employees if the Admiralty Overseer ordered Nos 5 and 6 tubes to be filled for purposes of 'trim'. Mr Wolfe responded by saying that the foreman fitter of the Engineering Department (Mr Robinson) would give his orders to a particular man to perform the operation. Mr Wolfe said that the man might be Eccleston. He went onto say that Eccleston was the man he believed to be familiar with filling torpedo tubes. He suggested that, in all probability the tubes would be flooded from the WRT tank, but that, if the matter was urgent, it was possible that they might be flooded from the bow caps.

Summary of Part 2.
An account of the disaster as witnessed by the survivors.

At 10.00 on Thursday 1 June 1939, His Majesty's Submarine *Thetis* made her way out of Cammell Lairds's Shipyard at Birkenhead. Now flying the White Ensign, *Thetis* was under the command of her captain, Lieutenant Commander G. H. Bolus RN, and was crewed by officers and men of the Royal Navy, many of whom had been 'standing-by' the submarine during the lengthy fitting out period, immediately following her launching. Also on board that day was Captain H. P. K. Oram RN, Commanding Officer of the Fifth Submarine Flotilla. After formal acceptance of the vessel from Cammell Lairds, *Thetis* would be attached to the Fifth Submarine Flotilla. The main purpose of Oram's visit was to see for himself, at first hand, just how the officers worked—as a group and also as individuals; war with Germany was imminent, and there would doubtless be many opportunities for promotion for capable officers.

Because, technically, the submarine was not as yet a Royal Naval vessel, staff from Cammell Lairds and other sub-contractors were on board. It was Cammell Lairds's staff who would have responsibility for the machinery and other equipment during the sea trials, under orders from naval officers. It was a delicate situation, both legally and operationally.

In total there were 103 persons on board as the *Thetis* left the shipyard. There were several trials which needed to be carried out that day, but the principal one was the diving trial.

It was stipulated in the contract that Cammell Lairds, the contractors, would provide a pilot during the sea trials and also an attendant tug. On the day, a well-experienced Mersey Pilot, Mr N. D. Willcox, took charge of piloting. The tug in attendance was the *Grebe Cock*, one of ten *Cock* boats owned and operated by the Liverpool Screw Towing and Lighterage Company, and under the command of Captain A. E. Godfrey—an experienced tug master, having worked on tugs for thirty-five years, many of which as master. For the last two years he had been in command of *Grebe Cock*, a relatively new steam tug, having a gross tonnage of 171 tons. *Grebe Cock* was fitted with the latest radio telephony which enabled communication to other vessels or land facilities within a radius of seventy-five miles. In addition to the seven-man crew, *Grebe Cock* had four other people on board, Lieutenant Coltart, Crosby, Mr Randles, an employee of Cammell Lairds and Mr Southey, a friend of Mr Randles.

On the day before the sea trials, Captain Bolus contacted Lieutenant R. E. Coltart, RN—standing-by HMS *Trident* during her fitting-out at Cammell Lairds—and asked him to be in attendance on *Grebe Cock* during the trials. Coltart's role during the trials would be two-fold. Firstly, he would be responsible for ensuring that other vessels did not enter the area of the dive trial site; and secondly, he would have overall responsibility for any necessary communications between the submarine and *Grebe Cock* during the trials.

When discussing methods of communication if the submarine was submerged, Coltart had two suggestions; they could tap on the tug's hull and hope that the sounds would be heard by those on the submarine, or they would drop small explosive charges overboard which, again, would alert those on board *Thetis*. Bolus was not impressed by either of these suggestions, and stated that, before diving, he would do a 360° sweep with his periscope. He added that, in the event, he would not be remaining below periscope depth long enough for any vessel to come close enough to cause any undue alarm. Bolus then issued Coltart with the detailed trials programme:

HMS *Thetis* Programme for Dive

Take draughts. F. A.
Disembark men not required for dive.
Open up for diving. Make diving signal.
Test H.P. blows on main tanks fitted. L.P. blowers on all tanks.
Vacuum test. Slow G.U
Submerge and obtain trim.
Test battery ventilation outboard trunks, W/T deck tubes, all T. T. drains, W.C.s and look through ship for leaks.
Surface and blow main tanks on blowers.
Stop. G.U slow.
Dive to periscope depth. Time.
Lower periscopes.
Dive to 60 feet. Close WT. doors at 60 feet.
Auxiliary drive.
Fire smoke candles.
Periscope depth 4–5 knots. Cheek by log.
Raise & Lower W/T mast.

Blow main tanks to put forward casing just awash (15 foot on gauges.).

Full speed. Cheek on log. 380 revs.

Forward Hydroplane trials.

Dive to periscope depth.

Stop end obtain trim.

Release indicator buoys.

Surface with L.P. air—take time for each tank.

Take draughts and condition of all tanks.

Before their discussion ended, it was agreed that both vessels, *Thetis* and *Grebe Cock* would fly a red flag. This would aid recognition, especially when *Thetis* was at periscope depth.

To assist Lieutenant Coltart with communications, Wireless Telegraphist Victor James Crosby—a submariner of seven years' experience, and also standing-by *Trident*—was detailed to take an Aldis lamp and attend on *Grebe Cock*. Coltart was also informed that an employee of Cammell Lairds, Mr E. J. Randles, would also be on board *Grebe Cock*. He would have responsibility for the safe transfer of staff from *Thetis* to the *Grebe Cock* immediately before the dive trials commenced. He also carried responsibility for liaison between Lieutenant Coltart and Captain Godfrey. Randles was accompanied on the day by a friend, Mr Southey.

As previously agreed, both *Thetis* and *Grebe Cock* arrived at their rendezvous, the Bar Lightship, at mid-day. It was at this point that the Mersey pilot, Mr Willcox, was supposed to leave the *Thetis* and join the waiting pilot cutter. Willcox did not disembark. Shortly afterwards, *Thetis* communicated with *Grebe Cock* in order to inform the crew on the tug that nobody would be disembarking from the submarine. *Grebe Cock* was requested to then follow *Thetis* at a speed of nine knots.

As the vessels proceeded to the dive site, some steering trials were conducted and the main tanks were 'blown' as a test before the dive trials began.

The time came for persons who would be 'surplus to requirements' during the dive trials to disembark from *Thetis*. Bolus made it known to everyone on board that, if they were leaving before the dive trials started, they should make their way to the bridge—nobody came. The signal was then given for *Grebe Cock* to close. Then, when the tug was within hailing distance, Bolus called through his megaphone that nobody would be disembarking. He then informed *Grebe Cock* that his diving course would be 310°, and that they should station themselves at a distance of half a mile behind on the port quarter.

As was protocol before any dive, Lieutenant Commander Bolus was required to inform Captain S5 and the Admiralty Commander-in-Chief at Plymouth of his intentions. The communication was sent at 1340 hours, and was as follows:

From HMS *Thetis* to Captain S5 and Admiralty C in C Plymouth ASCBS.
Important. Diving in position 5335 North 0400 West, for 3 hours.

As soon as Bolus received acknowledgement of his message from the Naval
Wireless Station at Plymouth at 1356 hours, he shut off the submarine.
Having received this critical message, Bolus then made his way to the control
room accompanied by Captain Oram, and ordered that the main tanks should
be flooded in pairs and in 'slow time'. He also gave orders for the submarine
to move ahead at a speed of five knots.

Whenever diving trials are carried out at sea, it is customary for the person
acting as the Chief Admiralty Overseer to provide a statement of trim. Because
the trim statement is of such importance, it is usually prepared in conjunction
with a senior employee of the contractors. In essence, the trim statement
informs the commander as to the amount of ballast in the boat before diving
commences, and the additional amount required in the ballast tanks before a
state of neutral buoyancy can be attained.

The sequence of events which then occurred was critical. The main water
tanks had been flooded, as was standard practice, and, under normal conditions,
this would have enabled the submarine to begin diving, as the hydroplanes
had been set for diving. However, *Thetis* did not dive, and many on board
attributed this to the light trim of the vessel. More water was introduced to the
ballast tanks and, again with the hydroplanes set, the submarine was forced
into a dive, but only to a depth of about twenty feet, where she remained.
At this depth the submarine's bridge was still out of the water. It was evident
that the lightness was towards the forward end of the vessel—this condition
persisted, even when most of the for'd auxiliary tanks had been filled.

During the ensuing discussion between senior officers, First Lieutenant
Chapman, addressing Lieutenant Commander Bolus, queried whether tube
numbers five and six were full. At the subsequent Inquiry, Captain Oram
testified that:

> Somebody, I cannot recollect who, answered and said I do not think they
> should be full, to which Lieutenant Chapman, the first lieutenant, replied
> that they should be by the trim statement.

Captain Oram went on to say that Lieutenant Woods, who was the Torpedo
and Gunnery Officer, was then despatched to that area and asked to report
back on the state of the tubes. Oram went on to say that, after hearing the
conversation, he was inclined to think that it was in fact the empty condition
of tube numbers five and six that was causing the failure to dive.

Lieutenant Woods had been standing-by *Thetis* for most of the fitting-out
period, joining her as Torpedo and Gunnery Officer in October 1938. He had

Captain H. P. K. Oram, commander of the Fifth Flotilla and one of the four survivors of the disaster, on his way to the Tribunal together with his wife. Captain Oram was the first witness at the Tribunal. (*From* SOS *Thetis, Hans Müller Verlag, Dresden, 1943*)

actually joined the submarine branch of the Royal Navy in May 1936. His immediate subordinate was Petty Officer E. Mitchell who was designated Torpedo Gunner's Mate. Next when moving down the chain of command was Leading Seaman W. L. Hambrook, Mitchell's immediate subordinate. Hambrook had been standing-by *Thetis* for the last two months. These three crew members, Woods, Mitchell and Hambrook, had all been on board during the earlier trim dive which was successfully conducted in Cammell Lairds's wet basin.

Sometime before the dive trial was due to commence, Woods gave his last, thorough, check in the tube and torpedo compartments. He also checked the adjacent crew space to see that everything was as it should be. Returning to the control room, Woods then held a brief conversation with First Lieutenant Chapman. Chapman was holding the 'trim chit', on which was written the names and numbers of all of the auxiliary and compensating tanks, together with the state of flooding in each of these compartments. Just below these figures, there were similar readings for numbers five and six torpedo tubes. Against both of these lines was written, 'FULL'.

After examining the 'trim chit', doubts were sown in Lieutenant Woods's mind about the condition of tubes number five and six, especially as the submarine was experiencing considerable difficulty in diving. It was known that the for'd end was light, and that, perhaps, a state of neutral buoyancy had not been achieved. Woods needed to satisfy himself that the tubes were full, as was recorded on the 'trim chit'. He went through to the torpedo tube compartment and first checked number six tube. Moving the lever on which the test cock was located from the locked position to the unlocked position, he found that only a dribble of water came from the test cock, indicating that there was some water in the tube, but that it was not under any pressure.

When moving to the rear door of tube number five, where the test cock was located, and carrying out the same check, Woods found that there was no issue of water, not even a dribble. Logic dictated that, if there was any water in the tube, then it was at a level below the test cock. Unfortunately, it came to light at the subsequent forensic examination of the salved submarine, that the test cock was blocked by bitumastic enamel, thus yielding a totally incorrect reading.

As a result of Woods's checks, it was evident there was a discrepancy between what was recorded on the 'trim chit' and what was the actual state of number five and six tubes. Returning to the control room, he conferred with First Lieutenant Chapman, and asked him if number five and six tubes were meant to be full. Chapman confirmed that both tubes should be flooded, whereupon Woods categorically stated that both tubes were not full—he had only just re-checked the situation. First Lieutenant Chapman was now in a quandary himself, as the evidence as written on the trim chit and the actual situation as Woods had reported was at variance. Turning to Mr Robinson, Cammell Lairds's foreman engineer, Chapman asked a direct question as to whether tubes five and six were meant to be full. At the Inquiry, Woods testified that Robinson had answered No. He also stated that there was a further conversation between Chapman and Robinson, the import of which he could not recall.

Once again, because of the growing concern on the submarine as to exactly why she was not diving, Woods returned to the tube compartment. He decided to re-check his earlier findings. Going first to number six tube, he opened and then closed the lever and, once again, there was a small leakage of water, but certainly not enough to indicate that the tube was full. Woods then conducted the same test on number five tube, and once again no water came out of the test cock. A report of this was communicated to the control room, stating that number six tube was half full of water. The condition in tube number five was not reported, as the result was exactly the same as it had been just a few minutes ago. Woods was now completely satisfied that there was no water in tube number five.

As the situation was constantly changing, Lieutenant Woods saw that 'A' tank was just about full. From this evidence he concluded that *Thetis* was still light at the for'd end. Accordingly, he asked First Lieutenant Chapman whether filling the torpedo tubes would help *Thetis* to dive. Chapman replied,

Yes. Having sought this guidance, Woods then asked Cammell Lairds's foreman engineer, Mr Robinson, if there was power on the bow cap motors. When informed by Robinson that there was no power to the bow caps, Woods asked Mr Shaw, another Cammell Lairds employee, if power could be put onto the bow cap telemotors. Shaw went from the torpedo stowage room to the tube room where he instructed engine fitter, Mr H. Eccleston, to put on any power as might be required by naval officers. Again, there was the delicate legal situation between contractors and representatives of the Admiralty.

At the Inquiry Shaw, one of the four survivors, was unsure as to when he issued this directive, but he thought that it was before *Thetis* began to dive.

As soon as Woods knew that power to the bow caps was available, he went to the tube compartment and ordered Leading Seaman L. S. Hambrook to ensure that power was now being delivered to the bow caps. At this point Woods was not sure if all of the tubes would need flooding in order to be certain that *Thetis* could dive as required. Hambrook complied with this order. And then, as a further check, Woods asked if the levers were in the shut position, to which Hambrook replied 'Yes.' Woods then asked Hambrook if everything was correct. Hambrook again replied in the affirmative.

Before issuing any further instructions with regards to the bow caps, Woods carried out a check on the insides of the tubes. He had been aware that there was a slight leakage on one of the bow caps, and wanted to satisfy himself that everything was in order before the dive was made. Lieutenant Woods took this action of his own volition, and failed to inform the control room of this proposed action. Moving between the tubes, he made a visual inspection of all of the bow cap indicators. All six pointers were in the 'SHUT' position. By way of thoroughly checking everything, his next action was to open the test cock lever on number one tube. When there was only a small release of air, Woods instructed Leading Seaman Hambrook to open the rear door of number one tube, in order to check if there was any leakage from the bow cap. The space was meticulously inspected before the rear door was closed again. Lieutenant Woods then carried out exactly the same procedure on tubes two, three and four in turn. All of the tubes were dry. Whilst these checks were being carried out by Woods and Hambrook, there was another rating stationed between numbers one and two tubes; his task was to observe the vents on the tanks. Lieutenant (Engineer) Jamison from *Trident* was also in the compartment, and, standing just outside were Petty Officer E. Mitchell and Engine Room Artificer E. Howells.

Continuing with their systematic checks, Woods and Hambrook started to open the rear door of number five tube, after Woods had first checked number five test cock; again, finding no traces of any air or water. It was at this point that Hambrook tried to engage the lever which operates the mechanism to open the tube's rear door, but it proved to be very stiff. At the Tribunal of Inquiry, Lieutenant Woods stated:

> With the final movement of No. 5 lever, water commenced to issue from the bottom of the tube. Before I could take any action, the door was flung back and a large volume of water commenced to flow into the tube space. At the time I was so positive that the bow caps were shut, I considered that there must be a fracture in No. 5 tube. Had I realised, as I did soon afterwards, that No. 5 bow cap must have been open, I might possibly have been able to get at No. 5 bow cap operating lever to inspect its position, and move it to shut if it was in the open position. The tube compartment commenced to fill rapidly and I had some difficulty in gaining the port door. Leading Seaman Hambrook was between me and the door and was in some difficulty, as he appeared to be thrown about by the water. I had to assist him out of the compartment which meant that some time was wasted before the port water tight door could be closed. While I was by No. 5 door and the water was coming in I shouted to Mitchell to tell the control room to 'blow' (the main tanks) and he passed this order by telephone.

Continuing with his evidence at the tribunal, Lieutenant Woods said that he could not recall exactly what happened next, as his memory was hazy, and everything happened so quickly. When Mr Shaw, an employee of Cammell Lairds, came to give his evidence, he declared that:

> I felt a rush of air coming aft and the ship began to develop a list and she went down very quickly. I felt a bump and I was flung against the water tight door of 69 bulkhead. I heard an order given to 'blow' tanks and then an order to close all watertight doors.

Next to give evidence was leading stoker Arnold who, at the time, was standing just aft of number 40 bulkhead. He stated:

> There was a terrible rush of air from the foremost compartments and I heard people shouting from forward to the control room to surface. I realised that it was a torpedo tube open, because it is the biggest hole in the ship forward, and it must have been a big hole to have had such a terrible rush of air. A few seconds afterwards by the time the water had started rushing in the men were trying to shut the water-tight door of No. 25 bulkhead.

Strenuous efforts were made to close number five rear door, once the men inside the torpedo tube compartment had escaped. But there was a considerable delay in achieving this. The door itself opened forward, and was held in position by a latch. The latch had to be released first before the door could be closed, and this meant that Lieutenant Jamison and Engine Room Artificer Howells had to get around the door, and into the water, before this could be achieved. Having released the catch, there was a further delay because one of the 'turnbuckles' or butterfly nuts had fallen between the door itself and the coaming. It was at this point, when *Thetis* was diving at a steep angle, that the lights failed in the tube compartment. The situation was now becoming critical; it was now imperative that the watertight door between the tube compartment and the stowage compartment was closed as soon as possible. This was because the groups of batteries were located directly under the deck plates in this area. All attempts to close the watertight door in number twenty-five bulkhead ceased, and orders were given to clear the stowage compartment. Lieutenant Woods managed to get out of the torpedo storage compartment—with extreme difficulty. By now, because of the steep angle that *Thetis* was inclined at, all of the tables and stools which had been set up for the celebration 'big eats' were strewn all over the place in a completely random fashion. When Petty Officer Mitchell scrambled through shortly afterwards, he confirmed that he had secured one of the clips on the watertight door in number twenty-five bulkhead—just what the value of this was will never be known.

The race was now on to close the watertight door in number forty bulkhead, and thus prevent any water from reaching the banks of batteries directly below the deck plates. Fortunately, the door was closed just in time—seconds after Woods and Mitchell had crawled through.

It was time for Lieutenant Woods to report to the control room exactly what had happened, but, before doing so, he checked with Leading Seaman Hambrook to see if all of the bow cap operating levers were parallel to each other, as they should have been. Hambrook replied that they were.

As Woods was making his way to the control room, those inside were experiencing a sudden and significant rise in pressure. Lieutenant Commander Bolus, reading the situation, ordered that the main tanks should be 'blown' immediately. However, his orders came too late. *Thetis* lurched into a sharp dive and, just seconds later, struck the seabed with some force.

Captain Oram, one of the four survivors, stated that when *Thetis* struck the bottom, she was resting at an angle of 40° from the horizontal. It was known that the depth of water in the area was about 160 feet at low water. A few days later, on 3 June, a diver noted that at high water the depth was about 132 feet. Making some simple geometric calculations, if *Thetis* was 275 feet in length and her angle was 40° as Oram had suggested, then, even in 160 feet of water, *Thetis*'s stern must have been at least 24 feet out of the water.

As 'blowing' the tanks had not yielded the desired result—positive buoyancy—Bolus ordered 'blowing' to cease and all watertight doors to be closed. He then ordered the engines 'half astern', but this too did not have the desired effect, but merely increased the submarine's angle. As the afternoon wore on, *Thetis* settled on the seabed at an angle of about six degrees bow down.

As had been stated earlier, *Thetis* would release a smoke candle and an indicator buoy at an appropriate time, but none of the survivors could say exactly when they had been released, but there was consensus that they had been released when *Thetis* was resting on the seabed.

With *Thetis* having stabilised, albeit on the seabed, attention was focused on how to overcome the deepening problems. As the flooding was towards the for'd end of the submarine, it was considered that if access could be gained to the torpedo storage compartment via the forward escape chamber, then it might be possible, even at this stage, to close the rear watertight door of number five torpedo tube. Then, by utilising the submarine's pumps in conjunction with opening a number of valves, it might be possible to clear the floodwater from these compartments.

The first person to volunteer to attempt this high-risk strategy was First Lieutenant Chapman. It was gone four o'clock in the afternoon when he donned the Davis Submarine Escape Apparatus and ventured into the for'd escape chamber. Flooding of the chamber then commenced, as was standard procedure. But, when that particular operation was almost completed, Chapman signalled that he needed the chamber to be drained down. The flooding was stopped and the chamber drained. Whilst in the escape chamber he had felt nauseous and dizzy, and was not able to continue. The next to volunteer for the attempt was Lieutenant Woods. This time, the approach was modified somewhat, in that, rather than make the attempt on his own, there would be two people involved. In this way they would have a back-up, just in case Woods failed to return to the chamber. Petty Officer Mitchell, the Torpedo Gunner's Mate, volunteered to be the second person. His role was to remain in the chamber after Woods had ventured towards the flooded compartment. Then, in the event of Woods not returning, he was ordered to close the escape chamber's exit door and have the chamber drained, ready for another attempt.

When both Woods and Mitchell were inside the escape chamber, the flooding commenced once again. But, as had been the case during the previous attempt, the flooding had to be stopped, as Mitchell was experiencing severe pain in his inner ears.

It was decided that a third attempt should be made, as clearing the flooded torpedo compartment was seen as being critical to everyone's chances of survival. Again, Lieutenant Woods volunteered to make another attempt himself. This time he would be accompanied by Petty Officer C. Smithers, the second coxswain. But, yet again, when the escape chamber was almost totally flooded, Smithers complained of intense pain, and the chamber had to be drained down. It was clear that this approach was not going to work—another solution had to be found.

When the floodwater was being drained during all three attempts—a total weight in excess of four tons of water—it was carried by bucket chain to the after end of the submarine. The reasoning here being that, under no circumstances, could water be allowed to enter into the battery flat, as if water came into contact with the batteries there would be a chemical reaction, causing deadly chlorine vapour to be released.

It was becoming clear that this escape strategy was not going to work, and, as time was going on, conditions within the submarine were becoming increasingly difficult to cope with. The proposed solution which gained most support was to try to secure help from outside. Without suitable surface support, any attempt at escaping via the Davis Escape Apparatus would be futile, as anyone subjected to the cold seawater could only survive for a very short time unless given assistance from rescue vessels.

Commissioned Engineer R. D. Glenn, *Thetis's* engineer officer, wrote out the agreed plan for raising the submarine. It was written as follows:

From *Thetis*.
On Bottom. Depth 140 feet. 16° bows down. Fore end and torpedo stowage compartment flooded, number five bow cap and rear door open. Compartments evacuated. H.P. air required to charge submarine through either recuperator connection or whistle connection on bridge. Diver required to tighten down fore hatch, so that blow can be put on forward compartments without lifting hatch. Strongback required on hatch as soon as possible. Keep constant watch for men escaping through after escape chamber.

The conception of the plan was simple in principle. Firstly, divers would secure and tighten down *Thetis's* fore hatch. After successfully completing this operation, a compressed air line would be connected to *Thetis* from the surface vessel, and high-pressure air would be pumped into the submarine. By opening certain valves in the boat, compressed air would then force the water out of the flooded compartments, and the submarine would be able to achieve positive buoyancy once again.

During the long hours of the night, whilst conditions on board were still just about bearable, a number of activities were undertaken, all in an endeavour to assist in the ultimate rescue attempt. After the rescue plan had been agreed, the first decision that was taken was to wait until dawn before trying to send anyone to the surface—it was known that, to date, there were no rescue vessels in the immediate area. Next, a number of Cammell Lairds's workmen, working throughout the night, managed to raise the after escape chamber nearer to the water's surface. This action would have the effect of reducing the water pressure on anyone in the escape chamber—a problem which had been encountered previously. Also during the night hours, Petty Officer Telegraphist J. Hope, working with a telegraphist colleague, practiced sending distress messages by tapping on the boat's hull.

The period of enforced captivity was beginning to take its toll. Because of the number of people on board—almost double the intended figure— the air was now becoming contaminated and difficult to breathe. The air compressors which were in almost constant use, keeping the air pressure tolerably low and the air reasonably fresh, were becoming overheated because of overuse and had to be stopped. Also, there was very little food available, as most of the provisions were being stored in the now flooded torpedo stowage compartment. It was clear time was rapidly running out—if there was to be a successful outcome, rescue was needed, and fast!

Through the valiant efforts of Cammell Lairds's workmen, by four o'clock in the morning *Thetis's* angle of inclination had become 16°, and by seven o'clock that angle had increased to 34°. *Thetis's* stern was now above water level. However, the condition of the air had now deteriorated quite significantly, and many men were in a very weak state. Some rough calculations were made. Making the assumption that it took between ten to fifteen minutes for two men to escape through the escape chamber, there would not be enough time for all of them to escape before the air condition had deteriorated to such an extent that it would be impossible to support life. Something else had to be done.

Perhaps a degree of frustration was now beginning to creep into those stranded on board, so much so that just before eight o'clock Captain Oram decided that, even though there was still no evidence of any rescue vessels in the area, he would take his chances and hope that a passing ship might spot him. He was also conscious of the need to get the escape plan delivered to the authorities ashore. As it was considered better if two people went into the escape chamber, volunteers were requested. Two seamen volunteered, as did Lieutenant Woods. Woods was chosen, the rationale being that he had intimate knowledge of the submarine, having been standing-by for much of the fitting-out period.

Thetis was now inclined at a relatively steep angle, so a degree of difficulty was experienced by Oram and Woods as they made their way to the after escape chamber. Once inside the chamber, First Lieutenant Chapman had it flooded. But, no sooner had the chamber been flooded when Chapman ordered it to be drained. This action was taken in the mistaken belief that the top of the escape chamber was above sea level. In fact, the top of the chamber was about twenty feet below the surface. Before Chapman had the chamber flooded again, there was a loud cheer from the crew's quarters—this was because they'd heard charges being fired, presumably from a warship.

Oram and Woods successfully escaped from *Thetis* and were picked up almost immediately by a boat which had been sent from HMS *Brazen*. It was quarter to nine on 2 June when they were taken on board *Brazen*.

Unsure as to whether *Thetis* was totally or only partially submerged, Lieutenant Commander Bolus ordered that readings should be taken on the after depth gauge. The results obtained after several observations had been made showed a zero reading. From this Bolus deduced that *Thetis's* stern was now above sea level. Having gained this information, by way of doing a double check, he ordered 'Z' outboard vent to be opened and 'Z' inboard vent to be tested for water.

Before any further escape attempts could be made, the escape chamber had to be drained down following Oram and Woods's exit. But, during this process, a small amount of water ran over the coamings and onto the main engines and the switchboard. This leakage caused a reaction, and smoke came into the steerage compartment. Some put on gas masks whilst others donned their Davis Escape Apparatus. The bulkhead door was also closed for some time.

Knowing that time and oxygen were fast running out, First Lieutenant Chapman, in an attempt to hasten the escape operation, suggested that four men at a time should try to escape together. As all of the men on board were now suffering from lack of oxygen in the submarine's atmosphere, time was

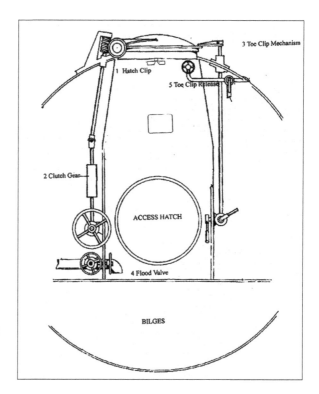

Escape chamber arrangements as installed on *Thetis*. (*By kind permission of Pamela Armstrong*)

of the essence. Chapman's suggestion was accepted. Accordingly, Leading Stoker Kenney, and Stoker Hole, both crew from *Thetis*, electrician Mr Smith from Cammell Lairds, and another of Lairds's employees entered the escape chamber. Leading Stoker Arnold then flooded the chamber whilst another rating operated the hatch wheel and removed the safety clip, thus ensuring that the escape hatch was free to open. When the chamber was completely flooded, the men inside needed to release any air remaining in the chamber, push open the hatch and escape. But the hatch cover could not be pushed up for some reason. They made several attempts to open the hatch, but after a quarter of an hour the chamber was drained. Three of the men were dead and the fourth, Mr Smith, was near to death. None of the men had been wearing the nose clips as stipulated. Before dying, Smith whispered to one of Cammell Lairds's charge hand fitters, Mr Shaw, that they could not open the hatch at the top of the escape chamber.

Quickly realizing that four men escaping at once was not feasible, they returned to the original strategy. After removing the four men from the escape chamber, Leading Stoker Arnold and Mr Shaw entered. By opening the outboard vent, Arnold allowed the chamber to flood. Shaw then tried to open the hatch but found that it was firmly fixed. Fortunately, he was successful on his second attempt. After he'd escaped Arnold followed shortly afterwards.

Two of the survivors, Mr Frank Shaw (Cammell Lairds's Fitter) and Leading Stoker Walter Arnold, on their way to the Tribunal. (*From 'SOS Thetis', Hans Müller Verlag, Dresden, 1943*)

His escape was not without some difficulty as he got caught on some clips on his way out of the chamber, but managed to kick himself free. Both men were picked up shortly after reaching the surface.

Immediately before Arnold and Shaw entered the escape chamber they observed that there were upwards of twenty men in the steerage compartment; all were showing signs of serious distress. Arnold said that he had a bad headache and was experiencing some difficulty in breathing. Shaw was later to comment that as he entered the escape chamber, the air in the submarine was very thick and, like the other people on board, he was finding difficulty in speaking as he had a choking sensation in his throat.

Arnold and Shaw had escaped from *Thetis* at about ten o'clock on Friday 2 June 1939.

Summary of Part 3.
A detailed account of the events which occurred outside the *Thetis* relating to her loss and the attempts to render assistance.

During this time of intense activity aboard the troubled *Thetis* whilst she was submerged, there was also much activity relating to rescue attempts being organised. *Grebe Cock* had moved her position about half a mile from the stern of the *Thetis* on her port quarter; this was in compliance with the orders issued by Lieutenant Commander Bolus immediately before leaving their earlier rendezvous at the Bar Lightship. Lieutenant Coltart was aboard *Grebe Cock* and paying strict observation to the movements of *Thetis* and also any other vessels in the near vicinity of the submarine. Coltart testified later that he watched *Thetis* submerging, a manoeuvre which took upwards of fifty minutes, and, even then, it was only a partial dive which *Thetis* made, her deck-mounted gun was still at water surface level. At this time, *Thetis* was making about four knots on an even keel. At the Inquiry, Lieutenant Coltart went on to say:

> About two minutes to three o'clock her bow came up, just broke the surface, and I saw a splash of air just forward of the bow. The *Thetis* dived horizontally and fairly fast, and completely disappeared about a minute to three.

Coltart went on to describe the splash of air as a lot of foam forward of the bows; like an air bubble which might have been caused when the bow broke the surface. Coltart was adamant that *Thetis* did not dive at an angle, but went below on an even keel. Coltart did not see the submarine's stern once the bows had disappeared. Leading Telegraphist Crosby later testified that *Thetis* was on an even keel when she dropped down very quickly. He did however say that he saw a slight disturbance in the water, perhaps caused by air escaping before *Thetis* disappeared. Captain Godfrey gave a similar testimony, adding that when he saw the puff of air on her port bow, he thought that they were 'blowing' tanks.

As an experienced sub-mariner, Lieutenant Coltart suspected that something was amiss in the dive. It appeared to him that *Thetis*, from being very light, had quickly become very heavy. He wasn't too concerned, knowing that if they gained a little speed and if the tanks were 'blown', or the pumps used, then they should be re-appearing soon some distance ahead. It was for this reason that he did not ask Captain Godfrey to take the tug any closer; there was a distinct possibility that *Grebe Cock* might 'over-run' *Thetis*. The next intense minutes were spent, by all hands on the *Grebe Cock*, in looking for indicator buoys, smoke candles or *Thetis's* periscope to suddenly appear. Nobody saw anything. Again, because of his experience in submarines, Lieutenant Coltart assumed that things must be going according to plan, as no distress signals had been seen. *Grebe Cock* stopped her engines and remained, as far as possible, on the station she had held before *Thetis* dived.

When Coltart had been given his instructions from Lieutenant Commander Bolus the day before the dive trials, he had also been presented with a detailed dive programme. According to the programme, *Thetis* was to partially submerge in order to determine trim. She would then 'blow' main tanks and surface. Following this she would dive to periscope depth, then lower her periscope and dive to a depth of 60 feet. On reaching this depth she would fire smoke candles. However, by this time, it was patently obvious to Lieutenant Coltart that *Thetis* was not adhering to her programme. Thinking through a range of possibilities, Coltart considered that the most likely explanation for this apparent deviation from programme might be that *Thetis* had surfaced again at such a distance from the tug that the periscope and red flag were impossible for those on board *Grebe Cock* to observe.

Those on board *Grebe Cock* kept their vigil for some time, but there came a point when Coltart considered that he needed to take further action. He ordered Leading Telegraphist Crosby to send a radio telephonic message to Fort Blockhouse seeking further information regarding the submarine's dive programme. The message was simple and succinct, phrased in such a way that it raised concern but not anxiety. The message, as transmitted to Fort Blockhouse, was as follows:

15.45. From tug attending *Thetis*. What was duration of *Thetis* dive?

Adhering to normal Royal Naval practice, *Thetis* had sent a wireless message to Fort Blockhouse at 1340 hours, stating that she was diving for three hours.

However, *Grebe Cock* did not have compatible systems on board, and did not therefore receive the message. The sequence of events in transmitting *Grebe Cock's* message was as follows:

15.46 GMT	Seaforth heard from pilot boat that the *Grebe Cock* was calling her.
15.56 GMT	Seaforth receives *Grebe Cock's* message.
16.03 GMT	Message sent on to Liverpool.
16.19 GMT	Liverpool message sent to London.
16.38 GMT	Message received at Gosport.
17.07 GMT	Message left Gosport with a boy on a bike.
17.15 GMT	Message received at Fort Blockhouse.

A question was raised at the time, querying whether *Grebe Cock* was operating on British Summer Time (BST) or Greenwich Mean Time (GMT), which, even from the transcript of the official Inquiry, appears to show a complete misunderstanding of the difference between BST and GMT. This difference might have influenced a different rescue attempt and a different outcome; but this is speculation and conjecture.

For reasons that he couldn't understand at the time, Coltart did not receive any information relating to his Inquiry to Fort Blockhouse. Faced with the decision as to what to do for the best in the absence of any specific orders in such an event, he decided that the tug should hold station at anchor. But, even this was not as straightforward as might have been expected. *Grebe Cock* was in waters twenty-two fathoms deep, much deeper than waters in which she normally anchored. In fact, *Grebe Cock* only had the equivalent of fifteen fathoms of anchor cable on each of its two anchors. The only viable solution was to join the two cables together, end-to-end—a process which, in itself, took upwards of an hour's hard work. But, now anchored in a position where they thought *Thetis* had dived, the intention was that *Grebe Cock* would act as a marker buoy. In actual fact, *Grebe Cock* was some four miles west-north-west from where *Thetis* had dived.

In an attempt to get an accurate 'fix' on *Thetis's* position, Captain Godfrey spoke to the pilot vessel which was stationed just off the Bar Lightship. The message from the pilot vessel was that they had not seen any trace of *Thetis*.

As Coltart had not had any response to his earlier message, he instructed Wireless Telegraphist Crosby to get a message to Seaforth radio station, stating that *Thetis* had not yet surfaced from the earlier dive. Unfortunately, because of weak signals between *Grebe Cock* and Seaforth, Crosby could not transmit his message. He made no further attempts at sending messages from *Grebe Cock*.

The breakdown in communication between *Grebe Cock*—and Fort Blockhouse, or, more correctly, the inability of *Grebe Cock* to be able to directly communicate with Fort Blockhouse, meant that no executive orders were issued from Fort Blockhouse to launch any rescue attempt. In effect, *Thetis* and *Grebe Cock* were isolated with little or no means of effective communication between themselves and shore-based authorities. It was not until 1822 hours that any orders were issued from Fort Blockhouse to initiate any form of assistance for *Thetis*, almost four hours after she had dived.

The protocols at Fort Blockhouse ensure that the dive times for every submarine are recorded, as are the times of surfacing. *Thetis* had dispatched a message to Fort Blockhouse at 1340 hours, stating that she would be diving for a period of three hours. The message was sent at 1340 hours and is recorded as being received by Fort Blockhouse at 1405 hours. The message was not transmitted directly to Fort Blockhouse, so there is a degree of uncertainty as to exactly when the communication from *Thetis* was acknowledged, and also the exact time when she started her dive. But, it is clear that it was sometime between 1340 hours and 1405 hours. From this information, it was known that *Thetis* was scheduled to surface, at the latest, at 1705 hours. Had this been the case, a message stating that *Thetis* had surfaced should have been received by Fort Blockhouse no later than, say, 1730 hours.

At Fort Blockhouse, it is the direct responsibility of the Chief Yeoman of Signals to record, for every submarine under their jurisdiction, accurate details relating to precise dive and surfacing times. Accordingly, at 1645 hours, the Chief Yeoman of Signals reported to the senior officer in command of the Fifth Submarine Flotilla that *Thetis*, due to surface at 1640 hours had not, as yet, sent any surfacing signal.

The chain of command at Fort Blockhouse was complex, especially due to a number of extraordinary circumstances pertaining on that particular day. However, it is important to give a brief explanation of the convoluted chain of command. Rear Admiral (Submarines) B. C. Watson had overall command of Fort Blockhouse. But, on this particular day, he was at home on sick leave. Watson's second in command was the Duty Staff Officer, who on that day was Commander G. B. Hamley Fawkes. However, before Fawkes received any information regarding the delayed surfacing signal, the information would have been passed through several levels of staff; only arriving on Fawkes desk when and if affirmative action was required. It was the direct responsibility of the Duty Submarine Commanding Officer to handle everyday routine matters. A different flotilla leader was nominated every day, and on this particular day, that officer was the commanding officer of the Fifth Submarine Flotilla— Captain Oram—who, at that time, was on board *Thetis*. Having anticipated his absence, Captain Oram had made arrangements for his colleague Commander Lancelot Milman Shadwell to stand-in for him. But, as Shadwell himself was engaged on an exercise in the English Channel, responsibility rested on the shoulders of Lieutenant Commander Lipscombe until Shadwell returned.

The business of the day was routine for Lipscombe; several communications, including Bolus's, were received. Lipscombe, after taking a cursory glance, arranged all of the messages, and awaited Shadwell's return.

It had been anticipated that *Thetis* would send a communication to Fort Blockhouse at approximately 1640 hours, shortly after she had surfaced. Shadwell returned to his office at 1615 hours.

As was the case for every other eventuality, the Admiralty had a Fleet Order protocol stipulating, in very precise detail, exactly what procedure to adopt in the case of a submarine failing to surface in home waters. Being fully conversant with this protocol, when the Chief Yeoman of Signals informed Shadwell at 1645 that no surfacing communication had been received from *Thetis*, he immediately telephoned the Admiralty Operations Division in Whitehall. Firstly, there was the requirement to inform them of the situation; and secondly, to inquire if any knowledge regarding *Thetis's* whereabouts had been communicated to them. It was confirmed that the Operations Division only held the same information as Shadwell. Next, Cammell Lairds was contacted, but they too had had no direct contact with *Thetis*.

But, even at this stage, there was no immediate panic, as the Admiralty was well used to submarines surfacing sometime after their scheduled time. Apart from anything else, it was the submarine's first dive, so *Thetis* might have encountered any one of a number of possible 'teething troubles'. It was, however, considered prudent for a wireless operator at Fort Blockhouse to send messages to *Thetis* every ten minutes. In order to ensure that all bases were covered, Shadwell informed his superior, the duty staff officer, Commander Fawkes.

As Rear Admiral (Submarines) Watson was not available to take important decisions, it fell to Commander Fawkes to initiate any action. At 1730 hours, in the absence of any messages from *Thetis*, Fawkes decided that action was now called for. After studying a chart of Liverpool Bay, Fawkes decided to alert the Admiralty and other relevant authorities of the situation. He also communicated the information to Rear Admiral Watson. In light of the gravity of the situation, Fawkes also endeavoured to contact Watson's chief, Captain Ian Agnew Patterson Macintyre. Having made several calls, all of which were unsuccessful, Fawkes decided that he needed to take responsibility and initiate some action.

At 1738 hours, Gosport post office received a telegram from *Grebe Cock* in Liverpool Bay. The communication was delivered to Fort Blockhouse but with no great urgency, as it was not marked either urgent or important.

Amongst his other calls, at 1750 hours Fawkes made contact with Duty Officer Bayne at Plymouth. He related his understanding of the events which were unfolding in Liverpool Bay, stressing that he didn't believe that anything untoward had happened, but that he did have some anxiety. Later, Baynes suggested that his understanding of the conversation was somewhat different from Fawkes's. Bayne's understanding was that Fawkes had said that there was no cause for anxiety, and that a surfacing signal was imminent.

Because of his role at Plymouth, Baynes was aware that HMS *Brazen* was somewhere near Liverpool Bay, as she was returning to Plymouth following gunnery trials in waters off Belfast. Baynes knew that *Brazen* was fitted with the latest ASDIC submarine detection equipment. He suggested to Fawkes that *Brazen* could be re-tasked and be in the area in the next hour or two, adding that the ASDIC equipment would soon locate *Thetis*. Fawkes was however reluctant to have the destroyer re-tasked before seeking higher authority.

Fawkes made another call to the Admiralty in Whitehall seeking further information, but none was forthcoming. Meanwhile Baynes, knowing that *Thetis* was now more than seventy minutes late in re-surfacing decided, on his own initiative, to re-task *Brazen*. He drafted a signal, re-directing her to *Thetis's* last known position.

It was 1810 before Coltart's telegram was received by Fort Blockhouse. Shadwell was instructed to telephone Seaforth with the information that Coltart had requested, namely that *Thetis* had stated that she was diving at 1340 hours for a period of three hours. The message did not convey any concerns, from either Plymouth or Fort Blockhouse, about *Thetis's* well being.

In actual fact, Coltart, because of his experience on submarines, was now fully aware that the matter was out of his hands, and any action that needed to be taken would be initiated much higher up the chain of command.

As time passed and still nothing positive had been heard from either *Thetis* or Coltart on the *Grebe Cock*, Fawkes began to question whether some catastrophic event had befallen the submarine. He contacted Bayne once again concerning the re-tasking of *Brazen*. Bayne immediately had another signal sent to *Brazen*, this time ordering the destroyer to proceed at top speed. The significant difference between the two signals being that the first was little more than a routine locate-and-communicate message, whereas the second signal inferred that the re-tasking might be to mount a rescue attempt.

Now that the plight of *Thetis* was assuming more significance, Fawkes contacted the Duty Commander of the Admiralty in Whitehall, informing him that there was a possibility that *Thetis* had met with some sort of accident. Officers in the Admiralty then contacted the Air Ministry, so that an airborne reconnaissance of the area could be mounted. It was at this point that the situation escalated to a completely different level. It was stipulated in Admiralty fleet orders that in a case such as this, overall authority and responsibility for all aspects of the operation would be under the direct control of the Commander-in-Chief of the home port, in whose area the sinking happened. This meant that the Commander-in-Chief Plymouth, Admiral Sir Martin Eric Dunbar-Nasmith VC assumed total command; all other personnel who had been involved to date, principally Bayne, Fawkes and Macintyre were now accountable to him.

Being conversant with fleet orders, paragraph five, Fawkes suggested to Admiral Dunbar-Nasmith that the time might have arrived to launch a full-scale search and rescue operation; the operation code-named in the Navy as 'Subsmash'. The suggestion was adopted, and the Sixth Destroyer Flotilla was ordered to join 'Subsmash'. Similar orders were dispatched to the mine sweeping flotilla and HMS *Tedworth*—a specialised diving vessel. Unfortunately, *Tedworth* was berthed on the Clyde, and did not have sufficient fuel to make the journey down to Liverpool Bay. It was almost seven o'clock in the evening when the operation 'Subsmash' swung into action.

Macintyre, Rear Admiral Watson's chief of staff, returned to Fort Blockhouse at 1940 hours, after spending the day with the First Lord of the Admiralty on board HMS *Enchantress*. He conferred with all relevant staff at Fort Blockhouse before ordering the duty destroyer HMS *Winchelsea* to be made ready for sea. His judgement was that he should be present at the dive site itself, so that he could have a direct input into the rescue operation. Just why he opted to travel by sea, rather than air, car or train is open to conjecture. It was estimated that a successful 'Subsmash' rescue operation should be effected within a twenty-four hour time-frame, but six valuable hours had elapsed since the time when *Thetis* was scheduled to re-surface.

Seafaring communities are relatively small and close-knit, and on this occasion that small world proved useful. Whilst there was little that those on board *Grebe Cock* could do, save keeping a vigilant lookout, there were other Liverpool-based resources that could be deployed. Liverpool's Marine Surveyor and Water Bailiff, Commander Hubert Viner Hart was known, personally, to Admiral Dunbar-Nasmith. One of Hart's primary responsibilities was to salvage any sunken vessels within a prescribed area around Liverpool, thus ensuring that access to the Mersey and the vital port of Liverpool was always clear. Hart had an impressive record; over his twenty-three year career he had been involved in over fifty successful salvaging operations in the waters in and around the River Mersey. Commander Bayne contacted him sometime after eight o'clock in the evening and explained the situation. The upshot being that Admiral Dunbar-Nasmith was requesting that, because of the situation with *Thetis*, and the knowledge and salvage equipment that he (Hart) had, could he proceed—as soon as possible—to the dive site. Following a well-tried and tested system, Hart contacted the Shore Superintendent at Liverpool and asked that all relevant personnel, including Charles Brock—the Liverpool Wreck Master—and divers, join him aboard the Mersey Harbour vessel, *Vigilant*, berthed at Princes Landing Stage. The *Vigilant*, a multi-purpose vessel, was a salvage vessel, a hydrographic tender and buoy tender; added to which, because of the various duties which she was called upon to perform, the vessel had enhanced pulling power. Accepting the urgency of Dunbar-Nasmith's request, Hart decided to sail without a full crew. He was under no illusion as to the gravity of the situation, ordering that the port's other salvage vessel, *Salvor*, should be deployed, and that *Vigilant's* missing crew should be ferried out on the tug, *Crosby*.

It was not beyond the bounds of possibility that *Thetis* might have to be salvaged, so Hart gave orders for three of the port's 'camels' to be made ready for towing to the dive site. A 'camel', in this context, is a type of barge, having no motive power of its own, but being equipped with various types of salvage gear. When a salvage operation is being attempted using 'camels', two 'camels' are generally used. They are positioned either side of the sunken vessel, then wires are strung between them and passed under the hull of the vessel being salved, and secured. This operation is conducted at low tide. Then, as the tide rises, the vessel is lifted from the seabed. The 'camels' are then towed inshore as far as possible, any slack in the wires taken up, and the process repeated until the sunken vessel surfaces.

Important as the 'camels' were, they couldn't be taken to the dive site immediately for a number of reasons. First of all they had to wait for the high tide, so that they could leave Liverpool's Albert Dock; also, there was no definite knowledge that *Thetis* was in difficulty or had met with some sort of accident.

At 2145 hours *Vigilant* sailed from Princes Landing Stage, little more than an hour after having been contacted from Plymouth. Commander E. W. Harboard from the Mersey Docks and Harbour Board deputised for Hart. Also on board were Charles Brock, the Liverpool Wreck Master and Frederick Orton who was a diver. So, the authorities at Liverpool had responded straight away, and other rescue services, being directed from Plymouth, were also heading towards the dive site. Knowing how vital any information relating to the submarine was, a search was made for the captains of submarines HMS *Trident* and HMS *Taku*, both of which were being built at Cammell Lairds, and both of their captains were standing-by during the fitting-out period. In the absence of any other personnel with vital information about the detailed workings of the submarines, their input would be of great value.

The official Inquiry listed, in strict chronological order, the exact timings of all messages sent and received, and also the actions which were ordered and initiated. The message which Lieutenant Coltart had sent from *Grebe Cock* requesting to know the duration of the dive was received at 1815 hours. This request served to increase anxiety levels at Fort Blockhouse. It was at this point that the staff officer, Commander Fawkes, thought it necessary to communicate with both the Admiralty and the Commander-in-Chief at Plymouth. The procedure to be adopted in just such an event as this was clear, and was put into operation immediately.

At 1822, HMS *Brazen* was ordered to proceed to the dive site. And later, at 1830 hours, Fort Blockhouse contacted Cammell Lairds informing them of the possibility that an accident might have befallen the submarine. It was also reported to Cammell Lairds that *Brazen* had been re-tasked, and was now heading for the dive site. The next action, at 1850 hours, was to organise an air search of the area around the dive site. Knowing that *Brazen* would take some time to steam to the area, Admiral Dunbar-Nasmith considered what might be possible immediately. Accordingly, at 2015 hours, a call was put through to the Marine Surveyor and Water Bailiff at the Mersey Docks and Harbour Board, Captain Hart. At 2145, the Mersey Docks and Harbour Board's salvage vessel, *Vigilant* sailed from Liverpool to assist in the rescue attempt.

Later that same evening, at 2140 hours, a flotilla of torpedo destroyers sailed from Portland for Liverpool Bay, and arrived the next morning at 1040 hours.

Because the *Vigilant* had sailed from Liverpool without her full complement of crew, the Mersey tug, *Crosby*, left Liverpool at 2315 hours that night, carrying the said missing crew-members. Earlier, HMS *Tedworth*, equipped with deep-sea diving gear and experienced divers, had left her base on the Clyde, but didn't arrive at the dive site until 0300 hours on Saturday 3 June 1939.

Captain Macintyre, wishing to be on hand, had ordered HMS *Winchelsea*, the duty destroyer, to be ready to sail for Liverpool Bay. She left Portsmouth later that evening, arriving the following day at 1700 hours.

Locating the actual site where *Thetis* was located was proving elusive. In fact, *Brazen* and *Vigilant*, having spent many long hours searching the area where they thought *Thetis* had dived, did not locate her until just before 0800 hours the following morning. The difficulty had arisen because the underwater signalling equipment on *Thetis* had been disabled when she struck the seabed; and, secondly, *Brazen* and *Vigilant* had been searching in the wrong area.

Lieutenant Avent, on duty up in Scotland, was informed of the situation *vis-à-vis Thetis* at 1925 hours. Given an area fifteen miles from Great Orme Head, on a bearing between 335° and 340°, he was ordered to search for a marker buoy or, failing that, any air bubbles or oil deposits which might give some indication of the submarine's whereabouts. In actual fact, *Thetis* was fifteen miles from Great Orme Head bearing 349° from the Head.

Four aircraft, under Lieutenant Avent's command, set off just before 2000 hours on the evening of 1 June 1939, reaching the search area about an hour later; just before sunset, which was at 2104 hours that night. No orders had been issued for them to locate *Grebe Cock* before starting their search—their task would, arguably, have been made somewhat easier had this order been given. As darkness was approaching, Avent spotted a buoy, and, directly below the water's surface, a long, dark object—perhaps twenty-five yards in length and a couple of yards wide. He immediately dropped to an altitude of less than fifty feet above the water's surface in order to check his reconnaissance. After his navigator had checked the position relative to Great Orme Head, Avent sent the following wireless message at 2125 hours:

Important. Marker buoy observed in position 322° Orme Head 13 miles.

Next, as there was a trawler at a distance of about two miles, he fired four green Very lights, but, for some reason, the trawler chose to ignore these signals.

At 2200 hours, Avent sent another message:

Cancel my 21.25 position of marker buoy. 303° Orme Head ten and a half miles.

A third message was sent at 2325 hours:

Yellow conical marker buoy. Impossible to detect anything.

As it was now far too dark to continue any meaningful reconnaissance, and with onboard fuel getting lower, the aeroplanes withdrew from the site, ready to resume the search at first light in the morning. The aerial search continued at 0415 hours the following morning, and continued for almost four hours. Visibility was much reduced that morning, due to a heavy smoke haze drifting over from Liverpool. Avent saw nothing. Speculation suggested that the buoy observed on the previous evening might well have been a marker buoy from a fishing vessel.

As *Brazen* was returning to Portsmouth, a message was received at 1845 hours, re-tasking her to a location 53° 35' N and 4° W; her task, to locate *Thetis*. Towards 2100 hours *Grebe Cock* was sighted. A message was sent to the tug asking if she was at the location where *Thetis* dived. *Grebe Cock* replied, stating that she was some distance from the submarine's dive site, but gave her proposed course as 310°. *Brazen's* captain, Lieutenant Commander Mills, immediately started his search, which, initially, was three miles to the west of *Grebe Cock*, Mills having made the assumption that the tug would be to the east of *Thetis*. In fact, *Grebe Cock* was about four miles NW of *Thetis*. It was during this initial search that another communication was received from Fort Blockhouse:

Aircraft report marker buoy in position 322° Great Orme Head 13 miles.
Investigate.

Mills headed for the new given position, but again, unknown to him, this station was about six miles south west of where *Thetis* actually was. At 2253 hours, another message was received, correcting the earlier position and giving a new position of 303° and ten and a half miles from Great Orme Head. This new search also found no success. Aided by the equipment on board, a searchlight and two signal projectors, *Brazen* continued her search throughout the night. With all of *Brazen's* search equipment, and, given that it was a clear moonlit night, it seems inconceivable that she would have missed spotting a marker buoy and flag, had there been one. At 0300 hours, *Brazen* went to investigate a report of oil on the water's surface on a bearing of 310° at a distance twenty-one miles from Great Orme Head. Again, the search proved fruitless. *Brazen* was in fact at least twenty-three miles west from *Thetis*.

Beginning to question the marked lack of success in the areas which he had already thoroughly searched, Captain Mills decided that, as he'd already searched the area to the south and west of *Grebe Cock*, he should now focus his attention on the eastern and northern side of her. This decision was taken shortly before 0700 hours on 2 June 1939. Less than an hour later, and two points on *Brazen's* starboard bow, *Thetis* was spotted at a distance of approximately three miles. By a rough estimation, her stern was proud of the water by about eighteen feet. Mills steamed to the vicinity and fired twelve underwater charges—thus alerting those on board *Thetis* that help was at hand. And then, less than ten minutes later, Captain Oram and Lieutenant Woods were seen to surface from the submarine. A boat, lowered from *Brazen* picked them up. Close to the protruding stern of *Thetis*, there was a small red spherical indicator buoy with a flag attached to it. It later transpired that the indicator buoy was the after indicator—the forward indicator buoy having completely disappeared. Mills went on to state that, with the search equipment on *Brazen*, he would have been able to spot the buoy at a distance of half a mile at night, and during daylight hours, at a distance of one mile.

The salvage plan, the content of which had been agreed before Oram and Woods had entered the escape chamber, was strapped to Oram's wrist together with a water-tight covering. The plan was given to Lieutenant Coltart. Captain Oram also gave orders for a message to be sent to the Commander-in-Chief at Plymouth. It read:

9.43 a.m. Immediate. Intercept. Please pass general situation to RA(S) and Cammell Lairds. *Thetis* is flooded to 40 Bulkhead. No. 5 tube bow cap and rear door presumed open. Port door of 25 bulkhead is believed to have only one clip on both compartments therefore being common S/M is lying with bows on bottom in 130 feet and by pumping fuel the stern has now been raised above water. Air is urgently needed and crew are expecting diver to connect armoured hose to whistle or gun recuperator when they will endeavour to lighten bow with salvage blow on 40 bulkhead. Before this can be done fore hatch must be strengthened with strong-back as it is feared any pressure in torpedo compartment will lift hatch off its seating. All on board are alive and endeavouring to escape by after D.S.E.A. which is near the surface but air in submarine is getting very foul.

After the Commander-in-Chief at Plymouth had contacted Captain Hart in Liverpool at 2030 hours, Hart set about having the salvage vessel SS *Vigilant* prepared for sea. *Vigilant*, a twin-screw steamship of 344 gross tonnage was owned by the Mersey Docks and Harbour Board and was fitted, specifically, for diving and salvage work. Just over an hour later, the vessel was leaving Princes Landing Stage in Liverpool, with Hart in command. Also on board were Commander Harbord, Hart's deputy; Mr Brock the Liverpool Wreck Master, Mr Orton the Board's diver, Mr Watters from Cammell Lairds, and Lieutenant Commander Bittlestone, the Naval Liaison Officer at Liverpool.

Vigilant searched for *Thetis* throughout the night of 1 June, but, as incorrect information had been given regarding *Thetis's* position, she was unable to locate the stricken submarine. However, *Vigilant* was able to rendezvous with *Grebe Cock* shortly after three o'clock the following morning. It was at this point that Lieutenant Coltart transferred to *Vigilant* to discuss search strategy with Captain Hart. Coltart confirmed that *Thetis* was within a mile of *Grebe Cock's* anchored position. After a number of marker buoys had been placed, Hart decided to make a sweep at a radius of one mile and through 360° around *Grebe Cock*. Shortly after 0400 hours, Hart received a message from the Admiralty stating that, following the airborne search, a marker buoy had been sighted 303° true, ten and a half miles from Great Orme Head. *Vigilant* curtailed her current search around *Grebe Cock* and made for the new search area. Captain Hart made a search in that area for at least two hours, but to no avail. It was towards 0630 hours that he decided to head back towards *Grebe Cock*. *Thetis's* stern was sighted just before 0800 hours, shortly after *Brazen* had appeared on the scene.

Hart observed that a continuous stream of air bubbles could be seen to be coming from the mid-ships area of *Thetis*. He ordered that a boat should be lowered and a messenger wire made fast to the submarine. Men on board the lowered boat then tapped continuous messages, in Morse code, against *Thetis's* hull: 'Come out', but they did not receive any response from those on board the submarine.

Just before nine o'clock in the morning, a message was sent from *Vigilant* to Mr Rowland at the Mersey Docks and Harbour Board, requesting that burners and burning gear be sent to *Vigilant* straight away by tug.

With Lieutenant Commander Bittlestone now on board *Vigilant*, he and Lieutenant Coltart both transferred to *Brazen* to confer about Oram's rescue plan before returning to *Vigilant*. Now, being conversant with the proposed plan, Hart knew exactly what additional equipment was needed to effect the rescue bid. He sent a detailed message to the Mersey Docks and Harbour Board:

Please send out with a tug with utmost dispatch, portable motor air compressor connections for air pipe to compressor. Burners and burning gear, Foreman Fitter and from Cammell Lairds 400 feet of air pipe for air compressor with suitable connections to attach to the hose connections on Gun Recuperator. Send Foreman Fitter Black, also send diver and tender from the Liverpool and Glasgow Salvage Association, but do not delay gear if diver and tender are not ready.

Oram's plan involved strengthening the fore hatch of the submarine with a strong-back, but *Vigilant* wasn't carrying any suitable material. Hart intended to improvise using some timber weighted by fire bars.

It had been some time since Oram and Woods had been picked up following their escape, and there appeared to be little prospect of any other men surfacing using the Davis Escape Apparatus, but then, shortly before ten o'clock, Leading Seaman Arnold and Mr Shaw—a Cammell Lairds employee—were seen on the water's surface. Further, they reported that, although only four men had escaped during the last two hours, it was believed that, given time, everyone on board *Thetis* would be able to escape and that the submarine herself could be saved. The safety and well being of any men escaping was paramount, and to that end, all vessels in the immediate vicinity of the escape hatches were ordered to keep well clear.

Part of Oram's plan involved attaching a line under the forward end of *Thetis* to assist the divers when locating the fore hatch and the gun recuperator valve. Working under these conditions, it was only possible for a diver to go down just before high water mark, and even then, it was only possible to remain below for a maximum time of half an hour.

The flotilla of torpedo destroyers which had sailed from Portland on the previous evening arrived on station at 1040 hours, under the command of Captain Nicholson. Upon his arrival, Captain Hart joined him aboard HMS *Somali* to apprise him of the situation. Nicholson said that the 400 feet of hose which Hart had requested to be sent out could be supplied from the flotilla.

There was a distinct lack of activity coming from *Thetis* following the escape of Arnold and Shaw, apart that is for what sounded like some hammering coming from inside the submarine. But, there were certainly no more men escaping from the stricken submarine. Also at that time, Mr Brock, the Mersey Docks and Harbour Board's Wreck Master, saw some air bubbles coming from *Thetis*. He'd also observed that before Arnold and Shaw's escape, similar air bubbles had been seen coming to the surface.

As time passed, it became clear that Oram's escape plan would not be able to be put into operation for some time. A number of factors prohibited its execution; the depth of the water that the divers would have to work in; the strength of the current—running at about two to two-and-a-half knots; not all of the necessary rescue equipment being available; and, perhaps most important of all, the fact that the diver who had come out on the *Vigilant* had no experience of working at such depths. However, as the situation was fast becoming more critical, he did venture down to *Thetis* and managed to secure guide wires to the submarine at high water—about 1130 hours. There was little chance of much more progress being made until low water at 1730 hours.

Following a series of conversations between Lieutenant Woods and Captain Nicholson, and later between Nicholson and Captain Hart on board *Vigilant*, it became evident that other, more radical, action needed to be taken—and with a degree of urgency. A decision was taken to try to raise the stern of *Thetis* a little higher out of the water, high enough for the cover plate of the manhole towards the stern to be removed and then a hole cut into the hull. This would enable a new escape route to be secured for the men remaining on board the *Thetis*.

The next stage of the rescue attempt was to gain access to the submarine through the outer cover plate located in the submarine's stern. This necessitated raising the stern of *Thetis* a little higher than what she already was. A three-and-a-half-inch wire rope, firmly fixed to the bows of *Vigilant*, was secured around *Thetis*. At 1310 hours *Vigilant* began the towing operation. In an effort to focus more power into the attempt, two tugs were linked to the stern of *Vigilant*. The combined pulling power enabled *Thetis's* stern to be raised a little more, just enough to make sure that the propellers were now clear of the water. Having reached this point, the next step was a rather precarious one. Mr Brock, the Mersey Docks and Harbour Board's Wreck Master, had to climb onto the protruding stern, and try to gain access to the submarine by removing the outer cover plate and then removing the inner cover to the manhole.

At 1330 hours, Brock estimated that the stern was some fourteen to fifteen feet out of the water, thus making access to the rear manhole cover relatively easy. As Brock eased the nuts following a standard pattern of procedure, he found that, as they were being unscrewed, an amount of air pressure was also being released from the outer cover. This unexpected release of pressure prompted the wreck master to tighten up the nuts again and await further instructions as to how to proceed—after having informed personnel on the *Vigilant* of this occurrence. He was told to continue unscrewing the cover plate. But, shortly before 1500 hours, as the tide was turning, *Thetis* pivoted around, and was no longer being held up by the force of the tide. In fact, the submarine was now being forced down by the tide, which meant that Brock could no longer maintain his position on the submarine, as it had now become impossible to continue work on removing the cover plate. He transferred from his precarious position, back to the boat which had brought him alongside *Thetis*.

There then followed what could only be described as crisis talks between Captain Nicholson and Captain Hart aboard the *Vigilant*. Nicholson's view was that the situation, owing to the passage of time, was now rapidly becoming desperate, and that something needed to be done at once. A number of alternatives were discussed, but, in the final analysis, a strategy suggested by Hart appeared to be the most feasible under the circumstances. His idea was for *Vigilant* to hold *Thetis* in position until low tide, and then attempt to ease the stern out of the water again. And, when the stern was sufficiently clear of the water, to cut a hole in the stern of sufficient size to enable the trapped crew to make their escape. The logic of Hart's proposal seemed irrefutable, but Nicholson, being the officer in command, insisted that there just was not the time to wait for low tide, and that a rescue attempt must be made forthwith. Against his better judgement, Hart reluctantly agreed to make the attempt. He had argued that by making the attempt at this time, with the water as high as it was, there was a distinct possibility that *Thetis* might cant around, thus causing irreparable damage. But, like Nicholson, he was conscious of the men inside *Thetis* and the desperate state that they must now be in.

Once again, *Vigilant* went alongside *Thetis*, and the tugs were secured to *Vigilant* so that the operation could commence. Also, on this occasion, *Somali* was positioned alongside *Vigilant*, so that the cutting equipment which she carried could be used to drill a hole in *Thetis's* hull. But, just before the operation was due to start, the tug *Crosby* arrived on the scene, carrying the much-needed oxy-acetylene gear. She changed places with *Somali*. When the operation did start, the forces being exerted on the hull of *Thetis* were too great, causing the submarine to cant. The tow wires could not withstand the tension and, at 1510 hours they broke. *Thetis* sank beneath the waves.

A number of events then occurred within a relatively short space of time, further intensifying the rescue bids. At 1720 hours, HMS *Winchelsea*, which had steamed up from Portsmouth, carrying on board Captain Ian Agnew Patterson Macintyre arrived. Then, at 1800 hours, one of the 'camels' which had been sent from Liverpool arrived. But then, another setback. *Thetis's* indicator buoy broke adrift, and, at the same time, the wire attached to the submarine slipped—*Thetis's* position underwater was now unknown. Fortunately, at about 2030 hours the same evening, another of the Liverpool and Glasgow Salvage Association's salvage vessels, *Salvor* arrived on station, and assisted *Vigilant* in trying to locate the stricken submarine—a mission which they accomplished at midnight.

Elsewhere, up at Scapa Flow in Scotland, another drama relating to the rescue attempt was unfolding. At ten o'clock in the morning, Mr Thomas McKenzie, Metal Industries Chief Salvage Officer was at work, when he heard of the developing situation in Liverpool Bay. As possibly the most experienced man in the whole country regarding this type of emergency, he immediately sent telegrams to both the Admiralty and Cammell Lairds offering his services. The replies which he received were, interestingly, very different. Cammell Lairds, the first to reply at 1230 hours, were courteous but definite in their reply; thanking him for his generous offer of assistance, but declining that offer whilst assuring him that the submarine had been located and that all of those on board were safe and well. The Admiralty's response, which was received some hours later at 1500 hours, was very different however. The message received expressed gratitude for his offer of assistance, and requested him to make an immediate start for Liverpool, giving the co-ordinates of *Thetis*. At the same time, McKenzie received specific information from the King's Harbour Master at Scapa Flow. The message was as follows:

> *Thetis* position is desperate. There is aeroplane waiting at Longhope to take you and three or four divers to Liverpool, changing at Inverness to be at Speke Aerodrome at 5 p.m.

At the time, McKenzie and his men were working on the *Derfflinger*, which was sunk in one hundred and forty feet of water. McKenzie sent an emergency message to his divers asking them to come up. The small party then went by launch to Lyness—taking off their diving gear as they went. They then transferred to car for the journey to Longhope, where an aeroplane was waiting to take them to Inverness. Unfortunately, the plane which was to take them on their next stage was only designed to carry five persons, but McKenzie's was a party of seven; three divers, two attendants, an assistant salvage manager, Mr Robertson, and McKenzie himself. The party took off for Inverness, but, because of the load restrictions, could not afford to take the diving gear with them. Upon reaching Inverness in safety, they were transferred to a larger and faster aircraft which would take them down to Speke Aerodrome, on the southern edge of Liverpool. Upon reaching Speke, there was a fast car waiting for them, taking them the seven or eight miles to Princes Landing Stage at Liverpool's Pier Head. HMS *Matabele* completed the final stage of the incredible journey, reaching *Thetis* at 2215 hours that evening. There was little or no time to spare so, at 0055 hours on the morning of 3 June, an hour after high water, and just a few hours after arriving following his exhausting journey down, Sinclair McKenzie borrowed diving gear from one of the salvage vessels and went down to assess the situation for himself. He was only able to stay below for fifteen minutes, but during that time he banged on *Thetis's* hull with a hammer—he heard faint tapping in response. Unfortunately, the tide was running too strong at that time for any further work to be attempted. He returned to the surface.

HMS *Tedworth* arrived at 0300 hours together with her experienced divers and diving equipment. Also, shortly after, two more 'camels' arrived from

Liverpool. But, it was left to the divers Taylor and Thompson, from Scapa Flow, to make another reconnaissance dive at 0600 hours. Then, as it was now low water, they were able to stay down for an hour. And, like Sinclair McKenzie, they hammered along the hull of *Thetis*, but this time they failed to illicit any response. They did however manage to secure a 2½-inch wire cable to the hull. Later that day, at 1200 hours, another attempt was made to lift the stern of *Thetis* out of the water using the camels. The attempt failed. Later that day, the Admiralty signalled to the Commander-in-Chief at Plymouth, who was now on station in Liverpool Bay. The signal was short and to the point, it said:

It is regretted that hope of saving lives in the *Thetis* must be abandoned.

After fifty hours of being submerged, it was clear that all life on board had ended, and so now the operation changed from one of rescue to one of recovery.

CHAPTER 9

The Report of the Public Inquiry
(Parts 4 & 5)

The first three parts of Mr Justice Bucknill's report, which were detailed in the previous chapter, gave:

1. An explanation of the structure of the *Thetis* (the section also gave a detailed account of certain work done on *Thetis* before the vessel left Birkenhead on 1 June 1939).
2. An account of the disaster as witnessed by the survivors.
3. A detailed account of the events which occurred outside the *Thetis* relating to her loss and the attempts to render assistance.

The fourth part of the report aimed to give a description of the state of the ship after being salvaged, so far as it threw light upon the causes of the loss. And then, in the fifth and last part of the report, Mr Justice Bucknill sought to attribute the causes of the loss.

Summary of Part 4.
A description of the state of the ship after being salved, so far as it threw light upon the causes of the loss.

Following the protracted period for the submarine to be raised, a forensic examination was made by a series of experts to ascertain whether there was any more material evidence to be gained regarding the disaster. Obviously, the Admiralty sent a number of senior personnel to make their investigations, as did the contractors, Cammell Lairds. The Amalgamated Engineering Union was represented by the eminent Marine Surveyor, Mr T. C. Rolland. Nobody had entered either the torpedo tube or the stowage compartments before these surveys were commissioned, so it was reasonable to assume that everything had remained as it was on 1 June. There was obviously the damage which had been caused by the seawater during that intervening period to be considered, but, in essence, everything had remained the same as it was before disaster struck *Thetis*. A significant part of the investigations were the discussions held with the divers, and just what they had observed during the salvaging of the submarine.

When detailing the findings of his Inquiry, thirteen key facts emerged. It was on these key facts that Mr Justice Bucknill based his findings. These facts were as follows:

1. The test cock hole in the rear door of No. 5 tube was blocked by bitumastic enamel. The hole in the rear door could not be seen from inside, because the enamel was smoothed over it. The obstruction was knocked out of the hole from the outside by using the rimer.

2. The rear door of No. 5 tube was fully open and engaged in its hold back position.

3. The bow cap of No. 5 tube was fully open. The bow caps of the other five tubes were shut and their bow cap shutters were indented from contact with the ground. The bow cap shutter of No. 5 tube had no indentation.

4. The position of the control lever for the bow cap of No. 5 tube was $5/_{32}$ of an inch or five degrees towards the open position. Both the opening and closing valves were fully open. The valves of the other five levers were fully open. The positions of the six levers were as follows:

Starboard	Port
No. 1 3/32 inch towards open	No. 2 2/32 inch towards shut
No. 3 5/32 inch towards open	No. 4 5/32 inch towards shut
No. 5 5/32 inch towards open	No. 6 8/32 inch towards shut

5. The mechanical indicator of the bow cap of No. 5 tube was approximately at the fully open position. The pointer was just to the left of the word 'OPEN' on the dial. The mechanical indicators of the other five tubes were at 'SHUT'.

6. The port bulkhead door in the bulkhead abaft the torpedo tube was closed. It was properly seated and no turnbuckle was between the door and the coaming. One turnbuckle at the top of the door was very tightly screwed up in the securing position. Of the remaining seventeen turnbuckles twelve were hanging loose including one at the bottom of the

door and five were in their stowage spring clips. The ventilation valves in No. 40 bulkhead were closed.

7.

i. The external clip of the hatch cover of the after escape chamber was 1½ inches clear of the periphery of the hatch cover. The hatch cover was on its seating and could be raised by hand about four inches. The cover was prevented from being fully opened by the position of the external clip. This position of the clip was caused by the fact that the hatch closing gear had not been put to the position in which the hatch spindle was free to revolve by reversing its wheel the necessary number of times, but had only been turned about one revolution. The external clip was subsequently moved by means of its operating gear to its full extent and was in proper working order. Some of the bodies were then removed through this hatch.

ii. Both drains of the after escape chamber were shut.

iii. The forward master flood valve of the after escape chamber was shut in the engine compartment. On the after side of the chamber, in the steerage compartment, the master flood valve and the flood valve of the chamber were wide open. Through the open condition of these valves the escape chamber was open to the sea.

iv. The inboard and outboard vents of the escape chamber on each side, forward and aft, were shut.

v. The forward door of the escape chamber was open, so that water from the chamber which was open to the sea freely flowed from the sea through the chamber into the engine room. At twenty-five feet depth the rate of inflow would be about three quarters of a ton a minute. The body of a man was caught by its clothing to the latch of the forward door of the escape chamber.

vi. The after door of the escape chamber was shut and the locking arrangement was just engaged.

8. The signal ejectors were clear. Two stoke candles and four torpedo indicator lights were found in the locker in the steerage compartment.

9. The two indicator buoys had been released. Both wires were completely unwound from the drums.

10. There was no evidence of the shifting of any machinery, or other heavy material owing to the steep angle of the *Thetis* during the morning of the 2nd.

11. There was no evidence of a serious fire. There was evidence of a slight fire in the engine room electrical machinery, as spoken to by Leading Stoker Arnold.

12. The bodies of the 99 men were distributed as follows:

67 were in the engine compartment and 32 bodies were in the steerage compartment. Everyone had therefore left the control room and the forward mess space. The bodies of four men, two of whom had certainly died in the escape chamber before Arnold and Shaw made their escape, were lying in the machinery space below the steerage compartment. The body of Lieutenant Poland was with them. It was necessary to remove a deck plate before these bodies could be taken out. The escape sets of the four men had been apparently taken off their bodies and were found in the engine room but an escape set was strapped to Lieutenant Poland's body and had been apparently effectively used by him. In the steerage compartment four bodies were wearing escape sets which had been apparently effectively used. In the engine room two bodies were wearing escape sets which had been apparently effectively used. Out of the 99 bodies, 50 bodies had escape sets fastened to them.

13. Obstructions were found in the test cock holes of Nos 3 and 4 rear doors—bitumastic enamel in No. 4 and probably mud in No. 3.

A great deal of time was spent by the various interested parties in surveying the submarine, so that, as much information relating to the reasons as to why the disaster had occurred could be gleaned. When all of the observations had been completed to the satisfaction of each surveyor, it was generally agreed that the position of the bow cap control ever for number five torpedo tube was of particular relevance. For this reason, the bow cap control lever panel was disconnected and taken away for further testing. The result of this test would influence the ultimate findings of the Tribunal of Inquiry. When the bow cap control lever for number five torpedo tube was first examined during the surveys, it was found to be $^5/_{32}$ of an inch from the shut position; but, significantly, it was subsequently proved that the lever had to be opened a further $^7/_{32}$ of an inch, that is, a total movement of $^3/_8$ of an inch, before oil started to pass through the opening valve and activating the telemotor systems. The results of this test were seen as conclusive evidence that, at the time of the disaster, the bow cap control lever for number five torpedo tube was in a safe position.

Throughout the total period of exhaustive surveying of *Thetis*, no documentary evidence came to light relating to the key questions as to who, when and why the bow cap to number five torpedo tube was opened. The chronology of part of the Diving and Diesel Electric Trials was found in the notebook of one of the navigating officers. It stated:

0940 hours. Slipped and proceeded.
1330 hours. Steering trials completed. Stopped.
1400 hours. Vacuum test.
1420 hours. Dived Course 310.

The wireless and A/S log has an entry

1340 hours. Dived to 30.
1458 hours. Mast under water
                          A/S gear damaged
2110 hours. White smoke candle fired
              Searching periodically only to save power.
              Fire a smoke candle.

2426 hours. L/S above us.

0500 hours. No answer to smoke candle

In searching for answers, some of the critical questions to be asked related to the draught of the submarine, as there were apparent inconsistencies and irregularities here. Chief Stoker H. J. Dillon-Shallard had an entry in his notebook, but it apparently referred to the previous, abortive, dive trials at Gare Loch. The entry appeared to make reference to the trim before the dive as recorded by one of Cammell Lairds's senior staff, Mr A B Robinson. The note records the condition of the various tanks and then, before giving the submarine's draught, states that tubes five and six are full and the remainder empty. Then below:

Draught 13 feet 7 inches F.
            14 feet 7 inches A.

The significance here is that the draught is one eighth of an inch more forward and one inch more aft than the draught immediately before leaving the wet basin. These are, in all probability, the draughts taken immediately before the dive commenced; indicating that water ballast had been taken on board in the period after leaving the wet basin and before attempting the dive trial. If ballast had been taken in Liverpool Bay, the trim would, conceivably, have been less, because taking on the more salty water in the bay would have affected the buoyancy, and hence the trim.

The notebook of Mr A. A. F. Hill, one of the Admiralty's Overseeing Officers on board, was found. He recorded the draughts required for the Gare Loch trials as:

13 feet 8½ inches F.
14 feet 7 inches A.

The notebook also recorded the dive programme for the Gare Loch trials, which was exactly the same for the Liverpool Bay trials. But, a draught of

13 feet 7 inches F.
14 feet 7 inches A.

would mean that *Thetis* was about twenty-one tons light of main ballast trim. On the same page in Mr Hill's notebook, which also recorded the amounts of water for the tanks, was an entry used for the trim chit. The entry was simple:

1 June 1939. Leave 0930 hours. Draughts 13 feet 8½ inches

these draught figures were struck out in the notebook.

Summary of Part 5.
The causes of the loss.

The findings of the Tribunal of Inquiry listed six major contributory factors which caused the disaster:

1. The blocking of the test cock hole of number five rear door.

2. The opening of the rear door of number five tube when the bow cap was open.

3. The failure to effectively close the port watertight bulkhead door.

4. The failure of those on board the *Thetis to refloat her.*

5. The failure of assistance from outside.

6. The failure to escape from *Thetis*.

The findings of the Inquiry, in the very first paragraph, state that the blocking of the test cock with bitumastic enamel, and the failure of anyone to notice this, undoubtedly played an important part in the ultimate outcome. The work of applying the bitumastic coating was done by the specialist company of Wailes Dove Bitumastic Ltd. who were, specifically, sub-contracted by the Admiralty. Additionally, Cammell Lairds had stipulated in the contract that the work must be finished to the complete satisfaction and approval of the Admiralty—who had supplied the rear doors and the test cocks in the first place.

When questioned, the enameller stated, unequivocally, that he had placed a plug in the hole in the rear door. But, after *Thetis* was raised and surveys made, it was found that both number five and number four test cocks were blocked with bitumastic enamel. If the enameller did put in the plug to avoid any blockage, then it must have fallen out sometime during the smoothing over of the enamel with the blow-lamp.

Because the Admiralty had stipulated that a specialist company should be contracted to carry out the bitumastic process, employees of Cammell Lairds played no part in the process. In fact, Lairds's charge-hand painter, Mr Taylor, when asked to comment, said that he did not consider that there was any chance of the bitumastic entering the test cock holes in the rear doors, and for that reason, he took no steps to avoid them becoming blocked.

On completion of the work, it was then the responsibility of the Admiralty Overseer, Mr Grundy, to check that the work had been carried out to Admiralty specification and, if so, to pass it. Mr Taylor, the Cammell Lairds employee who had overview of work in that area, then asked Mr Grundy to make the necessary checks before giving the work his—and the Admiralty's—approval. Mr Grundy testified that when he was asked to examine the work, he was in the process of 'gauging' the tubes—an all day job, after which he did not normally do anything else that day. He also declared that working on *Thetis* was his first experience of examining work on torpedo tubes. And, when questioned, he also agreed that he was aware of the test cock hole in the rear door and, perhaps of greater importance, just why a rimer was always supplied with the test cock. Again, with hindsight, if Grundy had have examined the interior of the doors, he would have observed that the test cock hole was blocked under a layer of bitumastic enamel. It was thus a perverse catalogue of chances that the man who did the job in the first place, the enameller, did not take enough care to ensure that the test cock hole was kept clear of bitumastic; then the Admiralty Overseer, Mr Grundy, did not use the rimer; Lieutenant Woods—in overall charge of that area during the dive trials—did not use the rimer; nor it would seem that anyone else, from the time that the initial work was done on 15 May 1939, until the day of the dive trials, on 1 June 1939, used the rimer on the test cocks.

The issue of riming the holes on the day of the dive trials falls once again into that delicate legal area as to who should shoulder responsibility. Lieutenant Woods declared that there was no specific routine in the Royal Navy relating to the clearing out of test cock holes in the rear doors. He did however state that it was his normal practice to order the Torpedo Gunner's Mate to rime the holes on a regular and frequent basis, but on this occasion he had not issued those orders to Petty Officer Mitchell as, in his considered view, he did not carry responsibility for the tubes at that time, adding that on 1 June, he believed that Cammell Lairds should have made sure that the test cock holes were clear. Next, the Inquiry considered the opening of the rear door of number five tube when the bow cap of that tube was also open. When the bow cap was closed, it was allowable to open the rear door in complete safety. However, with the bow cap open, opening the rear door would result in disaster, as it most certainly did.

Giving evidence at the Inquiry, Lieutenant Woods said that he ordered the rear door of number five tube to be opened in order to satisfy himself that the tube was completely empty and that the bow cap was watertight. He was confident that the bow cap for number five tube was closed because:

i.   No water came out of the test cock when it was checked (it wouldn't because it was blocked—unknown to Woods)

ii. The Cammell Lairds foreman on board, Mr Robinson, had previously informed him that tubes numbers five and six were not meant to be full.

iii. He had seen that the mechanical indicator was in the 'SHUT' position.

iv. Leading Seaman Hambrook had informed him that the control levers were also at 'SHUT'.

Lieutenant Woods declared that he had not informed any senior officers in the control room that he intended to open the number five rear door. Also in evidence, Captain Oram stated that he'd heard First Lieutenant Chapman request Lieutenant Woods to report on the condition of numbers five and six tubes. Lieutenant Woods later denied hearing any such instructions.

It was abundantly clear as to the actions taken, and by whom, to have the rear door of tube number five opened. However, the Inquiry drew a complete blank when trying to elicit evidence as to why, when or by whom the bow cap for number five tube was opened. There was certainly no recorded evidence available following the extensive surveys completed after *Thetis* was raised to the surface. Theories abound, but only three assumptions could reasonably be made:

i. That the bow cap telemotor operating mechanism and the bow cap mechanical indicator were both in working order. The mechanisms had proved to be effective prior to the accident; and, when tested after *Thetis* had been raised, they were also found to be in good working order.

ii. It could reasonably be assumed that number five tube was empty and the bow cap closed before any trim corrections were made on *Thetis* in the wet basin, before she sailed for the dive trials.

iii. A third, and, in some respects, irrelevant assumption which the Inquiry forwarded, was that skilful and careful men working under normal conditions, without the stress of undue haste or fatigue, would carry out their duties with skill and care.

A number of questions, specifically relating to the opening of number five bow cap were then asked; the first question being: why was the bow cap open? In considering this most fundamental of questions, the Inquiry decided that the only feasible reason for taking such an action was to trim the submarine in preparation for the diving trial. The trim, being a critical safety measure, was adjusted in the presence of Mr Bailey, the Admiralty Constructor and Mr Hill, the Principal Ship Overseer. Assisting in the operation were Mr Robinson, the contractors' foreman, and his subordinate, Mr Eccleston. Trim adjustments were made before *Thetis* sailed from the wet basin. When the trim adjustments had been made in accordance with the usual practice, the trim statement was completed by Mr Hill, or one of his colleagues, and then given to the commanding officer, Lieutenant Commander Bolus. It was also recorded in the trim statement that tubes numbers five and six were full and that the others were empty.

When *Thetis* was raised, number six bow cap was found to be shut. The Inquiry concluded that if number five bow cap was also opened before *Thetis* sailed from the wet basin, it would be highly unlikely that it would have been left open all morning. It must be assumed that number five tube was filled before leaving the wet basin by opening the bow cap, but that it was closed again before leaving, as indeed were the valves to the levers, and the lever left either at 'SHUT' or put to 'NEUTRAL'. One apparent, significant, anomaly here being that when Lieutenant Woods asked Mr Robinson whether number five and six tubes were meant to be full, he replied 'No.' There was an obvious misunderstanding between those finalising the trim of the boat and those responsible for the dive. The question whether tube number five was meant to be full, if it was indeed full, or if it was empty was still to be answered. It is just conceivable that sometime before Lieutenant Woods ordered the rear door to be opened, somebody opened the bow cap in order to fill tube number five for trimming immediately prior to diving and without the knowledge of Woods—and further, then omitted to close the bow cap following the trim adjustment, but this is speculation. If this is not the reason why the bow cap was opened, and left open, the only other explanation that the Inquiry could forward was that the lever had been moved in the direction towards the open position, when power was actually being applied to the bow cap, or it could have been a gradual creeping open of the bow cap—again, when the power was on the bow cap.

The Inquiry then went on to consider when the bow cap was opened. It was concluded that, immediately before the accident, Lieutenant Woods gave orders for power to be turned on to the bow caps—so that they could be opened prior to diving. Following this logic, it is highly unlikely therefore that the bow cap for number five tube was open before that time—Lieutenant Woods and his junior colleagues would have had sufficient indications if this were the case. Woods gave testimony that he inspected the mechanical indicator of number five tube and noted that it was indicating 'SHUT'. The Inquiry accepted this evidence. Woods's inspection of the mechanical indicator for number five tube occurred after he had asked for power onto the bow cap, therefore, at that time, the bow cap could not have been open. Lieutenant Woods was considered to be a completely honest witness. When the *Thetis* was raised, Woods's earlier observations relating to the condition of the test cocks on the other rear doors was confirmed as being accurate. It was considered by the Inquiry that, for obvious safety reasons, the indicators relating to the bow caps would have been checked to ensure that they were closed, and prior to the rear doors being opened. Again, it was noted that the number five indicator was difficult to observe because of its position on the panel, but Woods was adamant that this was checked and found to be 'SHUT'.

After much deliberation, it was recorded that Lieutenant Woods had examined the mechanical indicators, and that they were at 'SHUT', and that this observation was made after he had requested power to be turned on to the bow caps.

In the highly detailed questioning that followed, reference was made to the conversation which Woods had with Leading Seaman Hambrook. The conversation confirmed that the power had been turned on, and that the levers were at 'SHUT'. Woods actually saw the evidence of the mechanical indicators, but he did not see either the position of the control lever or that of the valve wheels. It is probable that Leading Seaman Hambrook either left all six levers at the 'SHUT' position or in the position of approximately 'NEUTRAL'—the position in which they were found when *Thetis* was raised. Again, on this particular point, Lieutenant Woods testified that when bow caps were 'SHUT', the lever was generally returned to the 'NEUTRAL' position, and that this was the normal position for the levers to be kept in. Woods was asked, directly;

'Have you any doubt that when Hambrook reported to you, that the levers were in the shut position?' In response, Woods could only answer, 'I am not sure of that. This is what I intended.'

It must be understood that, at that time, there was no Admiralty guidance or order relating to the use of the 'NEUTRAL' position. The position of 'NEUTRAL' was designed 'To provide an instantaneous method of locking pressure in the bow cap telemotor control system, so that if a pipe leaks it would not be necessary to shut one of the valves to lock the pressure in to the system.'

It was therefore established, in the consideration of the Inquiry, that the mechanical indicator to number five tube was in the 'SHUT' position, and that the bow cap was opened after Woods had made his inspection and then requested that the power be put on. But, the Inquiry also concluded that that was all that had been established. The Inquiry could find no other evidence relating to when the bow cap was opened. Lieutenant Coltart's evidence was then examined. Being, at the time of the disaster, aboard the support tug *Grebe Cock*, he had stated that he had seen air bubbles which appeared to be coming from just forward of *Thetis's* stern, immediately before she finally disappeared. The sudden appearance of air bubbles on the surface would indicate that an empty, or partially empty, tube was being filled by the opening of the bow cap. Lieutenant Coltart suggested that there might have been other reasons for the sudden appearance of air bubbles. Apart from the reasons already forwarded, air bubbles could have been caused by the bow of the submarine breaking the surface, or by the forward tanks being 'blown', or by air in the torpedo tubes. It was not considered that Lieutenant Coltart's testimony added anything further to the investigation. And therefore, in answer to the question, 'When was the bow cap opened?', the Inquiry could only conclude that it was opened sometime after the power was turned on, just before the accident occurred, but considered that there was no reliable evidence which could corroborate the precise time of opening.

The next question was, perhaps, the most difficult question of all to answer: 'Who opened the bow cap?' From the verifiable evidence available, Leading Seaman Hambrook was the last man to attend the control lever, but that doesn't, definitively, confirm that he was indeed the last man attending the control lever for number five tube. Lieutenant Woods actually asked Leading Seaman Hambrook if all the levers were shut, and Hambrook replied in the affirmative. Again, Hambrook might have thought that the 'NEUTRAL' position was the correct position to find the lever in when the bow cap was shut—hence his reply to Woods's question. It must also be remembered that Hambrook did have experience of working levers of this kind of lever before.

There was a period, of about ten minutes or so, when both Woods and Hambrook were away from the control levers, and this was when Hambrook was opening numbers one, two, three and four tubes; an operation carried out under Woods's watchful eye. It was conceded during the Inquiry that, during this time, the lever could have been moved by somebody—either on purpose or inadvertently. If this was the case, then the lever must have been returned to the 'NEUTRAL' position, as this was the lever's position when *Thetis* was raised.

But, it has to be said, this sequence of events is highly improbable, when one considers that Petty Officer Mitchell, Engine Room Artificer Harold G Howells and Lieutenant (Engineer) Jamison were all in that vicinity at the time, and any one of them would have observed anybody entering the tube compartment. Again, if orders had been given from the control room to flood number five tube, then the orders would have, in all probability, been given to Lieutenant Woods and, failing that, he would certainly have known of any such order, as indeed would everyone in that compartment.

After the accident, it appears that Lieutenant Commander Bolus did not inquire of the crew who were in the vicinity at the time, if they were aware that the bow cap was open. The four survivors who were able to give testimony at the Inquiry categorically stated that there was no immediate investigation by Bolus into the cause of the accident.

The evidence, scant though it was, was beginning to point towards Leading Seaman Hambrook as the person who, possibly, caused the bow cap to open. The action of pushing the lever to 'OPEN' might have been made inadvertently, before returning it to the 'NEUTRAL' position. But, the Inquiry concluded, it could not be stated with one hundred percent certainty that Leading Seaman Hambrook did cause the bow cap to open; and, as he couldn't answer any questions relating to either the accident or the actions which he had taken regarding the levers, it would be unjust to name him as the person who caused the bow cap to open.

Another possibility was forwarded, and this was considered to be the least improbable by the Inquiry—the possibility that the bow cap crept open and that the creep started when Lieutenant Woods ordered the power to be turned on, and continued until the bow cap was fully open. Then, the lever was put into the 'NEUTRAL' position—the position in which it was found when *Thetis* was raised.

Finally, the Inquiry concluded that, although other theories and explanations were possible, the truth may indeed have escaped all of those who had tried to answer this question—in other words, they just didn't know.

Attention then turned to what, in the Inquiry's view, was the third cause of the disaster, and that was the failure to effectively close the port watertight bulkhead door. The function of the watertight door is to do just that, i.e. when closed, it forms a watertight barrier and this prevents any water flowing from one compartment to another. *Thetis* had a series of watertight doors throughout her length, but the specific watertight door in question here was the door at bulkhead number twenty-five. When the tube compartment became flooded—because of the opening of the rear door—extreme difficulty was experienced in closing the watertight door. Because of its purpose, the door is necessarily very heavy, and this particular door opened forwards, which added another degree of difficulty when closing. Both of these factors caused delay in securing the door. Then, when Petty Officer Mitchell attempted to close the door, one of the lower turnbuckles fell down between the door and the coaming, when taken from its catch. The turnbuckle then had to be retrieved before the operation could be completed. But, whilst this was happening, an order was given from the control room to surface—an order which necessitated 'blowing' the main tanks. Then, for a short while, *Thetis* remained on an even keel. Water was continuing to rise in the tube compartment and—as the watertight door was not closed—also in the stowage compartment. As a result of the increased weight of water in the forward compartments of the submarine, the bows canted downwards and put the lower part of the door coaming under water. With the increasing angle of *Thetis* anything that was not firmly secured, including furniture and fittings, slid downwards into the bulkhead and the doorway. This movement ensured that the lower turnbuckles on the watertight door could not be secured. An order was given to evacuate the stowage compartment, but Petty Officer Mitchell, realizing the gravity of the situation, remained at his station, valiantly trying to secure the watertight door. With sustained and stoic efforts he managed to secure one turnbuckle fast. It was beyond human capability to secure any more. Although it is conjecture, it was speculated that if another turnbuckle could have been secured at the bottom of the door, then the flood might have been stayed, allowing water to be pumped out of the stowage compartment and then 'blown' from the tube compartment in front. If this could have been achieved, then *Thetis* would have been able to re-surface. This didn't happen, but the securing of one turnbuckle significantly reduced the inflow of water to the stowage compartment, although there was still a substantial volume of water entering through the bottom of the door where it had proved impossible to secure any turnbuckles.

When *Thetis* was raised, one of the eighteen turnbuckles at the top of the door was tightly secured. Of the other seventeen, five were in their stowage spring clips and the other twelve were hanging loose.

The Inquiry then considered the failure of those on board the *Thetis* to refloat her, but little evidence relating to efforts to refloat *Thetis* seems to have been forthcoming. The report of the Inquiry appeared to focus more on the tonnage of water in various compartments of *Thetis*, and the difficulty of removing it. The Inquiry considered that it was not possible to determine the exact volume of water flowing into the tube stowage compartment after Petty Officer

Mitchell had partially secured the port watertight door. The best estimate of the volume of water in the tube stowage compartment was forwarded by Captain Oram at the Inquiry. He went into the forward escape chamber about half an hour after the accident occurred, and he estimated that, at that time, the tube stowage compartment was about three quarters full. It was known that the total capacity of that chamber was about ninety tons of water. So, if most of the water flooded into that chamber after the watertight door was partially closed, a realistic estimate would be that the rate of inflow into the chamber was somewhere in the region of one hundred and thirty-five tons an hour. But, given the depth at which *Thetis* was now at, the maximum capacity of the pumps at that depth was closer to seventy tons an hour. And, even with the pumps operating at full capacity, it would not have been possible to stem the net inflow of seawater—and that calculation also pre-supposed that the valves could be configured in such a way as to enable the tube stowage compartment to be cleared of seawater.

The torpedo embarking hatch was not designed to resist any great internal pressure, so it was not possible to blow the water out of the two flooded compartments through the number five tube. After some deliberation on *Thetis*, it was agreed that applying air pressure in the tube stowage compartment would cause the hatch to lift, thus allowing air to bubble out, and thus wasting limited supplies of high-pressure air. After an initial, brief, attempt to clear the tubes using this approach, the method was not used again.

The Inquiry then concluded that it would have been virtually impossible for anyone, however great his endurance or courage, to get through to the torpedo tube compartment, close the tube door, return to the stowage compartment and open the two valves which would have enabled the pumps to clear that compartment of seawater.

But three attempts were made to do just that. But, on each occasion, the men had to leave the chamber because of the intolerable pain they experienced. The Inquiry had been told that men could be saved using this apparatus and at much greater depths than *Thetis* was at. Indeed, Lieutenant Chapman, Petty Officer Mitchell and Petty Officer Smithers had all been trained in the use of the apparatus. Also, on the two occasions that Lieutenant Woods had made the attempt, he was able to withstand the pressure, which indicated that the chamber was not flooded up too quickly. The Inquiry concluded that, in all probability, Lieutenant Chapman, Petty Officer Mitchell and Petty Officer Smithers had all failed to use their sets correctly. Further, they had failed to relieve the pressure on their ears—a phenomenon which is inevitable under such circumstances—by one of the recognised methods of either swallowing or holding the nose and blowing. In mitigation, the Inquiry heard that, because of the limited time available to the volunteers, the chamber might have been flooded too quickly. Some concluding remarks in the final report however did acknowledge the peril that Lieutenant Chapman, Lieutenant Woods, Petty Officer Mitchell and Petty Officer Smithers had placed themselves in.

The Inquiry's findings regarding the failure of assistance from outside efforts to save the lives of those on board the *Thetis* was very clear. The Inquiry found the main reason for this to be the failure to locate her position during the sixteen and three-quarter hours from 3 p.m. on 1 June to 7.50 a.m. on the 2nd. During this time, the air in the *Thetis* became very foul. This was, in part, due to the unusually large number of men on board, and also partly due to the fact that a considerable amount of hard manual work was done, using up much valuable air.

After the three escape attempts when the *Thetis* was on the sea bottom, about four tons of water had to be carried away by hand when the forward escape chamber was being emptied. And, it must be remembered that Cammell Lairds's men worked overnight to make the necessary pumping connections to clear the flooded compartments. This was arduous work carried out under difficult conditions. The Inquiry nonetheless concluded that the work had been carried out patiently and meticulously.

Although the support tug *Grebe Cock* was on station when *Thetis* disappeared, it was concluded that Lieutenant Coltart, in all probability, had difficulty in deciding a proper course of action. There was a strong tide running, and *Grebe Cock* was in deeper waters than she normally operated in. There was no marker buoy on board to indicate where *Thetis* had gone down, and nor did anyone think to improvise one.

When giving evidence, Lieutenant Coltart said that, from his experience, his first thoughts were that *Thetis* might have suddenly become too heavy. One explanation forwarded was that one of the vents to the main ballast tank might have stuck, thus causing undue lightness; then, whilst she was trimming down, the vent opened causing the main ballast tank to flood, and hence making *Thetis* too heavy. Coltart went on to say that he considered that this situation could be easily remedied without too much difficulty by pumping out her auxiliary tanks. From this observation, Coltart concluded that there was not sufficient reason for believing that a serious accident had happened. His view was, if that was the case, *Thetis* would either fire a smoke candle or release an indicator buoy—neither happened. Also, nobody came to the surface using the Davis Escape Apparatus.

Later, Mr Godfrey, Master of the *Grebe Cock*, Lieutenant Coltart and Wireless Telegraphist Crosby all testified that they had kept a vigilant look out for *Thetis* but saw nothing. Further, there was no evidence on board *Thetis* when she was raised that a smoke candle was discharged until some considerable time after she sank. *Thetis's* first recording of the firing of a candle is not recorded in *Thetis's* log until 2110 hours. A series of twenty-one indicator lights were also fired, but probably sometime after the candle. A forward indicator buoy was released at 1530 hours, but it is possible that this may have broken adrift. When *Thetis* sailed from Birkenhead she had three candles on board. Evidence showed that when she was raised, there were still two candles intact on board.

Understandably, when Lieutenant Coltart did not see either a candle or an indicator buoy to show any signs of distress, he was reluctant to contact Fort Blockhouse and suggest that *Thetis* might be in some sort of distress—especially if she should resurface in the near future. It was late in the afternoon before *Grebe Cock* contacted Fort Blockhouse by radio telephony, but there was nothing in the words of the message to create anxiety. The message was received at Fort Blockhouse at 1815 hours. The very fact that there appeared to be no urgency in the words of the message, which talked about the length of the dive rather than *Thetis's* sudden disappearance, perhaps contributed to the message not arriving sooner at Fort Blockhouse. Another factor which was taken into account at the Inquiry, was that, by the time that *Grebe Cock* anchored, she had in fact moved some four miles from the area where *Thetis* sank, and this possibly accounted for *Grebe Cock* not seeing the smoke candle, the indicator lights or the indicator buoys that *Thetis* had released.

Grebe Cock's anchorage undoubtedly accounted for both *Brazen* and *Vigilant* initially searching for *Thetis* in the wrong area—and wasting valuable time. A further complication and time delay occurred when the search aircraft sent a report of the sighting of a buoy. Again, this sighting was some miles from *Thetis's* actual position. The net result was that neither *Brazen* nor *Vigilant* were able to locate *Thetis* during the night of 1 June. Later on the morning of the 2nd, at 0700 hours, it was decided that *Brazen* and *Vigilant* should renew their searches to the east of *Grebe Cock*. At 0750 hours, the stern of *Thetis* was observed protruding out of the water. It was shortly after arriving on station that both Captain Oram and Lieutenant Woods were picked up following their escape from *Thetis*.

The Inquiry then went on to consider whether there was any undue delay in sending any vessels or aircraft to search for *Thetis*. It was considered that, as the submarine was not scheduled to surface until 1700 hours, and, in the absence of any message to the contrary from Lieutenant Coltart, there was no reason for concern on the part of those in charge of operations at Fort Blockhouse. However, after 1700 hours, there was perhaps some cause for concern, irrespective of whether any messages had been received or not from *Grebe Cock*. But, it was not until 1820 hours that an order was despatched for HMS *Brazen* to proceed to the dive area and search for *Thetis*; but, the message was sent in code and took some time to decipher, causing more un-necessary delay. Later, at 1850 hours, a message was sent from Fort Blockhouse for an airborne search to be made. Because of the distances involved, no searches were able to commence before 2100 hours, and, by this time, the day's light had almost gone. Sunset that day was 2104 hours.

The Inquiry found that, Royal Naval protocol being as it is, there was some initial difference of opinion between the staff officer at Fort Blockhouse and the staff officer at Plymouth. The decision to order a search is a command which is only given after much deliberation. At 1750 hours, personnel at Fort Blockhouse considered that it was too early to order a search, especially as, at that time, there had been no message from the tug attending *Thetis* that anything untoward had occurred, and there was elaborate and complex machinery to set in motion when dealing with a submarine search. The Inquiry considered what facts were known at 1750 hours. It was known that:

i.   *Thetis* was doing her diving trials in Liverpool Bay

ii. The trials were in open water and out of sight of land

iii. There were strong tidal currents in that area

iv. She had on board a number of men largely in excess of her normal complement

v.   She would be short of air reserve when submerged for a long time

vi. She only had a tug standing by—a vessel without wireless and without means of underwater signalling to *Thetis*

vii. The tug only had a junior Royal Naval officer on board

viii.   It was now late in the afternoon

When taking all of these factors into consideration, the Inquiry adjudged that there had indeed been some unnecessary delay in ordering a sea and air search for *Thetis*. But, the Inquiry also concluded that the delay was not caused by any lack of vigilance on the part of responsible staff ashore. There was a number of reasons for the delay:

i.   There was no reason to suppose that such an accident would occur

ii. There was a desire not to cause unnecessary alarm, and

iii. There was a reluctance to set a number of ships and men in motion as required by the procedure laid down for such a case, if it proved to be a false alarm

The report of the Inquiry found that the procedures to be adopted in the event of a submarine sinking in home waters were too elaborate, and the situation could have been dealt with far more effectively by despatching an aircraft to search for *Thetis*, together with HMS *Brazen*, and then communicating this information to *Grebe Cock*. The decision-making process was not made easier because of the fact that the Admiral in command of submarines at Fort Blockhouse was on sick leave at the time.

As soon as Lieutenant Coltart's belated message was received at Fort Blockhouse, the plight of the stricken submarine and the subsequent rescue attempt was treated with utmost urgency, and everything was done as could reasonably be expected to be done.

Thetis's underwater signalling apparatus had been irreparably been damaged when the accident occurred, otherwise, with the equipment on board *Brazen*, the submarine would have been located as soon as *Brazen* reached the area of the dive site, but this was not to be; and, in the words of the Inquiry report: That was one of the many mischances which almost conspired to lose the *Thetis* in a sea of trouble.'

When considering the reasons why the stern of the *Thetis* had not remained above water, a number of reasons were forwarded, but all were prefaced with the caveat that nothing relating to the stern losing buoyancy was known for definite. It was uncertain if the stern would have remained above water if no towage had taken place or if the stern received no support. It was also speculated that whilst the stern was still above water, air could have escaped from the after main tanks to be replaced by seawater, thus further reducing the submarine's buoyancy. Another possible reason for the loss of buoyancy could have been the opening of the forward door of the after escape chamber, whilst the after flood valves of the chamber were open. This would have resulted in water pouring into the engine room compartment. The Inquiry considered that it was doubtful if anyone on board could have climbed through into Z tank, even if they had been able to open the manhole door in the bulkhead. It was an almost impossible task to get through the manhole on the top of Z tank which was above the rudder head—the space between the deck and the rudder head being nine inches. The advantage of removing the manhole doors on Z tank and the bulkhead would have meant that there could be direct communication with those on the outside—the plight of the men inside might then have been better understood.

When Captain Oram and Lieutenant Woods escaped, there was some small chance of a rescue being effected, as Oram had a rescue plan strapped to his wrist under a protective watertight covering. The salvage vessel *Vigilant* made an attempt to carry out the plan, but found it to be unworkable. There was a lack of necessary materials available, and, added to which, it was known that there was very little time left for the submarine to be able to sustain life.

There were twenty-nine Davis Escape Sets stored in the torpedo stowage compartment, but they were not available as that compartment had been flooded. Also, by a complete oversight, nine sets which would normally be on the submarine were somewhere in Cammell Lairds, as they had been taken ashore for overhauling. *Thetis* had actually sailed from Birkenhead with only one hundred and twenty-two sets, but, as twenty-nine of these were now unavailable, that left a total of ninety-three sets available for use—but *Thetis* had sailed with one hundred and three people on board. As this availability was known to the senior officers it is not inconceivable that they would have made every attempt to raise the submarine, and thus save all lives.

It may be that, if those in charge of the rescue operation when the stern was above water had focused their attention on keeping the stern out of the water and obtaining oxy-acetylene equipment sooner, then it's just possible that, with a hole cut into the stern, more lives might have been saved. The obvious danger here being that, if a hole had been cut in the stern and then buoyancy was lost in the stern, both Z tank and the steerage compartment would have become flooded. Those conducting the Inquiry held that if the stern of *Thetis* had been lashed to the *Vigilant* then this obvious danger could have been avoided.

The Inquiry then heard that the reason why this method of escape had not been pursued with more vigour was for the simple reason that senior personnel in charge of the rescue attempt believed that the Davis Escape Apparatus would be used for the escape of most of the men on board. Then, and only then, would the submarine be salvaged—and, hopefully, the men remaining on board at that time would be saved. However, when no other men after Arnold and Shaw appeared on the surface, those in charge realised that, because of the air condition on *Thetis*, time was rapidly turning against them, as very soon the submarine's air supply would not be able to support life. It was decided to tow the submarine to safer waters, but keeping the stern out of the water, and then for an opening to be cut in Z tank. However, the oxy-acetylene apparatus did not arrive on station until 1430 hours, and, before the hole could be cut, the tow rope failed, *Thetis's* stern sank, and there was nothing left that could be done—*Thetis* and her crew were lost.

There is little evidence relating to the reasons why no more men save for Oram and Woods, then Arnold and Shaw, came to the surface using the Davis Escape Apparatus. When giving evidence at the Inquiry, Leading Seaman Arnold testified that there were at least a dozen men who were in a fit enough state to escape using the escape apparatus, as he had done. But the reasons why they, and others, didn't escape using this method can, at best, be reasoned conjecture. It was known that there had not been a fire or other major incident of that kind following Arnold and Shaw's escape. Apart from the rapidly deteriorating air condition, the other major change was the angle at which *Thetis* was resting. As the tide rose, the buoyancy in the stern, and the flooding in her bow compartments caused the angle to the horizontal to increase. Both Captain Oram and Lieutenant Woods testified that they had experienced considerable difficulty in climbing through the engine room compartment because of the inclination of the boat. They also commented that they were given helping hands, literally, from men who were lying in that area. Before Arnold and Shaw used the Davis Apparatus to escape, *Thetis's* angle had again increased. Shaw reported that Lieutenant Commander Bolus was having difficulty in standing upright and was having to support himself against the bulkhead door whilst issuing his orders.

It must be appreciated that whilst rescue attempts were continuing outside of the submarine, the condition of the men inside the boat was now becoming critical. The air supply was becoming noxious and, consequently, the men were becoming weaker. On the ebb tide, when the depth of water was falling, the angle of the submarine tended to diminish, but those on the outside, wanting to burn a hole in Z tank towed the stern, and thus increased the boat's angle again. Unbeknownst to them, this was totally counter-productive, as, with the increasing weakness of the men, and now the increasing angle of the boat, it was highly unlikely that any of them would have had the strength to climb as far as the after escape chamber.

Before Arnold and Shaw escaped, it had been suggested that, in order to speed up the escape process, four men rather than two should enter the escape chamber. Four men did in fact enter the after escape chamber but, perhaps due to the extreme overcrowding, found it impossible to open the escape hatch. Three of the men had died in the attempt, and the fourth man was near to death when he was taken from the chamber. Speculating as to what might have occurred when the four men were in the escape chamber, Shaw, relating to his own experience, said that he felt claustrophobic and trapped inside the chamber. He had instinctively put his hand up to try to push the hatch open. The hatch would not open, and he had to wait until the pressure inside had equalised with the outside pressure. He added, 'If one is not patient one loses one's head. I do not think I would have been here today to give evidence but for Leading Stoker Arnold.' Leading Stoker Arnold had experience of escape techniques, but the men on board who were employed by Cammell Lairds, and Shaw was one of them, had only attended a lecture about the use of the Davis Escape Apparatus, and had not had any practical experience of its use in a tank.

The Inquiry report, making reference to experimentation conducted by Professor Haldane, stated that the men in the chamber might have felt desperately ill when they started to breathe oxygen, and were unable to wait to operate the escape hatch. Also, it must be remembered that the escape chamber was only designed to accommodate two men, and this overcrowding would have in itself created difficulties for each man in using the apparatus correctly. The angle that the boat was now at, the exhausted condition of the men, and the fact that they had not eaten for some considerable time, all led the Inquiry to conclude that it was not surprising that the men had failed to use either the escape apparatus or the escape chamber effectively. The Inquiry did not question the logic of the reasoning behind four men entering the escape chamber at once, rather than just two.

As the forward escape chamber of *Thetis* was about 150 feet below sea level at high water, it was obvious that this chamber would not be used for mounting any escape attempts. This was confirmed when *Thetis* was raised.

In his evidence to the Inquiry, Mr Brock, the Mersey Docks and Harbour Board's Wreck Master, stated that he saw bubbles of air coming from *Thetis*, which indicated that two separate efforts to leave the boat by the after escape chamber had been made soon after Arnold and Shaw surfaced. Both attempts failed, perhaps because the escape hatch could not be opened. This evidence was supported when *Thetis* was raised. It would appear that when Mr Brock was heard working on the boat's stern, men assembled in the two after compartments. But, when *Thetis* suddenly moved, forcing Mr Brock to leave the boat, it seems that one final effort was made for two men to escape from the submarine. It was impossible to open the hatch because of the partially engaged position of the outside clip. It would appear that they then either opened the forward door of the escape chamber, or the door was opened by accident, but, one way or another, water came pouring into the engine and steerage compartments. The after main valve of the escape chamber was not closed. Consequently, *Thetis* slowly lost buoyancy in the stern, and when the tow-rope to *Vigilant* failed due to the increasing tension on it, *Thetis* sank shortly afterwards.

One of the concluding statements in the Inquiry report suggested that, in the absence of so many who could have explained the precise reasons for the initial disaster and the subsequent actions taken to rectify the situation, much remains doubtful and obscure.

One final statement was made in the report, which were words spoken at the Inquiry by Captain Oram who said; 'I would like to make known the excellent behaviour of all the men on board the *Thetis*. I saw no signs of panic at any time. Whenever there was any work to be done, men sprang to help. I heard men talking and joking until the foul air caused them to keep quiet; and they showed a quiet bravery which is a memory which will live with me for ever.'

The report was dated 31 January 1940.

It can be observed in the foregoing sections that Mr Justice Bucknill assiduously avoided addressing and answering difficult questions in the body of the report, which was significantly different from the way in which Raikes had approached his report. As to whether this was his brief, or whether this was his personal preference is open to conjecture.

CHAPTER 10

Litigation

In August 1939, immediately before the outbreak of war with Germany, the Amalgamated Engineering Union instructed the law firm of Evill & Coleman to act on behalf of the families of their former members who had been lost in the tragedy; some twenty-five writs were issued. Also, the Electrical Trades Union assured the families of their former members that they too would meet all of the legal costs in pursuing any claims for their loss. Finally, there were another six claims which were being brought and paid for privately. Indeed, as a direct result of the, now public, Bucknill Inquiry, it was now known, for certain, that at the time of the fateful dive Lieutenant Commander Bolus was in overall command of the submarine; that contractors to Cammell Lairds, Messrs Wailes Dove Bitumastic Ltd, had inadvertently blocked the test cock, and further, that senior inspection personnel, acting for and on behalf of both Cammell Lairds and the Admiralty, had signed papers to the effect that *Thetis* was seaworthy. It also transpired during the course of the Inquiry that Leading Seaman Walter Hambrook was in the tube space and near to the lever in question, and that Lieutenant Woods was the officer in charge of the torpedo space. Although it had clearly not been Bucknill's intent to apportion blame in his report, this, in effect, appeared to be exactly what he was doing. Subsequently, it was the collective view of Evill & Coleman that, given the circumstances and the information which had now been publically verified, there was a strong case for pursuing the claims. Writs were issued against Mrs Sybil Bolus as wife and personal representative of the late Lieutenant Commander Bolus; Lieutenant Woods; the representatives of Leading Seaman Hambrook, and Messrs. Cammell Lairds & Co. Ltd. But, having studied the implications of both the report itself and the possible fall-out which might result from any successful writs, the British Government, at the very highest levels, took steps to ensure that this possibility did not become a reality.

Following much detailed discussion between the Solicitor-General Sir William Jowett, Treasury Solicitor Sir Thomas Barnes and the First Lord of the Admiralty Albert Victor Alexander, and with the knowledge and tacit agreement of the Attorney-General Sir Donald Somerville, the strategy adopted was, in essence, to convince the General Secretary of the Trades Union Congress, Sir Walter McLennan Citrine, that it was in the wider interests of the Trades Union Congress in general to drop the writs which had been issued on behalf of their former members. It was further reasoned that, if this could be achieved, then, almost by default, the other private writs would, in all probability, also be withdrawn. The evidence which leads to this conclusion is somewhat fragmented, but, whichever way it is cut, it does not show the Admiralty in a particularly favourable light—apparently having scant regard for the deaths of serving personnel and their grieving families. It was becoming clear that the Admiralty considered that it was a distinct possibility that the cases, if brought, might well go against the defendants, most notably Lieutenant Woods and Leading Seaman Hambrook and, almost by definition, against the Admiralty themselves.

The First Lord of the Admiralty, Albert Victor Alexander, himself having his roots in the Co-operative movement and being a Labour party sympathiser, decided that by far the best approach would be to contact the union leaders, informally, and try to persuade them to withdraw their claims. The Treasury Solicitor, Sir Thomas Barnes, had suggested to him that that there were at least three valid reasons for this stance. Firstly that, currently, it may be difficult to mount a defence of the cases, in that some of the key witnesses had already forfeited their lives; secondly, there was no reason to suppose that the plaintiffs would actually lose, and thirdly, and perhaps most importantly at the moment, it was not a good idea to have details of submarine construction discussed openly in court, in the current hostile climate. Having said that, the Admiralty could actually claim privilege relating to details of evidence involved. It was also suggested by the Admiralty that, assuming Alexander's intervention was successful, they, the Admiralty, would meet any outstanding legal fees and, additionally, would give a significant sum to the Lord Mayor's fund which had been started for the benefit of those who were dependents of the disaster's victims. However, this last point was considered to be somewhat distasteful under the circumstances, as it could conceivably be viewed as being accepting of a degree of Admiralty liability.

With reference to the strategy which had been sketched out between the Treasury Solicitor Sir Thomas Barnes and the First Lord of the Admiralty, the next step was for the First Lord to hold a meeting with the Solicitor-General Sir William Jowett concerning these matters. Indeed, if informal discussions were to be held with the General Secretary of the Trades Union Congress, Sir Walter McLennan Citrine, it was probably advisable for the Solicitor-General himself to make contact, rather than the First Lord. He suggested that the only way for the respective union leaders to accept the proposition was to hear it from Sir Walter himself. And, if that was accepted, it would still be possible for the Admiralty and, it must be said, the Government itself, to rid themselves of any culpability in the matter. Accordingly, sometime before Jowett was scheduled to meet with Citrine, Sir Thomas Barnes, the Treasury Solicitor, was in contact with the Permanent Secretary to the Board of Admiralty, Sir Henry Markham, seeking clarification as to what the terms of any settlement might be. The two major points being the overall cost of the legal fees and also the amount which was to be placed in the Lord Mayor's *Thetis* fund. Earlier, with regards to the Lord Mayor's fund, there had been suggestions that a figure of perhaps £10,000 would be fitting, but the Treasury Solicitor considered that £5,000 would be more appropriate. It was difficult to appreciate that during this high level 'horse-trading', the men who had sacrificed their lives on board *Thetis* were still entombed in the boat, still resting at the bottom of Liverpool Bay.

It was now becoming evident that the Admiralty may be prepared to endeavour to stop the unions' cases from ever coming to court. Obviously, this action was dependent upon a number of factors, not least of which was the Treasury agreeing to meet the cost of the legal fees to date and also to made some sort of contribution to the Lord Mayor's *Thetis* fund. There were many confidential letters exchanged between the Treasury and the Admiralty, and it must be said that if the Treasury was reluctant to meet these bills, that in itself would be somewhat of an understatement. Indeed, there was a great reluctance to make any contribution whatsoever. There was an unsigned confidential memorandum sent from the Treasury stating

> I myself do not like very much the idea of paying these people anything, but in the circumstances it may be wiser to make a contribution to the fund for the benefit of all those who have suffered by reason of the disaster than finding ourselves having to meet judgments obtained by these particular plaintiffs. I hope moreover, that we shall be able to get all the actions withdrawn, although I agree that the Trade Unions do not represent all the plaintiffs. The non-Trade Union plaintiffs will not, I think, want to go on if the Trade Union support is withdrawn.

Many of the negotiations were dependent upon the General Secretary of the Trades Union Congress, Sir Walter McLennan Citrine, to discuss the issues with the relevant union leaders and to make an agreement such that the unions withdrew their cases. Although talks did take place, the unions however would not agree to this 'whitewash'. There was a test case arranged whereby the law firm, Evill & Coleman, suggested that Cammell Lairds were negligent in allowing for the sea trials to go ahead, and further, that they failed to provide suitable supervision and inspection after work had been carried out by sub-contractors. Evill & Coleman also suggested that the Wailes Dove Bitumastic Company Limited were also negligent, and that their negligence had in fact been the direct cause of the disaster.

It was also alleged by the law firm that both Lieutenant Woods and Leading Seaman Walter Hambrook were negligent; Woods because, as the Torpedo Officer on the submarine, it was he who had responsibility for the torpedo tubes and he had failed to check if the bow cap was open before he had the rear door of number five tube opened. Similarly, Hambrook was also cited as being negligent, in that, his responsibility was to control the levers for the bow cap which, it was alleged, he either opened or caused or allowed it to be opened. Evill & Coleman were relying on case law and quoted Donoghue v. Stevenson.

In the case of Donoghue v. Stevenson, it took three years and several court appearances for May Donoghue to finally win her case. The final judgement which was made in the House of Lords, the highest court in the land, hinged upon the fact that 'reasonable care must be taken to avoid acts or omissions, which would be likely to injure those closely and directly affected by such actions.' May Donoghue was awarded £200 compensation. Evill & Coleman,

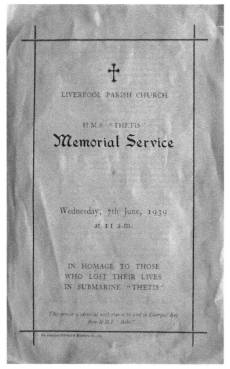

Order of the Memorial Service held at Liverpool Parish Church on Wednesday 7th June 1939. The service was identical with the one used in Liverpool Bay on HMS *Hebe*. (*By kind permission of Holyhead Maritime Museum*)

acting on behalf of the Amalgamated Engineering Union and their former members Lairds's Engineer's Fitter Archibald Craven and Brown Brothers' steering gear fitter, David Norman Duncan, suggested that there were similarities and direct comparisons which could be drawn between the case of Donoghue v. Stevenson and their current case, citing that Cammell Lairds and all those who had built the submarine had a duty of care to prevent serious injury or death. Evill & Coleman believed that Mabel Craven, Archibald Craven's widow, and Rose Duncan, David Norman Duncan's widow both had a very good case for compensation, based, primarily, on Cammell Lairds's negligence.

The test case went to the King's Bench Division of the High Court on 17 April 1940, and, to a large extent, the outcome was dependent upon case law, which, in turn, was dependent upon the production of several documents relevant to the case. Unfortunately, many of these documents were held by the various defendants, most notably Cammell Lairds, Messrs Wailes Dove Bitumastic Ltd and the Admiralty. In truth, the Admiralty held all of the trump cards, and were able to claim Crown Privilege as their reason for not allowing the documents to be released.

And now began a long and convoluted legal argument. It was the considered view of Evill & Coleman that they had a strong case for obtaining the document which the Admiralty were withholding, citing Crown Privilege. Evill & Coleman responded by stating

> It was urged before us that whatever the true principles upon which production of the documents should be refused on the ground of public interest, some of these documents could not validly be withheld because they had already been produced before the Tribunal of Inquiry into the loss of the *Thetis*, over which Mr Justice Bucknill presided, and because some reference was made to them in his report.

So, it was now up to the First Lord of the Admiralty, Alexander, to make a decision. He, understandably, decided against release, and communicated this decision to the Treasury Solicitor, Sir Thomas James Barnes, who in turn was instructed to convey this decision to Evill & Coleman. Being of a legal disposition, Barnes added that, if it became necessary to have this decision qualified, then he would obtain an affidavit from Alexander in order to formalise it. However, Evill & Coleman were not to be intimidated, and refuted the decision. Alexander's subsequent affidavit stated,

> 'All the said documents were considered by me with the assistance of my technical advisors and I formed the opinion that it would be injurious to the public interest that any of the said documents should be disclosed

to any person. I accordingly instructed the Treasury Solicitor to write on behalf of the Lords Commissioners to the Solicitors to the said Defendants not to disclose the documents set out in the said list, their contents to the Plaintiffs or either of them or to anyone on their behalf nor produce them for inspection in this action and to require them to claim privilege for the documents on the ground that it would be injurious to the public interest that the same should be disclosed or produced for inspection.'

It was now abundantly clear that the Admiralty was holding firm, but so too were Evill & Coleman. Without these documents there wasn't, realistically, very much chance of winning the case. Several appeals were made in an endeavour to release the documents, the final appeal ending in the House of Lords. After much deliberation, the Lords ruled against Evill & Coleman, and upheld the Admiralty's view that, in the public interest, the documents should not be released. It was alleged that, even though they, the Lords, were given the chance to view the documents, they never availed themselves of this opportunity, preferring instead to reach a decision without, apparently, assessing all of the available evidence. Following this setback, the case was nonetheless brought before Mr Justice Wrottesley in the summer of 1943. It was not until October of that year that he delivered his judgement, stating that:

> In no way were Lieutenant Woods and Hambrook negligent. They were attached to the ship for instruction. Neither of them could have been expected to be on guard against what happened in this case, when the hole [was blocked] in the test cock by being enamelled over before the *Thetis* sailed. I have been warned in this case about being wise after the fact. Lieutenant Woods and Leading Seaman Hambrook did not know the state of the test cock and there has not been established to my satisfaction the failure of any kind by them to take responsible care. The man of the Bitumastic Company who did this painting did a slovenly piece of work. Two of these holes were obstructed and a cursory inspection would have shown them to have been blocked.

Justice Wrottesley went on to declare that, in his view, the cursory inspection should not have been made by the Admiralty in the person of Admiralty Overseer Edward Grundy, but Cammell Lairds. Justice Wrottesley continued by saying,

> On behalf of the Wailes Dove Bitumastic Company it was said they were humble painters. This argument was not available to Cammell Lairds, who were not humble painters, but shipbuilders and engineers. In fact their

master painter inspected the work and should have been in a position to have noticed the blocked hole. Although primarily Cammell Lairds's obligation was to carry out their contract with the Admiralty I think it must be accepted that they owed a duty in the circumstances to those who set out aboard the *Thetis* to take reasonable care that the vessel was fit for the trial in question.

The horizon was beginning to look bleak for Cammell Lairds and its management team. Rather than ascribe any blame for the disaster to the Admiralty and more particularly the Admiralty Overseer, Edward Grundy, Wrottesley opted to place blame onto Cammell Lairds's management for failing to conduct a satisfactory inspection of the rear torpedo doors following the sub-contracted work which had been undertaken by the Wailes Dove Bitumastic Company. It was clear to Mr Justice Wrottesley that it was incumbent upon Lairds to make sure that the submarine was ready for her sea trials as, technically and legally, until those trials had been successfully completed, *Thetis* was not a Royal Naval ship, but still owned by its builders, Cammell Lairds. Wrottesley declared that, 'In my view each of the plaintiffs succeeds in establishing the liability of Cammell Lairds on the loss of their wage earners on the grounds of negligence. They failed to discover the defect in the test cock of Number Five torpedo tube. As against the other defendants the claims against them fail.' So, Lairds had lost! And, following that protracted and complex test case, others would now be enabled to go ahead with their claims 'on the back' of that case. There was little doubt that the pressure, a very great pressure, had now been placed upon Cammell Lairds, and more particularly, their management team. Needless to say there were several lengthy discussions in the management offices at Cammell Lairds, where all of the several options were duly considered and given a weighting value. Also, it didn't go unnoticed that war was being waged and Cammell Lairds's expertise and experience—a proud tradition of over one hundred years of shipbuilding—would be needed to assist in the war effort. There were a number of options open to Lairds. They could meet the claims and, in all probability, have to be declared bankrupt. In light of the earlier consideration with reference to the war, that option didn't appear to be viable, and not just because of the war, there was the well-being of all of Lairds's employees to be taken into consideration. The other options which were available at the time appeared to be either to lodge an appeal or to hope that Lairds's insurance would cover any liability. Again, the several insurance policies which the company had were detailed and complex, and contained many escape clauses in the small print. More problems lay ahead for Cammell Lairds.

Faced with the prospect of having to meet any number of claims, Lairds made a bid to mitigate their possible commitments. There was a clause in their

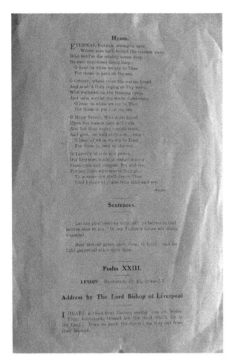

The Memorial Service included the naval hymn 'Eternal Father Strong to Save'. The address was given by The Lord Bishop of Liverpool. (*By kind permission of Holyhead Maritime Museum*)

insurance policy which stated that any amounts which they became liable to pay and which were not specified in the contract might be recoverable from the Liverpool and London Steamship Protection and Indemnity Association Limited and/or the North of England Protection and Indemnity Association; but, after extensive enquiries, it was accepted that neither of these Associations were liable for any claims. The Managing Director of Lairds also wrote to the Iron Traders' Association as a number of their members had been lost in the disaster, but he received the same response. Mr Johnson was now in a very difficult position as, without adequate insurance cover, Lairds would have to meet the total costs which Mr Justice Wrottesley adjudged.

But, the management of Cammell Lairds, supported by their legal team, still held to the view that they were not to blame for the disaster, but rather the Admiralty themselves. Indeed, Lairds had a body of evidence which, they believed, all pinned the blame on the Royal Navy, even from the time when *Thetis* went on her first sea trials up in Scotland, and the hydroplane gear was malfunctioning. There was also the question of the submarine's trim when she left Cammell Lairds's wet basin, and the central issues of the opening of the rear doors and the failure to use the rimer; all operations conducted, or not as the case may be, by navy personnel.

Cammell Lairds went on to cite many more errors which, cumulatively, led to the disaster. Further, their legal team was of the opinion that all of these errors occurred as a direct result of incompetence on behalf of the Royal Navy and not themselves as builders of the submarine. They made reference to the delay in sending the initial message—Coltart's responsibility; the delay in closing number twenty-five bulkhead door which caused the torpedo compartment to flood; the incorrect location of the submarine being given to the rescue vessels; not securing *Thetis's* stern to the *Vigilant*; the flooding to the engine compartment as a direct result of after escape hatch being open to the sea; the bow cap being open when, clearly, it should have been closed to the sea, and there were many more un-necessary mistakes in this catalogue of errors.

Because there was so much riding on the outcome of this case—not least of which was the very survival of Cammell Lairds as a shipbuilder, Messrs Laces & Company re-examined every shred of material evidence obtained to date, and every aspect relating to the swings and roundabouts of the legal arguments as they had been presented in court. There was certainly the outstanding question as to whether or not Lairds should have allowed the *Thetis* to sail from the wet basin, knowing that the trim was not as it should be; but, there again, the Admiralty was also obviously aware of the submarine's condition in this respect. But, maybe of even greater significance to them, was the fact that in the subcontract which was awarded to Messrs Wailes Dove Bitumastic Ltd there was a clause which stated that the work should be carried out to the satisfaction of the Admiralty—and that is why, presumably, they had an overseer, Grundy, to inspect and accept the work on their behalf. It is strange therefore that the blame was laid at the door of Cammell Lairds. It was however their responsibility to inform the Admiralty, in the person of Overseer Grundy, that the work had been carried out, and then it fell to him to accept the work as being to a satisfactory standard—which he did!

Lieutenant Woods's role in the disaster also came under the spotlight at this point. As the officer in charge of the torpedo compartment, it was his responsibility to ensure that everything within his sphere of command was in order. Woods had stated that, according to the indicator, number five bow cap was closed, but this was clearly not the case when further extensive examination was made sometime later when the submarine was taken to Holyhead. Laces then went on to allege that both Lieutenant Woods and Leading Seaman Hambrook were guilty of negligence, as it had been their duty to ensure that the bow cap was not open; it was patently obvious that this had not been the case and that the bow cap was, in fact, open. As the forensic examination of the evidence continued, there was one other significant clause which Laces were able to reveal, and that was to refute the current understanding that, until the final sea trials had been found to be acceptable to the Admiralty, then the submarine's owners continued to be Cammell Lairds. Laces were now calling this belief into question, stating that clause twenty-seven in the first schedule of the contract stated that 'After the first payment on account of the price, the vessel should vest in and be the absolute property of the Admiralty without prejudice to the right of the Admiralty to reject.' According to Lairds's legal representative, Mr Sellers KC, 'The first payment on account had been paid before the disaster and it seems clear that the ownership of the *Thetis* at the time that she sank was vested in the Lords Commissioners of the Admiralty.' In light of these revelations, it was the considered view of Lairds's legal team that they should not allow the case to drop, but should appeal Mr Justice Wrottesley's verdict. If Lairds's had not opted for this course of action, then the probable outcome was too catastrophic to even contemplate. They would fight on!

In addition to Cammell Lairds, there were others contesting the decision which Wrottesley had made. Many, including Mabel Craven and Rose Duncan believed that, given all of the facts of the disaster, the evidence was still pointing to Lieutenant Woods and his negligence which had caused the death of the ninety-nine men. When the case went to appeal, every aspect was, yet again, examined; indeed, Lord Justice Goddard was of the view that there had been a mis-reading of the mechanical indicator and that number five tube's bow cap was already open. The appeal court judges, on balance, considered Woods might be the guilty party.

Lord Greene, in delivering the decision which the Court of Appeal had reached, stated that their decision had been based upon two legal principles; firstly, that of *res ipsa loquitur* (In the common law of negligence, the doctrine of *res ipsa loquitur*—the thing itself speaks—states that the elements of duty of care and breach can be sometimes inferred from the very nature of an accident or other outcome, even without direct evidence of how any defendant behaved. Upon a proof of *res ipsa loquitur*, the plaintiff need only establish the remaining two elements of negligence—namely, that the plaintiff suffered harm, of which the incident result was the legal cause. Lord Greene then stated that: 'If this were not applicable, then because in my opinion an affirmative case is established, I feel constrained to hold that Lieutenant Woods was guilty of negligence. He failed to give the proper order to Hambrook to put the lever in the closed position and relied in part on the evidence of the test cock which he ought to have known was never intended to be relied on for such a purpose and was in any case wholly unreliable unless the rimer was used.' However, returning to his original statement in which he invoked the principle of *res ipsa loquitur*, Lord Greene then went on to state:

> The Court of Appeal have, however, put the blame on Lieutenant Woods for a more general reason. The case against these two defendants (i.e. Lieutenant Woods and Leading Seaman Hambrook), can, I think, be founded upon the doctrine of *res ipsa loquitur* since Lieutenant Woods was the officer in

Sir John Anderson, Minister of War. A book published by Count Michael Alexander suggested that Anderson had protected Cammell Lairds from bankruptcy. The allegations were never proved. (*From* SOS *Thetis, Hans Müller Verlag, Dresden, 1943*)

charge of the tube space, he was in sole control and an accident happened which in the ordinary course of things would not have happened if he had used proper care. But where the thing is shown to be under the management of the defendant or his servants and the accident is such as in the ordinary course of things does not happen if those who have the management use proper care, it affords reasonable evidence, in the absence of explanation by the defendants, that the accident arose from want of care.

But, following this decision by the Court of Appeal, rather than clarifying the issue, it only meant that, in effect, there were still many more legal battles to be waged. Lieutenant Woods, who was now being held responsible for the disaster could not, under any circumstances, meet the payments which he would be called upon to make. The Treasury could meet some of the financial shortfall on behalf of the Crown; but, here again, it was known by the lords sitting on the bench of the Court of Appeal that the Crown could not be forced to make any payments if they chose not to do so. Alternatively, it would be theoretically possible to bankrupt Lieutenant Woods, but this would be a costly process in itself and, even assuming that the bankruptcy was declared, there was no guarantee that the plaintiffs would be in receipt of any significant monitory reward. Woods could of course appeal to the House of Lords in an effort to change the Court of Appeal's judgement and re-establish Wrottesley's original verdict. Mabel Craven and Rose Duncan still held to their view that somebody was to blame, and again turned to the actual construction of the vessel, seeking to demonstrate that Cammell Lairds and the Wailes Dove Bitumastic Ltd had both been negligent, and that the submarine was unsuitable for sea-going duties.

In the latter part of 1945 and the early months of 1946, yet another reappraisal of the events surrounding the disaster, and also who was to be held responsible for the catastrophe, was held. Viscount Simon, one of the four lords charged with re-examining the evidence for the House of Lords—the highest court in the land—openly declared that it would be 'A complicated and difficult appeal.' In presenting his evidence, the Attorney-General, Sir Donald Somerville, who was acting on behalf of Lieutenant Woods, considered that the Court of Appeal's ruling, which had gone against Lieutenant Woods, was seriously flawed. Accepting that Woods had given an order for the rear door to be opened, Somerville nonetheless took the view that Woods had taken every necessary action which led him to the view that the bow cap was closed. He, (Somerville), argued that Woods could not have been expected to anticipate a case of triple negligence—which was, in actual fact, the case here. The negligence had started with the shoddy workmanship by employees of the Wailes Dove Bitumastic Ltd when they painted over the hole; then there was the failure of the Admiralty Overseer, Grundy, to identify this flaw in his subsequent inspection of the work; and finally, there was the actual unauthorised opening of the bow cap by a person or persons unknown.

As might be envisaged, there were several conflicting views expressed on behalf of the various plaintiffs involved in this increasingly complex case. Somerville, acting on behalf of Woods took a particular line, whereas Sir Walter Monckton KC, leading Mabel Craven's and Rose Duncan's legal team, took a diametrically opposing line. Somerville suggested that if Leading Seaman Hambrook had answered 'Yes', when Lieutenant Woods had asked of him whether the indicators were shut, then how could he, Woods, conceivably be accused of being negligent. The other doors had been opened without any difficulties, and further, the use of the rimer had never been incorporated into standard naval procedure and practice. Somerville's view was that a new vessel coming from a reputable manufacturer should be expected to be fit for purpose. However, Monckton, acting for Mabel Craven and Rose Duncan, stated that Woods had indeed been negligent, as he held ultimate responsibility for everything that occurred in the torpedo compartment. Monckton argued that Woods had not exercised adequate supervision and adhered to safety procedures when ordering number five torpedo tube's rear door to be opened. He also considered Leading Seaman Hambrook to be negligent, as he was directly responsible for the operation of the bow cap levers, stating that 'Their negligence (Lieutenant Woods and Leading Seaman Hambrook) was the direct cause of the accident and of the deaths of Duncan and Craven.'

Whilst seeking to attribute blame for the disaster, in addition to citing Lieutenant Woods and Leading Seaman Hambrook, Monckton also alleged that Cammell Lairds were negligent, in that they permitted *Thetis* to leave the wet basin in 'an unsafe and dangerous condition'. After the work had been carried out by Wailes Dove Bitumastic Ltd, Lairds had failed to carry out suitable checks and inspection of the work in order to ensure that the submarine was fully prepared and safe to go on her sea trials; and this was some time after experiencing the difficulties encountered during her first abortive sea trials in Gare Loch. Not only did Monckton lay the disaster at the feet of Cammell Lairds, he also sought to lay blame on Wailes Dove Bitumastic Ltd, again citing the fact that their employee had failed to do his job properly and that this negligence had led directly to the disaster. Monckton alleged that:

This may be a case where concurrent causes have combined to bring about the accident but these respondents are bound to recover, since if Woods was wrong in relying on the test cock to inform him as to the condition of the tube, he acted negligently and if he was right then failure was due to the negligence of Cammell Lairds and the Bitumastic Company. As regards the case against Woods, the doctrine of *res ipsa loquitur* applies. Not only was the bow cap open but he was in control of the torpedo compartment, and he himself opened the rear door.

By the time that Monckton was rehearsing his case in court, Bucknill's lengthy report had been published. What Monckton was unaware of, however, was the fact that Bucknill did not attribute any blame, whatsoever, on Leading Seaman Hambrook, as, in his view, the weight of substantive evidence did not support this conclusion. But, this adjudication was not to be found in the body of Bucknill's main published report.

Cammell Lairds had the services of two King's Counsel to mount their defence at the House of Lords hearing, Sellers and Nelson. They sought to have the blame for the disaster placed firmly on Lieutenant Woods and, to a lesser extent, on Leading Seaman Hambrook. Their contention was that, as officer in charge of that area, it was incumbent upon Woods to ensure that the tube was not flooded before the order for the rear door to be opened was given. Logically, this meant that he should have used, or had instructed to have used, the rimer, even though this may not have been strict navy protocol. They further asserted that, if Woods was not to blame for this omission, then Leading Seaman Hambrook must be to blame for not ensuring that the lever was in its correct position. They added that Lieutenant Woods should have issued an order, in clear terms, instructing Hambrook to make certain that the lever was in the 'SHUT' position, and not in either the 'NEUTRAL' or 'OPEN' position. This did not happen.

Sellers was also of the opinion that the Admiralty Overseer, Grundy, had to shoulder some of the blame for the disaster; it was after all his specific responsibility to conduct a thorough inspection of the submarine when all of the work had been completed, and pass the vessel as being seaworthy. He had indeed issued a certificate to this effect.

And so, on 27 February 1946, after almost seven years of legal to-ing and fro-ing, the stage was set to deliver the final verdict—there being no higher court in the land. As a direct result of this verdict, the finger would ultimately point as to who it was, and who would be 'picking up the tab'. But, before the adjudication was delivered, Viscount Simon prefaced his remarks by declaring the process whereby decisions had been arrived at. Obviously, the evidence submitted to Mr Justice Wrottesley had been examined in detail, and so too was the evidence presented in the Bucknill Inquiry. Viscount John Gilbert Simon of Stackpole then went on to declare that it was accepted without question that both Lieutenant Woods and leading Seaman Hambrook had a duty of care for all of those on board *Thetis*, and further that, depending upon interpretation, this might mean that they were negligent or, conversely, it might mean that they had not been negligent—it all depended upon context

Lord Quintin McGarel Hogg Hailsham, Secretary of War. According to Count Michael Alexander, it was Hailsham who brokered the agreement between the American bank of J. P. Morgan and Cammell Lairds. The allegations were never proved. (*From* SOS *Thetis, Hans Müller Verlag, Dresden, 1943*)

and, thus, interpretation. Simon asserted that Woods had made a reasonable assumption that number five bow cap was closed when the mechanical indicator actually indicated that it was shut. And further, even though Woods's commands to Hambrook were brief and to the point, they had not in any way been misleading. Being an experienced sub-mariner, Hambrook was fully aware of the need to ensure that the bow caps were shut. Irrespective of anything that Woods may or may not have said, Hambrook would not have opened the rear doors if he had thought for even a second that the bow cap for number five tube was open.

In addressing some further observations, Simon considered that, because there was no issue of water and that the indicator showed that the bow cap was shut, it was perfectly reasonable for Lieutenant Woods to assume that the bow cap for number five tube was closed; adding that it was not normal naval practice to use to rimer on every occasion when tests of this kind were being made. Simon opined the view that Lieutenant Woods had every right to assume that the mechanical workings of machinery within his sphere of responsibility was in good working order. However, when moving to consider whether or not Cammell Lairds could be found to be negligent in any area of what might be construed as being their responsibility as boat builders, he predicated his remarks by stating that, in order to establish any liability whatsoever, three legal aspects relating to the case had to be tested. Firstly, it had to be demonstrably evident that Cammell Lairds had failed to exercise due care; secondly, Lairds also had a duty of care to all of the men who were on board *Thetis* at the time of the disaster; and thirdly, it had to be shown that, if there was any failure by Cammell Lairds, then that failure resulted, directly, in the disaster and hence, the occurrence of the men's injury. Having outlined these three points, Simon went on to state that although Cammell Lairds had referred to a specific clause in the contract with Wailes Dove Bitumastic Ltd, whereby they were bound to complete the work to the satisfaction of the Admiralty, and not Cammell Lairds, and the fact that the Admiralty Overseer failed to observe the blockage, did not absolve Cammell Lairds from their responsibility and duty of care. The contract which Cammell Lairds had originally signed, bound them to build the submarine 'in a proper and workmanlike manner'. The pivotal point thus hinged on whether Cammell Lairds had a duty of care to David Duncan and Archibald Craven who were civilian workers on board at the time of the disaster. They were on board, by arrangement, because of their skills and experience. And, so it was argued, Cammell Lairds did indeed have a duty of care towards them.

Viscount John Gilbert Simon of Stackpole in making his final remarks stated that, 'The crucial question has to be answered whether Cammell Lairds's negligence can be said to be the 'cause' of the disaster.' He continued by saying that, 'After much reflection I have reached the conclusion that the Court of

Appeal is right in saying that blocking the hole with paint is not the cause of the accident and Cammell Lairds is therefore discharged from liability. These arguments also apply to the position of the Bitumastic Company ... its workmen painted badly, but remedies in contract, if any, are nothing to the point.' In conclusion, Simon declared that 'If it be thought remarkable that after so long and elaborate an investigation no one should have been found liable for this loss of life, the answer is that in order to recover damages it is necessary to prove liability against one or other of the parties sued. The key to what is uncertain may have been lost among the ninety-nine who perished in the disaster. I move that Lieutenant Woods's appeal be allowed and that the decision of the Court of Appeal as to the non-liability of the other defendants be affirmed.'

Lord Macmillan presented Lord Russell's decision in the peer's absence. Lord Russell concurred with the earlier decisions stated by Viscount Simon, in that he too accepted what Lieutenant Woods's question meant when he asked Leading Seaman Hambrook if the bow caps were shut, stating,

> I am not prepared to hold that in the circumstances he was negligent in not using the rimer, and, its use formed no part of the drill in regard to the opening of rear doors. He had never in his experience known a test cock to become choked. He was entitled to assume that the test cock was in order when the ship sailed from Liverpool with all the bow caps that closed. For the reasons which I have indicated, I am of opinion that the appeal of Lieutenant Woods should succeed. As regards the cross-appeal against the widow of Hambrook, I can see no evidence on which a case of negligence against Hambrook can be based. That cross-appeal must fail.

However, Russell was of the opinion that, making the assumption that Lairds were careless, and further, that this negligence did in fact cause the disaster, that still left the unanswered question as to whether they were in breach of their duty of care to Craven and Duncan, and this in turn begged the question as to whether the blocking of the test cock might place in danger those on board. In Russell's view, it was unreasonable to expect anyone to foresee such an eventuality. It was his considered opinion that the test cock was primarily there to be used during torpedo firing, and as such, this formed no part in diving trials. And continuing, Russell asserted:

> If this view is right, as I think it is, Cammell Lairds is under no liability to the plaintiffs. As to the case against Wailes Dove Bitumastic Limited, if Cammell Lairds are under no legal liability, neither can they be subject to any. I will only add this. The fact that no one can be made liable to the plaintiffs for the damages, which flowed from this disaster is, I doubt not,

due to the deaths of so many people, among whom might have been found the person capable of solving the mystery of how the bow cap came to open during the inspection of the tubes. To me it remains a mystery, and no good purpose can be served by suggesting possibilities which have no foundation in the available evidence.

It was then time for Lord Macmillan to forward his own assessment of the case before him. In fact, directly following on from the views which he had just expressed on behalf of Lord Russell, Macmillan concurred with the views of Viscount Simon and Lord Russell, by agreeing that Lieutenant Woods had not been negligent in any of his actions, and indeed had taken every reasonable precaution. With regards to the blocked test cock, Macmillan took the view that this aspect of the case did not impact, in any way, in the charge of negligence on his part; and further, that Woods had also checked with Hambrook; again, another precaution. Before moving to his overall assessment of the evidence placed before him, Russell stated: 'As to Hambrook himself, the case against him finds no support in the evidence.' Although Macmillan considered that Cammell Lairds were in breach of contract, he also considered that this was a very different concept from being liable for the catastrophe, stating that:

> Where the case against them breaks down is in the connection of their failure to observe and remedy this defect with the occurrence of the disaster. The chain of causation, to borrow an apposite phrase, would appear to be composed of missing links. The case against the Bitumastic Company fails even more signally for the same reason. I accordingly agree with the motion proposed by my noble and learned friend on the woolsack.

Lord Porter, whose judgements were delivered by Lord Simonds in Porter's absence, agreed that it had not been necessary to use the rimer in this instance, concluding that Lieutenant Woods's actions in ascertaining whether the bow caps were shut were exact in every detail.

It was becoming obvious from this summing up that it would be difficult, if not impossible, to prove negligence on the part of either Lieutenant Woods or Leading Seaman Hambrook. Porter completed his analysis by stating; 'The question, as I see it, is not, does the accident of itself point to his negligence, but is it right on the evidence as a whole to find him guilty of negligence?' He then went on to declare; 'It is true that the opening of the bow cap is difficult to explain without some negligence somewhere, but this is not a justification for concluding that Woods or Hambrook was the guilty party.'

Porter agreed that both Cammell Lairds and the Wailes Dove Bitumastic Company had a duty of care, but both could only be found to be guilty of negligence if their acts, or lack of, could be attributed or anticipated as being the ultimate cause of the loss of so many lives. Taking a purely legal stance, Porter stated that, unless a defendant knew that his decisions and subsequent actions would result in either misadventure or even tragedy, then he could not be declared as being negligent, and it was self-evident that Lieutenant Woods did not know that the bow cap was open when he decided to have number five torpedo tube checked. Similarly, Cammell Lairds had grounds to believe that the test cock would be clear; even though they had not had it inspected themselves. Their contract stipulated only that it should be ready for inspection.

In conclusion, Lord Porter declared: 'Then let the standard of care demanded of them be what it may, they owed no duty in respect of their careless act to the plaintiffs and cannot be made liable for it to them. In the result the appeal of Lieutenant Woods should, in my opinion, be allowed and the several appeals or cross-appeals of Mrs. Duncan and Mrs. Craven dismissed.'

And so, after almost seven years of bitter legal battles and recriminations, the families of David Duncan and Archibald Craven had finally lost their case in the highest court in the land. The tragedy was deemed to be officially recorded as 'a non-negligent accident'.

Epilogue

The life of His Majesty's Submarine *Thetis* was now over, but not that of the submarine herself, or the four survivors.

When the hull of what had been HMS *Thetis* was brought back from Anglesey to Cammell Lairds at Birkenhead, she was completely stripped. There was then a period of uncertainty whilst officials at the Admiralty pondered whether the hull should be dismantled for scrap, or whether the submarine should be completely re-fitted. After much deliberation the decision was taken to re-fit the vessel, as more submarines were constantly being required to assist in the war effort. Indeed, it was thought that, given reasonable progress, the re-fitted submarine—now to be known as HMS *Thunderbolt*—could be operational before the end of the year.

Up in Birkenhead, the mood was sombre and negative feelings towards the Royal Navy and its personnel were only just hidden below the surface. After all, many of Cammell Lairds's key workers had been lost in the *Thetis* disaster, and most of the yard's remaining workforce placed the blame squarely on the shoulders of the Admiralty. The overwhelming body of opinion in the town and the shipyard was that the navy's reaction to the disaster had been lethargic at best and criminal at worst. However, when crew for the newly-emerging submarine were being drafted to the shipyard there was no personal animosity towards them—in fact, it was quite the opposite, as they were given every assistance that they required.

Gradually, the transformation was taking place—a new submarine was emerging. The submarine was not re-launched, nor was there any formal naming ceremony; everything about the new submarine was kept deliberately 'low key' for obvious reasons. Lieutenant J. S. Stevens joined her in June as First Lieutenant. Shortly afterwards, in September 1940, Lieutenant Commander Cecil Bernard Crouch, RN was given the command of *Thunderbolt*, having previously seen service on the submarine HMS *Swordfish*. Petty Officer Telegraphist Yeates was next to join the growing body of men who were to be core members of *Thunderbolt's* crew. The view was taken at Fort Blockhouse that the submarine should be commissioned in the normal way, and without any undue ceremony. Also, the question of volunteering for service on the re-fitted submarine was no longer seen as an option—routine drafting, as was the normal practice, was adopted.

As commander-designate of HMS *Thunderbolt*, Crouch gave a short informal speech to his embryonic crew. He stressed that *Thetis* was in the past, and now they were members of the crew of the new submarine HMS *Thunderbolt*.

Progress on re-fitting the submarine had been good, and before the end of October *Thunderbolt* was ready for her acceptance trials. Again, and for obvious reasons, the acceptance trials—engine, steering and diving—were not conducted in Liverpool Bay, but up in Scotland. Because of the hostilities with Germany *Thunderbolt* was escorted to Gare Loch by a naval vessel. Admiralty officials and employees of Cammell Lairds, who were deemed to be necessary during the trials, joined the boat on a daily basis whilst up in Scotland, but none had travelled up with her. The engine and steering trials having been completed, it only remained for the dive trials to be held. The trials were completely successful, much to everyone's relief and satisfaction. *Thunderbolt* was now ready for war.

In early November *Thunderbolt* was alongside HMS *Forth*, the depot-ship of the 3rd Submarine Flotilla at Holy Loch. It was here that she went through her 'working-up' exercises where both the boat and her crew were 'brought up to speed' with regards to the various complex operations which needed to be conducted with speed, split-second timing and, above all, efficiency. The ghost of *Thetis* was finally beginning to recede. When all of the exercises had been completed satisfactorily, HMS *Thunderbolt* sailed from the Clyde on 3 December 1940, together with HMS *Tribune* and HMS *Cachalot*. They were escorted by the armed yacht HMS *Cutty Sark*.

Thunderbolt's patrol was near to the mouth of the River Gironde on the west coast of France. She then headed south into her main patrol area, the Biscay sector. As might be expected, tension was high during the first days of the patrol, but this reduced as time went on and confidence in each other's knowledge and skills developed. It was in these waters on 15 December, on her first patrol, that Crouch saw what he believed to be another submarine; he ordered 'diving stations'. They had found the Italian submarine *Tarentini* commanded by Alfredo Iaschi—a very experienced commander. Crouch ordered torpedoes to be fired from all six tubes, and, less than five minutes later, *Thunderbolt* had claimed her first victim. There were four survivors. *Thunderbolt* was safely home, back in the Clyde before Christmas. She then crossed over to Halifax, Nova Scotia, where she was assigned to convoy escort duties. Then, in July 1941 *Thunderbolt* was again transferred, on this occasion to the Mediterranean, being based initially in Alexandria and then in Malta.

Towards the end of January 1942, on passage to the west coast of Greece, *Thunderbolt* successfully attacked an escorted merchantman. She also sank a U-boat and an armed trawler by gun action. On the other hand, they were attacked by a number of destroyers and also an Italian seaplane. In addition, they were bombarded by in excess of sixty depth charges—and survived!

In March 1942 *Thunderbolt* returned to the Clyde, ready for a complete re-fitting at Blyth. The re-fit lasted until May. At the end of the year, *Thunderbolt* was again sailing for Malta.

In January 1943 *Thunderbolt* was part of 'Operation Principal', a mission which was being fought against Italian ships at Palermo. Before leaving Malta *en route* for Algiers, *Thunderbolt* had orders to patrol the Straits of Messina. It was here during the night of 12/13 March 1943, between Marittimo and Cape San Vito, that *Thunderbolt* spotted a convoy. It looked as though it was being accompanied by an Italian sloop. *Thunderbolt* manoeuvred in readiness for a torpedo attack; the torpedoes were fired and the steamer *Estorel* received a direct hit. But the Italian corvettes *Libra* and *Cicogna* were not easily thwarted, as the captain of *Cicogna*, Capitano di Corvetta Augusto Migliorini, had many years' experience as a submariner, and was fully aware of *Thunderbolt's* most probable move. The corvettes pursued *Thunderbolt* for a further couple of days. Then, after such a lengthy pursuit, Captain Migliorini decided on a different approach. He calculated that, after such a long period, *Thunderbolt* would be very low on battery power and would not be able to remain submerged for very much longer. The *Cicogna* took its first shots at *Thunderbolt* when her periscope was seen early on the morning of 14 March. Sometime later, after Captain Migliorini had received fresh orders, he decided to opt for a depth charge attack; an attack which proved successful. *Thunderbolt* was bombarded with a series of depth charges until, ultimately, her stern was seen to rise out of the water, only to plunge straight down again and disappear beneath the waves, taking all sixty-two men on board with her. Just to make sure, Captain Migliorini ordered more depth charges to be fired; the total being in excess of twenty. There was now no doubt about it; *Thunderbolt's* short but illustrious war career had ended.

Shortly after that date, the Admiralty posted a notice which read:

The Admiralty regrets to announce that His Majesty's Submarine *Thunderbolt* must now be considered lost.

Once it was generally known that Captain Oram was the first officer to escape from the stricken submarine, his action did not endear him to that many people, and, although not often openly stated, he became a defamed figure. After his recuperation, Oram did not go back to his role at Fort Blockhouse, but returned to General Service. He took command of the C-class cruiser, HMS *Hawkins*. But, as the strength of the Royal Navy was increasing during the conflict with Germany, the Admiralty had other plans for Captain Oram. In the summer of 1943 he was transferred from *Hawkins* to HMS *King Alfred* where he was instrumental in instituting training programmes in preparation for the Normandy landings.

After the war, there was a body of opinion that took the view that Oram was never adequately recognised for the service he had given to his country. Captain Oram died in his ninetieth year in 1986.

The only civilian survivor of the *Thetis* disaster, Mr Frank Shaw, opted to return to his former employment and Cammell Lairds, and returned once again into his role there—but chose never again to work on submarines. Lairds did however recognise his service to the company, so, soon after his return he was given 'staff' status, and was shortly to join the ranks of the house-owning middle classes. Frank Shaw was reluctant to discuss the events of 1 June 1939, although it was rumoured that the press did buy his story for a considerable, but undisclosed, consideration. Frank Shaw always attended the service commemorating the *Thetis* disaster which took place every year at Holyhead, but, other than that, preferred to keep his undoubtedly painful memories deep within his own bosom. He died in January 1981 aged seventy-three.

Immediately following his escape from *Thetis*, Arnold was hospitalised at Plymouth, where he was given specific orders that he must not, under any circumstances, engage in conversation or any other form of communication with people from the press or other media. It was also during this period that, because his pay-book was resting on the seabed in Liverpool Bay, he was unable to present it to the relevant authorities, which subsequently meant that he was refused any wages! He was in danger of being charged with mutiny if he remonstrated against the order. At that time mutiny was a hanging offence—not an avenue for Arnold to go down.

Even after all of his experiences on *Thetis*—both on 1 June and subsequently—Leading Stoker Walter Arnold took the brave decision to remain in the Submarine Service. In February 1940 he was drafted to HMS *Spearfish* at Blyth. But, unfortunately on her first dive his nerve 'carried', and he realised that submarines were no longer for him. Shortly afterwards, the Navy transferred him to HMS *Fiji* on compassionate grounds. As *Fiji* was a new vessel, she had to undergo 'working-up exercises' which were carried out in the West Indies. It was when she was returning to the Clyde later in the year that she was torpedoed, but managed to limp home. As soon as repairs

Leading Stoker Walter Arnold comforting relatives at the memorial service for all of the men who died on board *Thetis*. (*From SOS Thetis*, Hans Müller Verlag, Dresden, 1943)

had been completed, *Fiji* sailed for the Mediterranean. But, on 21 June *Fiji* was subjected to unremitting air attack, which resulted in her sinking. After clinging onto driftwood for several hours, Arnold was eventually rescued by crew from one of the escorting destroyers. Following that particular encounter, Leading Stoker Arnold returned to join the battleship HMS *King George V*. This posting was very different from the last, in that *King George V's* duties were to act as escort to the Russian convoys. Leading Stoker Arnold's last voyage was to the Mediterranean aboard HMS *Duke of York*. After twenty-two years in the Royal Navy, Arnold was never awarded any medals in recognition of his valiant service to his country.

It has to be noted that, after the war, even though they'd been through so much together on *Thetis*, Walter Arnold and Frank Shaw—who lived within a mile of each other—never formed any lasting friendship, yet they both attended the same commemoration services for many years, and they'd both faced disaster together.

Leading Stoker Walter Arnold died in 1974.

After his ordeal, Lieutenant Frederick Woods returned to General Service; but, although wishing to return to the Submarine Service, the Admiralty considered that it would be imprudent. They were conscious of the adverse publicity that this action might give rise to in a hostile press. Woods was drafted to HMS *Norfolk* and later to the destroyer HMS *Worcester*, where he found himself to be an object of derision and contempt, and the butt of many malicious jokes. He, more than any of the other survivors from *Thetis* was vilified and held in contempt by many, including the commander of HMS *Worcester* who would not even deign to speak directly to Woods. He was however held in high regard by 'lower deck' crew, but generally disregarded by fellow officers.

Woods was awarded the Distinguished Service Cross for his courage during the Dunkirk Landings.

Continuing his naval career, Woods joined the staff of the Commander-in-Chief (Mediterranean) at the end of the war. This appointment was made a little while after he learnt that he had been totally exonerated by the Law Lords, of any actions which he may or may not have taken on 1 June 1939. He died in May 1946, following a car crash in France.

Perhaps fittingly, Lieutenant Frederick 'Freddie' Greville Woods was buried at sea.

A naval rating lays a fitting memorial tribute in honour of the ninety-nine men who died aboard HMS *Thetis*. (*From* SOS *Thetis, Hans Müller Verlag, Dresden, 1943*)

Persons on board HMS *Thetis* on 1 June 1939

Officers and Men of HMS *Thetis*

Lieutenant-Commander G. H. Bolus, RN
Lieutenant H. Chapman, RN
Lieutenant W. A. W. Poland, RN
Lieutenant F. G. Woods, RN*
Mr R. D. Glenn, Commissioned Engineer, RN

Chief Petty Officer G. P. Cornish
Petty Officer E. Mitchell
Petty Officer T. T. Goad
Petty Officer C. E. Smithers
Petty Officer Telegraphist J. A. Hope
Petty Officer Cook J. C. Hughes
Electrical Artificer A. W. Byrne
Chief Engine Room Artificer W. C. Ormes
Chief Engine Room Artificer P. F. Jackson
Engine Room Artificer J. C. Creasy
Engine Room Artificer H. W. E. French
Engine Room Artificer H. G. Howells
Chief Stoker H. J. Dillon-Shallard
Stoker Petty Officer J. W. Wells

Leading Seaman W. L. Hambrook
Leading Seaman W. A. Luck
Leading Seaman J. A. Read
Leading Seaman A. H. Smith
Leading Seaman S. W. G. Stevens

Leading Signalman F. B. Batten
Leading Telegraphist W. E. Allan
Leading Telegraphist G. A. Harwood
Leading Steward F. N. Stock
Able Seaman J. Costley
Able Seaman S. Crombleholme
Able Seaman E. A. Kendrick
Able Seaman N. Longstaff
Able Seaman J. A. Morgans
Able Seaman F. Rogers
Able Seaman J. H. Turner
Able Seaman T. Wilson

Telegraphist C. T. W. Graham
Telegraphist T. W. Mortimer

Leading Stoker W. C. Arnold*
Leading Stoker R. S. Brooke
Leading Stoker D. Cunningham
Leading Stoker J. S. Feeney
Leading Stoker T. W. Kenney
Leading Stoker E. J. Youles
Stoker T. Bambrick
Stoker J. Craig
Stoker A. H. Dunn
Stoker L. E. Green
Stoker A. G. Hills
Stoker W. T. Hole
Stoker W. A. Matthews
Stoker W. Orrock
Stoker A. E. Yates

Officers of T class submarines being built at Cammell Lairds

Lieutenant-Commander R. N. Garnett, RN
Lieutenant-Commander T. C. C. Lloyd, RN
Lieutenant P. E. J. Ryan, RN
Lieutenant (Engineer) A. G. J. Jamison, RN

Other Naval Officers

Commander R. G. B. Hayter, RN
Commander L. G. Pennington, RN
Engineer Captain S. Jackson, RN
Lieutenant (Engineer) C. M. H. Henderson, RN
Captain H. P. K. Oram, RN*

Admiralty and Overseeing Officers

Mr W. H. Aslett
Mr F. Bailey
Mr E. Gisborne
Mr A. A. F Hill
Mr C. W. Horne
Mr H. Horsman
Mr L. W. Hunn

Employees of Cammell Lairds and Co., Ltd

Managers and Foremen

Mr J. I. Armstrong
Mr R. W. Crout
Mr R. Kipling
Mr W. Owen
Mr A. B. Robinson
Mr R. Rogerson
Mr F. Shaw*
Mr A. S. Watkinson

Caulker

Mr W. B. Beatty

Electricians

Mr S. Broad
Mr A. G. Chinn
Mr C. J. S. Hamilton
Mr E. H. Lewis

Mr W. H. Smith
Mr G. A. Summers

Engine Fitters

Mr F. R. Bresner
Mr W. Brown
Mr H. Eccleston
Mr J. Griffiths
Mr R. Homer
Mr J. A. Page
Mr P. L. Quinn
Mr C. Smith

Ship Fitters

Mr A. Craven
Mr G. L. Scarth
Mr W. Watterson

Employees of Vickers-Armstrong, Ltd

Mr T. Ankers
Mr H. T. Cragg
Mr D. V. Tyler
Mr J. Young

Employee of Brown Bros, and Co., Ltd

Mr D. N. Duncan
Mersey Pilot
Mr N. D. Willcox

Employees of City Caterers (Liverpool), Ltd

Mr W. G. Bath
Mr G. H. Dobells

*Survivor of the disaster

HMS *Thetis*—Configuration

Thetis was 275 feet long (about 84½ metres), and had a beam of approximately 26½ feet (just over 8 metres). But, the beam inside the submarine was considerably less than this—16 feet (just less than 5 metres) maximum diameter. This was because of the pressurised, double-skinned, construction which was necessary so that the submarine could withstand external water pressure when submerged.

   Thetis was divided into six main compartments, stem to stern, separated by watertight bulkheads:

1. Torpedo Tube Compartment
   The forward most compartment was the Torpedo Tube Compartment. *Thetis* was equipped with six torpedo tubes, which were configured in two tiers of three. The starboard side tier housed numbers 1, 3 and 5 tubes, with tubes 2, 4 and 6 on the adjacent port side. The forward end of the tubes were closed to the sea by a bronze plate, known as the bow cap. Numbers five and six torpedo tubes and bow caps were always below water level, even when the submarine was cruising on the surface. Each of the six bow caps were opened and closed by means of a telemotor system, activated by levers. The function of the bow caps was to allow the torpedoes direct access to the sea when fired.
   Apart from the torpedoes, the only other armament that 'T' class boats carried was a 4 inch gun which was mounted on the outside of the submarine near to the conning tower. The gun was brought into action when mounting a surprise attack or, conversely, as a last resort when the vessel was unable to dive.

2. Torpedo Stowage Compartment

   The after end of each of the six torpedo tubes came through to the Torpedo Stowage Compartment. Each tube had a rear door, which, after a torpedo had been fired, allowed access to the tube for reloading. The Torpedo Stowage Compartment, between watertight bulkheads numbers 1 and 2, was where the main arsenal of torpedoes was kept.

3. Mess Space

   The third compartment, between watertight bulkheads numbers 2 and 3 was the Mess Space. In this space there was the Seamen's' Mess, the Petty Officers' Mess, the Engine Room Artificers' Mess and the Wardroom. There was a series of batteries under the Mess Space.

4. Control Room

   The fourth compartment, known as the Control Room, was located between watertight bulkheads numbers 3 and 4 and was, as its name implies, the very centre of operations. The two periscopes were located in this compartment; the larger normal periscope and the smaller, 'attack', periscope. Also within the compartment were the hydroplane and helmsman posts, the gyro-compass, the ASDIC (Anti-Submarine Detection Investigation Committee—a British term for underwater-acoustic detection equipment.) listening posts, and the 'blowing' panel. Access to the conning tower, bridge and the gun turret was gained from the Control Room. The communications room and the galley were also located in the Control Room. There were more batteries directly under the Control Room.

5. Main Engine Room

   The fifth compartment, generally known as the Main Engine Room, was located between watertight bulkheads numbers 4 and 5 and was where the two main diesel engines were housed. There was a smaller Motor Room, which was where the two electric motors were located; these motors were for underwater propulsion.

   The shipyards which were engaged in building 'T' class submarines normally had their own preferences for the engines which they fitted; Vickers Armstrong normally fitted their own engines; Cammell Lairds used Sulzer engines, which were made in Switzerland; boats built by the Royal Dockyards always used Admiralty engines, and Scotts used German super-charged engines—these were later changed for Admiralty engines.

6. Steering Compartment

The sixth compartment, which was after-most compartment of the submarine, was the Steering Compartment. In addition to housing all of the necessary steering gear equipment, the compartment had a Torpedo Storage Area and the Stokers' Mess Room.

'T' class boats had six openings to the outside—the forward escape hatch, the torpedo loading hatch, the gun tower, the conning tower, the engine room hatch and the after escape hatch. There was also a 'soft patch' located directly above the engine room.

The submarine's ballast tanks were located on either side of the pressurised hull. These ballast tanks were filled with water when the vessel was required to dive. Also, throughout the length of the boat there was a series of 'trimming tanks', which were used to adjust the 'trim' of the submarine as and when required. The ballast tanks were 'blown' with compressed air when the submarine was required to surface.

Submarine Building Programme 1935-1942

Submarine Name	Submarine Builder

Group One

1935
Triton   (Vickers Armstrong, Barrow-in-Furness)
1936
Thetis
(Later to be re-named   (Cammell Lairds, Birkenhead)
Thunderbolt)
Trident   (Cammell Lairds, Birkenhead)
Triumph   (Vickers Armstrong, Barrow-in-Furness)
Tribune   (Scotts, Greenock)
1937
Taku   (Cammell Lairds, Birkenhead)
Thistle   (Vickers Armstrong, Barrow-in-Furness)
Tarpon   (Vickers Armstrong, Barrow-in-Furness)
Triad   (Vickers Armstrong, Barrow-in-Furness)
Truant   (Vickers Armstrong, Barrow-in-Furness)
Tuna   (Scotts, Greenock)
Tigris   (Chatham Dockyard)
1938
Tetrarch   (Vickers Armstrong, Barrow-in-Furness)
Torbay   (Chatham Dockyard)
Talisman   (Cammell Lairds, Birkenhead)

Group Two

1939
Trusty   (Vickers Armstrong, Barrow-in-Furness)
Turbulent   (Vickers Armstrong, Barrow-in-Furness)
Thrasher   (Cammell Lairds, Birkenhead)
Thorn   (Cammell Lairds, Birkenhead)
Tempest   (Cammell Lairds, Birkenhead)
Traveller   (Scotts, Greenock)
Trooper   (Scotts, Greenock)

Group Three

1940
Trespasser   (Vickers Armstrong, Barrow-in-Furness)
Taurus   (Vickers Armstrong, Barrow-in-Furness)
Tactician   (Vickers Armstrong, Barrow-in-Furness)
Truculent   (Vickers Armstrong, Barrow-in-Furness)
Templar   (Vickers Armstrong, Barrow-in-Furness)
Tally-Ho   (Vickers Armstrong, Barrow-in-Furness)
Tantalus   (Vickers Armstrong, Barrow-in-Furness)
Tantivy   (Vickers Armstrong, Barrow-in-Furness)
1941
Tradewind   (Chatham Dockyard)
Trenchant   (Chatham Dockyard)
Thule   (Devonport Dockyard)
Tudor   (Devonport Dockyard)
Tireless   (Portsmouth Dockyard)
Token   (Portsmouth Dockyard)
Telemachus   (Vickers Armstrong, Barrow-in-Furness)
Talent   (Vickers Armstrong, Barrow-in-Furness)
Terrapin   (Vickers Armstrong, Barrow-in-Furness)
Thorough   (Vickers Armstrong, Barrow-in-Furness)
Tiptoe   (Vickers Armstrong, Barrow-in-Furness)
Trump   (Vickers Armstrong, Barrow-in-Furness)
Taciturn   (Vickers Armstrong, Barrow-in-Furness)
Tapir   (Vickers Armstrong, Barrow-in-Furness)
Tarn   (Vickers Armstrong, Barrow-in-Furness)
Teredo   (Vickers Armstrong, Barrow-in-Furness)
Talent   (Vickers Armstrong, Barrow-in-Furness)
1942
Totem   (Devonport Dockyard)

Truncheon	(Devonport Dockyard)
Turpin	(Chatham Dockyard)
Thermopylae	(Chatham Dockyard)
Theban*	(Vickers Armstrong, Barrow-in-Furness)
Threat*	(Vickers Armstrong, Barrow-in-Furness)
Thor*	(Portsmouth Dockyard)
Tiara*	(Portsmouth Dockyard)
Tabard	(Scotts, Greenock)
Talent II*	(Scotts, Greenock)

*Submarine cancelled due to cessation of hostilities

List of Public Inquiry Witnesses

Captain H. P. K. Oram
Lieutenant F. G. Woods
Leading Stoker W. C. Arnold
Mr Frank Shaw
Mr Henry Bremner
Rear Admiral F. T. Tower, CB, OBE
Mr G. J. Stunden
Mr Ernest Sutton
Commander A. Maguire
Mr S. H. Abrahams
Mr Thomas Wolfe
Mr J. Lauder
Mr Edward Grundy
Mr James Watters
Mr John Rowe
Mr J. H. B. Stinson
Mr W. G. Taylor
Mr F. M. Black
Mr Charles Goodall
Mr A. N. Harrison
Mr L. C. Williamson
Lieutenant Commander E. R. C. Macvicker
Chief Petty Officer R. V. Rowkins
Lieutenant R. E. Coltart
Wireless Telegraphist V. J. Crosby
Mr A. E. Godfrey
Mr E. J. Randles
Mr D. F. Waller

Mr F. J. W. Legg
Commander C. S. Miller
Commander L. M. Shadwell
Commander G. B. H. Fawkes
Commander R. C. Bayne
Captain I. A. P. Macintyre
Acting Flight Lieutenant John Avent
Lieutenant Commander R. H. Mills
Captain R. S. G. Nicholson
Captain H. V. Hart
Mr Charles Brock
Mr Frederick Orton
Mr Robert Frederick
Captain P. Ruck-Keene
Admiral Sir M. Dunbar-Nasmith, VC, KCB
Mr Thomas Mckenzie
Mr Sinclair Mckenzie
Sir Stanley Goodall
Mr E F. Cox
Professor J. B. S. Haldane
Commander R. M. L. Edwards